To

CH: John Radford, who showed me Psychology.

PT: Michael Argyle and Bridget Bryant, for their pioneering
ideas, inspiration, and support.

Handbook of Social Skills Training

VOLUME 2

*Clinical Applications and
New Directions*

Edited by
CLIVE R. HOLLIN

and

PETER TROWER

PERGAMON PRESS

OXFORD · NEW YORK · BEIJING · FRANKFURT
SÃO PAULO · SYDNEY · TOKYO · TORONTO

U.K.	Pergamon Press, Headington Hill Hall, Oxford OX3 0BW, England
U.S.A.	Pergamon Press, Maxwell House, Fairview Park, Elmsford, New York 10523, U.S.A.
PEOPLE'S REPUBLIC OF CHINA	Pergamon Press, Qianmen Hotel, Beijing, People's Republic of China
FEDERAL REPUBLIC OF GERMANY	Pergamon Press, Hammerweg 6, D-6242 Kronberg, Federal Republic of Germany
BRAZIL	Pergamon Editora, Rua Eça de Queiros, 346, CEP 04011, São Paulo, Brazil
AUSTRALIA	Pergamon Press Australia, P.O. Box 544, Potts Point, N.S.W. 2011, Australia
JAPAN	Pergamon Press, 8th Floor, Matsuoka Central Building, 1-7-1 Nishishinjuku, Shinjuku-ku, Tokyo 160, Japan
CANADA	Pergamon Press Canada, Suite 104, 150 Consumers Road, Willowdale, Ontario M2J 1P9, Canada

First edition 1986

Library of Congress Cataloging-in-Publication Data
Handbook of social skills training.
(International series in experimental social psychology; v. 12)
Contents: v. 1. Applications across the life span
v. 2. Clinical applications & new directions.
1. Social skills — Study and teaching. 2. Social psychiatry.
I. Hollin, Clive R.   II. Trower, Peter, 1938–   .   III. Series.
HM299.H35   1986   302   86-5053

British Library Cataloguing in Publication Data
Handbook of social skills and training.
(International series in experimental social psychology; v. 12)
1. Social skills — Study and teaching
I. Hollin, Clive R.   II. Trower, Peter   III. Series
302'.07   HM132

ISBN 0-08-031297-7   v. 1 (Hardcover)
ISBN 0-08-031296-9   v. 1 (Flexicover)
ISBN 0-08-034049-0   v. 2 (Hardcover)
ISBN 0-08-034048-2   v. 2 (Flexicover)

ISBN 0-08-034160-8   (2 Volume Set Hardcover)
ISBN 0-08-034159-4   (2 Volume Set Flexicover)

Printed in Great Britain by A. Wheaton & Co. Ltd. Exeter

Introduction to the Series

MICHAEL ARGYLE

Social psychology is in a very interesting period, and one of rapid development. It has survived a number of "crises", there is increased concern with external validity and relevance to the real world, the repertoire of research methods and statistical procedures has been greatly extended, and a number of exciting new ideas and approaches are being tried out.

The books in this series present some of these new developments; each volume contains a balance of new material and a critical review of the relevant literature. The new material consists of empirical research, procedures, theoretical formulations, or a combination of these. Authors have been asked to review and evaluate the often very extensive past literature, and to explain their new findings, methods or theories clearly.

The authors are from all over the world, and have been carefully chosen, mainly on the basis of their previous published work, showing the importance and originality of their contribution, and their ability to present it clearly. Some of these books report a programme of research by one individual or a team, some are based on doctoral theses, others on conferences.

Social psychologists have moved into an increasing number of applied fields, and a growing number of practitioners have made use of our work. All the books in the series have been of some practical application, some will be on topics of wide popular interest, as well as adding to scientific knowledge. The books in the series are designed for advanced undergraduates, graduate students and relevant practitioners, and in some cases for a rather broader public.

We do not know how social psychology will develop, and it takes quite a variety of forms already. However, it is a great pleasure to be associated with books by some of those social psychologists who are developing the subject in such interesting ways.

Preface

We began with what seemed at the time a reasonably sane suggestion: a review of all the areas in which social skills training has been applied. Over the 2 years or so that it took to transform this suggestion into reality, the project expanded into previously unconceived dimensions. In its final form the work collected in two volumes contains contributions from 24 authors (excluding us), distributed over three continents and a range of disciplines — including education, linguistics, psychiatry, psychology and social work. As editors we wish to thank our contributors for the overall excellence of their manuscripts which made our task so much easier.

For preparation of the final manuscript we are indebted to Vivienne Doughty, who not only word-processed most of our work from handwritten drafts, but also somehow made sense of our editorial hieroglyphics to re-type sections of other manuscripts. Without her efforts the genesis from "in prep" to "in press" would have been so much longer.

Finally we wish to thank our respective partners for tolerating long absences when other, more enjoyable, activities were being forfeited. Their support is gratefully accepted, but not taken for granted.

CLIVE HOLLIN
PETER TROWER

May 1986

Contents

List of Contributors

Editors

Clive R. Hollin, Department of Psychology, University of Leicester, Leicester, England.

Peter Trower, Department of Psychology, University of Leicester, Leicester, England.

Contributors

David B. Abrams, Miriam Hospital & Division of Biology and Medicine, Brown University, Providence, U.S.A.

Michael Argyle, Department of Experimental Psychology, University of Oxford, Oxford, England.

Jody A. Binkoff, Providence YAMC & Division of Biology and Medicine, Brown University, Providence, U.S.A.

Thomas M. DiLorenzo, Department of Psychology, University of Missouri in Columbia, U.S.A.

David Good, Social and Political Sciences Committee, University of Cambridge, Cambridge, U.S.A.

Peter Maguire, Department of Psychiatry, University of Manchester, Manchester, England.

Johnny L. Matson, Department of Psychology, Louisiana State University, Louisiana, U.S.A.

Peter M. Monti, Providence YAMC & Division of Biology and Medicine, Brown University, Providence, U.S.A.

Geoff Shepherd, Department of Psychology, Fulbourne Hospital, Cambridge, England.

J. Mark G. Williams, Medical Research Council Applied Psychology Unit, Cambridge, England.

William R. Zwick, Providence YAMC & Division of Biology and Medicine, Brown University, Providence, U.S.A.

Clinical Applications and New Directions for Social Skills Training: An Introduction

CLIVE R. HOLLIN and PETER TROWER

In the introduction to Volume 1 of this Handbook the origins of social skills training (SST) were traced to three independent areas: the emergence of behaviour therapy, particularly the work of Wolpe; research into the relationship between social competence and mild to severe psychiatric disorder; and research in social psychology into verbal and nonverbal communication (Hollin and Trower, 1986). In the previous volume the application of the SST model was traced across the life span from children, to adolescents, young and middle-aged adults, and to the elderly. The various specialist uses of SST with the issues and problems prevalent at these stages of life-span development were reviewed in depth. Further, the use of SST with specific sub-groups within these age groupings was also included; for example SST with delinquents and adult anti-social behaviour received particular attention. It was also suggested that through its use in professional training programmes SST had once again been of influence across the life-span. Whilst adult professionals such as teachers and managers have been directly influenced, their client groups — across the full age range — will also have been influenced by their experience of, hopefully, improved professional services.

As well as these life-span applications, SST has a firm basis in clinical psychology. Indeed, as already noted, the research conducted in the 1960s linking social competence and rehabilitation following schizophrenia provided the basis for one of the first uses of SST. This volume begins with this theme: Geoff Shepherd shows in Chapter 1 how these beginnings have now expanded into a considerable literature on SST and schizophrenia. However, in the course of his discussion it becomes apparent that as well as the usual difficulties of assessment, training methods, and so forth associated with SST, there are intricate complexities with the concept of "schizophrenia". Shepherd discusses these issues in some depth and concludes that, despite the difficulties, SST can be an effective technique

1

for some of the social difficulties associated with schizophrenia. He also suggests possible future directions, including the use of cognitive techniques and family therapy, noting that these can be complementary rather than antipathetic to SST.

A second early impetus, again prompting one of the first uses of SST, came from the premise that poor social behaviour was related to social anxiety, and therefore if social skills could be improved, social anxiety would decrease. In Chapter 2 of this volume Peter Trower examines the use of SST with those individuals deemed to be "socially anxious". The number of studies is very large and reviews have been produced at regular intervals since the 1970s. Trower discusses these reviews in light of research findings from *both* social and clinical psychology. Whilst he points to conceptual problems with SST and "social anxiety", his conclusion is guardedly optimistic that there are openings for future research to develop the efficacy of SST in the treatment of social anxiety.

The enthusiasm with which practitioners adopted SST led to the application of the technique to further clinical populations. The mentally handicapped, perhaps more than any other population, have been traditionally associated with behavioural intervention. Thus it was not unexpected that SST should be used with this client group. In Chapter 3 of this volume Johnny Matson and Thomas DiLorenzo leave little doubt that this has been both an appropriate and successful application of the technique. Training programmes for verbal behaviour, personal hygiene, and self-help skills have all been implemented successfully. In looking to the future they note two developments: the first, in keeping with the move to community rather than institutional care, is "independence training". The second is the use of SST in the rehabilitation of those mentally handicapped as a result of organic impairment following physical trauma. Little empirical evidence is available as yet, but the seeds for further clinical growth have been sown.

In Chapter 4 of this volume Mark Williams charts the further expansion of SST to the treatment of depression. As with schizophrenia, the concept of depression is not simple: the term covers a wide variety of presenting behaviours and various subtypes are thought to exist. In reviewing the evidence, Williams arrives at the intriguing possibility that the depressed person may *elicit* social skills deficits in those with whom they interact; this process eventually results in their alienation from social interaction. The evidence indicates that whilst SST can be successful with depression, it does not appear to be any more or less so than other psychological or pharmacological interventions. However, any conclusions are limited as research has not elaborated on which treatment, or combination of treatments, is best suited to which subtype of depression.

In Chapter 5 Peter Monti and his colleagues address the use of SST with alcohol and drug abuse populations — a development of SST which was seen as following the pioneering work of the Sobells in applying a behavioural framework to the understanding of alcoholism (Hollin and Trower, 1986). This chapter shows that whilst SST faces the familiar problems of effective assessment, training and generalisation, there are grounds for cautions optimism for progress. The authors' confidence in meeting this assertion stems, perhaps, from a relatively sound empirical base: the evidence reveals that some individuals with substance abuse problems have social skills difficulties and so SST programmes can realistically go some way towards ameliorating alcohol related problems.

A further step in the application of SST within the clinical field was to the professionals themselves — those individuals responsible for the delivery of treatment. The application of SST to professional groups has over recent years considerably changed the training of health profession- als. The traditional method for medical students of learning by example, that is simply by watching qualified practitioners in action, has undergone some revision with the advent of interpersonal skills training. The case for this revision rested on the arguments that with improved communication between practitioner and patient more and better information could be gathered to plan treatment for the benefit of the patient's health: additionally, better communication would act to decrease the patient's anxiety. A large number of studies have been conducted on doctor-patient communication and the effectiveness of interpersonal skills training with health professionals. As these studies have been comprehensively re- viewed elsewhere (e.g. Pendleton and Hasler, 1983) we thought that it would be illuminating to see the detail necessary for such programmes to be constructed. Therefore in Chapter 6 of the present volume, Peter Maguire plots the course of a series of studies to design a training programme to improve doctor-patient communication. Case examples are presented to emphasise the need for good communication between doctor and patient, and from this basis the details of training programmes to improve the communication skills of medical students are presented. The detailed attention to the role of the various components of training shows how painstaking such research must be to construct better, more efficient training. The potential of the skills training approach is finally expanded with a suggestion to formulate training programmes to meet the require- ments of other aspects of health professional-client interaction.

Having spread to so many areas of clinical (and non-clinical) application, the expansion continued as researchers and practitioners developed new uses of the SST model. In Chapter 7 of this volume Clive Hollin discusses a number of unusual, "one-off", applications of SST. The range includes clinical applications such as with transsexualism and anorexia nervosa; physical handicaps such as blindness and diabetes; and adjustment to physical trauma resulting from severe physical injury, specifically spinal cord injury. The findings and methodological strengths and weaknesses of these studies are discussed. Finally, empirical research suggesting a role for SST with the facially disfigured illustrates that the field is not static and that new uses for SST will continue to emerge.

Whilst new developments in terms of client populations are underway, refinements and improvements in training techniques are also constantly demanded by practitioners. Therefore following new clinical applications the final chapters of the Handbook move to theoretical advances which may in turn influence the practice of SST. As we discussed in the opening to Volume 1, SST relies heavily on social psychology to provide the "raw material" from which to construct effective training programmes. Since the promulgation of the SST model in the late 1960s, there have been considerable advances in social psychology with some ramifications for SST (see Argyle, 1983). One particular movement within social psychology, which gathered momentum in the late 1970s and early 1980s, was the analysis of the types of situation within which social behaviour takes place (e.g. Argyle, Furnham and Graham, 1981). A summary of the research into situational analysis and its relevance for SST is presented by Michael Argyle in Chapter 8 of this volume. This approach maintains that whilst, of course, individual behaviour is one aspect of social functioning, all social behaviour occurs in social situations with different situations calling for different types of social behaviour. Thus an understanding and analysis of situations is important to the social skills trainer. This chapter moves through the various features of situations such as goal structure, rules, and types of setting, to consider the interaction between the difficulties posed by a given situation and the social skills it demands of the individual. The suggestion of "Situationally Focussed SST" is advanced; through understanding situational demands training goals can be formulated which aim to benefit the trainee as much by environmental management as by individual change.

When we refer to "social skills" the tendency can be to concentrate upon overt motor, or "nonverbal" behaviour such as posture, gesture, and eye contact; and perhaps also on the type of social setting in which the behaviour occurs. Whilst we do convey large amounts of social information by nonverbal communication, we also rely heavily on *verbal* communication in most social interactions. Thus linguistic research, particularly into conversation, provides a potentially rich source of information and data for practitioners of SST. Two approaches to understanding linguistic interaction are *Speech Act Theory* and *Conversational Analysis*. The applicability of Conversational Analysis to SST has been described recently by Coulthard (1984). In Chapter 9 of the present volume David Good examines the specific contribution which Speech Act Theory might make to SST. Good suggests how the analyses of conversation, following this theory, could be applied to SST; for example, trainers may need to attend more closely to the implicit rules of spoken language, which are not obvious at the "surface" level of words but nonetheless play an essential role in socially skilled behaviour.

In the final chapter Clive Hollin and Peter Trower seek to draw together the various strands evident throughout the book. Three broad areas are covered; technical issues and the technique of SST; the practicalities of the use and abuse of SST; and conceptual and theoretical issues concerned with SST. Whilst both editors agree that the concept of SST needs refinement, they differ in theoretical approach. Peter Trower has expressed his views in full elsewhere (Trower, 1984) and they are summarised here. Clive Hollin has drawn on a quite different approach, radical behaviourism, to attempt to analyse social behaviour with a view to refining the concept of SST. The suggestion is that SST be sub-divided into three distinct types of training from this radical behavioural perspective — social perception training, social cognition training, and social perform-ance training. Suggestions as to the content and evaluation of these types of training are given. Finally three scenarios for the future development of SST are presented: it is concluded that real progress will take place when all practitioners and researchers can agree on a common model of social skills.

References

Argyle, M. (1983) *The psychology of interpersonal behaviour* (4th ed.). Harmondsworth, Middlesex: Penguin Books.

Argyle, M., Furnham, A. and Graham, J. A. (1981) *Social situations*. Cambridge: Cambridge University Press.

Coulthard, M. (1984) Conversation analysis and social skills training. In: P. Trower (Ed.), *Radical approaches to social skills training*. London: Croom Helm.

Hollin, C. R. and Trower, P. (1986) Social skills training: A retrospective analysis and summary of applications. In: C. R. Hollin and P. Trower (Eds.), *Handbook of social skills training, Volume 1: Applications across the life-span*. Oxford: Pergamon Press.

Pendleton, D. and Hasler, J. (Eds.) (1983) *Doctor-patient communication*. London: Academic Press.

Trower, P. (1984) A radical critique and reformulation: From organism to agent. In: P. Trower (Ed.), *Radical approaches to social skills training*. London: Croom Helm.

Clinical Applications

1

Social Skills Training and Schizophrenia

GEOFF SHEPHERD

Schizophrenia is a relatively rare condition. It generally affects between 1 and 2% of the population at any one time. However, schizophrenics form the majority of long-stay psychiatric in-patients and, although there have been increasing efforts towards community provision, many still suffer frequent relapses and require repeated admissions to hospital over long periods of time. Whether in hospital or in the community, schizophrenia is a condition with potentially seriously disabling social consequences. Social factors seem to play a large part in its aetiology and they have a significant influence on the likelihood of relapse. In addition, social factors are important prognostically and if certain key aspects of patients' social adjustment could be improved, then their outcome might be considerably better. SST therefore has obvious potential. However, the extent to which such an approach will actually be helpful depends not only upon a realistic appraisal of its effectiveness and limitations, but also upon a clear understanding of the nature of social functioning itself. These are the issues to be addressed in this chapter. Let us begin by examining the symptoms of schizophrenia and the part that social factors play in its aetiology, course and outcome.

Schizophrenia and Social Functioning

Schizophrenia is not, of course, a single set of symptoms. Indeed, it is probably more accurate to talk of "the schizophrenias", rather than to imply a unitary syndrome. Neale and Oltmanns (1980) in their excellent discussion of the historical background to the classification of these disorders have shown how the term has been used to refer to widely different syndromes at different times and in different cultures. They suggest that schizophrenia is most properly regarded as an hypothetical "construct", with behavioural referents which can be observed and with considerable explanatory power, but which itself is not capable of direct observation. In general, it has been shown that American psychiatrists

9

have tended to use a much wider construct than their European counterparts (Cooper *et al.*, 1972). Thus, many patients whom American psychiatric professionals might regard as schizophrenic, European workers would regard as suffering from an affective or personality disorder. This is important to bear in mind when considering cross-cultural comparisons of the evidence, particularly regarding treatment outcome.

Despite differing interpretations of the construct of schizophrenia, there are still some features that are generally regarded as characteristic. After Leff (1982) we may divide these into two broad groups: *Positive* and *Negative*. The positive features may be seen as behavioural "excesses": they include disorders of thought (delusions); disorders of perception (hallucinations); mannerisms and posturing; and inappropriate or incongruous affect. The disorders of thought and perception are often known as "first-rank" symptoms to denote their diagnostic significance. Thought disorder is also not a symptom which can be directly observed, but it can be inferred from the form or the content of the patient's speech. This may contain new words (neologisms) or be constructed in such a way as to lack the normal redundancies and interconnections of conversational speech. In addition, the speech content itself may be bizarre containing palpably false beliefs, such as "they put a computer in my head and now it tells me when to lift my feet up and down"; or strange experiences, e.g. "thoughts come into my mind from people on the television". At a psychological level it has been suggested that some of these cognitive disorders reflect a breakdown of the "filters" that normally operate to select and process information (McGhie and Chapman, 1961). Hence, schizophrenics seem to have difficulties with concentrating and focusing their attention and are highly susceptible to distraction on tasks requiring higher-order cognitive processing (Oltmanns and Neale, 1982). At a social level it is clear that these kinds of problems are likely to give rise to difficulties in initiating and maintaining social interactions.

The negative features of schizophrenia may be seen more as behavioural "deficits": they include lack of emotional response; lack of energy and motivation; and social withdrawal. This negative syndrome is sometimes known as a "defect state" and was once thought to be most prominent in patients who had lived in dull and unstimulating social environments such as the "back" wards of long-stay psychiatric hospitals. Studies of the treatment of acute and chronic schizophrenic states suggest that while the positive symptoms are generally susceptible to neuroleptic medication, these negative features are much more sensitive to levels of social and environmental stimulation (Wing, 1982a). However, more recent studies of schizophrenics in the community have demonstrated that this so-called "defect state" can also occur outside the hospital (Gibbons *et al.*, 1984; Lamb and Goertzel, 1971; Ryan, 1979). This suggests that levels of social functioning and withdrawal are dependent upon features which are, in fact, intrinsic to the schizophrenic condition but which may be exacerbated by certain kinds of environments. As Gordon Paul (1969) noted some years ago, "institutionalism" is not therefore the *cause* of schizophrenic deficits, it simply contributes to the interaction between the schizophrenic and a particular kind of environmental setting. Indeed, the environment can be too stimulating. Thus, just as low levels of stimulation and structured activities in hospital are associated with high levels of symptomatology and withdrawal (Wing and Brown, 1970) so excessive, or too rapid, social change can also lead to withdrawal and symptomatic relapse (Hemsley, 1978; Van Putten and May, 1976). These findings have obvious implications for the setting up of active treatment programmes like SST since they suggest that the successful management of schizophrenia depends upon maintaining a balance between over- and under-stimulation which in turn depends upon the precise characteristics of the setting, not its location (e.g. hospital vs. community).

Further examples of the responsiveness of schizophrenics to social change come from the studies of the impact of life-events. Brown and Birley (1968) reported that some 60% of the schizophrenic patients in their study had experienced an independent or possibly independent life event in the three-month period leading up to a relapse of their symptoms. This compared with only 15% for matched controls during a similar period. Brown and Birley also note that some of these upsetting events involved apparently positive changes, e.g. getting married, as well as negative ones such as losing a job, or the death of a close relative.

Some of the most important research relating schizophrenia and social factors comes from investigations of the effects of certain kinds of family interactions on patients with established schizophrenic disorders (Brown, Birley and Wing, 1972; Brown *et al.*, 1962; Vaughn and Leff, 1976a). These studies showed that patients discharged to marital or parental homes where the relatives are characterised as being high on "expressed emotion" (EE) were at a much greater risk of relapse than those returning to non-high EE homes (51% vs. 13%). The expressed emotion which seemed to be the most important was direct criticism or hostility. Over-protection and over-involvement were also important, but to a lesser degree. These studies also demonstrated that the effects of high EE relatives could be significantly ameliorated: (a) by ensuring that the patient received regular medication; and (b) by attempting to reduce the amount of face-to-face contact between the patient and their relatives to less than thirty-five hours per week (through engagement in day care, sheltered work, etc.). Brown and Leff's work therefore provides some important clues as to how the social environment of schizophrenic patients might be successfully managed and symptomatic relapse prevented or postponed.

The next important set of studies concerns the prognostic significance of social factors in relation to long-term outcome. For some time it has been realised that the outcome of a first schizophrenic episode can be highly variable (Watt, Katz and Shepherd, 1983; Wing, 1982b). Generally speaking, between 15 and 25% of schizophrenics are likely to make a more or less complete recovery and not suffer a further episode within a 5-year period. A further third may suffer several episodes with only minimal impairments. The remainder are likely to suffer a chronic relapsing course with varying degrees of impairment and no real return to normal functioning. About 10% are likely to remain continuously severely disabled. A number of factors have been shown to consistently predict outcome and these include age, sex, marital status, social class, type of onset (gradual vs. acute) and pattern of symptomatology (paranoid vs. non-paranoid). These factors are not independent and hence it is possible to have a "worst case" combination, i.e. a young, single, working-class, male, with an insidious onset and undifferentiated delusional symptoms. Some of the most careful research on prognosis and outcome has been conducted by Strauss and Carpenter and their colleagues as part of a World Health Organisation (WHO) study of schizophrenia (Strauss and Carpenter, 1972; 1974; 1977; Strauss, Klorman and Kokes, 1977). In this they explain this kind of "worst case" scenario by reference to the interaction of a number of different aspects of social adaptation viewed within a developmental context. Thus, a slow onset of symptoms is likely to disrupt social adaptation leading to difficulties in forming peer relationships and spilling over into problems at work. These difficulties are likely to be greatest the earlier the age of onset and to be most acute in the period of late adolescence and early adulthood when friends and careers are being formed. Women are also likely to be relatively protected from some of these stresses as the social expectations to initiate relationships and find careers outside the home are generally less. (Of course, if these social expectations change, then the prognostic significance of these factors for female schizophrenics may also change.) The outcome of schizophrenia is thus very much dependent upon the social expectations and opportunities offered by a particular culture and this is reflected in another WHO study which compared outcome across a number of different countries (WHO, 1979). Here it was found that schizophrenics seemed to have a better outcome in non-industrialised as opposed to industrialised countries. Cooper and Sartorius (1977) suggest that this might be due to cultural differences whereby non-industrialised countries offer more tolerant and supportive extended family networks and less specialised employment roles. We will return to some of these ideas later when we consider the management of schizophrenia from a social perspective.

Strauss and Carpenter's work also underlines the specificity of outcome "systems". Thus, although different areas of functioning, e.g. symptomatology, employment record, social contacts, and hospitalisation showed some degree of intercorrelation, nevertheless this was by no means perfect and there was a much stronger relationship over time *within* outcome systems than *between* them. So, if one wishes to predict the outcome of a schizophrenic with respect to some specific aspect of their functioning, one needs to examine their history of performance in that specific area and not some plausible, although not necessarily highly correlated, domain. This raises questions of specificity with regard to social functioning which have implications for both the assessment and treatment of social difficulties which we will also consider later.

Social functioning is therefore so much a part of schizophrenia that it is virtually impossible to discuss this disorder without reference to its social implications. However, the theoretical and causal mechanisms are clearly complex. There is certainly some kind of genetic component (Rainer, 1982) and probably an associated biochemical abnormality (Rodnight, 1982), however, schizophrenics are also highly sensitive to interpersonal stress and environmental change. Schizophrenia is thus most accurately characterised as a stress-related, biological disorder. In addition, while the part that social factors play in determining the course and outcome of the condition is fairly clear, the part that they play in its aetiology is still somewhat obscure. Because of the complicated interactions of biological, psychological and social factors the effects of interventions at any one level are likely to be unpredictable. This means that we must be realistic in what we can expect from an approach like SST. Even if it is effective in changing certain fundamental aspects of social adjustment, it will still not be a panacea. The best we can hope for is the demonstration of reliable relationships between particular interventions and specific aspects of social adjustment. So, let us now begin to consider some of the problems raised by the need to provide specific assessments of social functioning, before going on to consider the question of treatment and outcome.

The Assessment of Social Difficulty

Before beginning the assessment of social difficulties we require some kind of overall conceptual framework to organise and direct our thinking. As the social skills model has developed over the past few years we have come to recognise that social functioning is not itself one "thing", rather it is a set of "things" (variables) which are often fairly loosely related to one another. Although loosely related, these variables still correlate more highly with one another than they do with other unrelated variables, e.g. measures of intelligence. In this sense social functioning, like schizophrenia itself, is a "construct" (Shepherd, 1983a). It has empirical reality by virtue of its internal correlation structure and it has explanatory value simply by virtue of its convenience. However, it does not have a simple, tangible reality. Its existence is inferred, but cannot be directly observed by a single measurement operation. A construct view of social functioning thus emphasises the multidimensionality of social performance and opens up the possibility of "desynchrony" between different elements. It also gives us a conceptual framework within which it is possible to relate the "micro-level" behavioural skills of social interaction to the "macro-level" indices of social performance and adaptation.

What are the major elements which comprise this construct? There are three clear candidates: (1) *Behavioural*, e.g. eye contact and speech volume; (2) *Cognitive*, e.g. attributions of control and expectations regarding the behaviour of others; and (3) *Performance*, e.g. frequency, range and duration of social contacts. (We could add a fourth element here — psychophysiological responses — but this is beyond the scope of the present discussion.) A central implication of a "construct" view is that we should assess each of these elements separately. Thus, we cannot assume a necessary correspondence between self-reports (cognitions) and behaviour; or between "micro-level" behaviour in one setting and "macro-level" performance in another. The specificity of responses is widely accepted in most areas of psychology (Mischel, 1968) but in social skills we have seemed reluctant to abandon a "lump" theory and have appeared persistently disappointed when our assessments fail to "generalise" across widely different situations or response systems. Situational specificity and response specificity should be expected, not deplored. The implication is simply that we must assess each component separately. Considerations of situational specificity also dictate that this should be done in the criterion situation if possible, or at least some close approximation to it. With this in mind, let us consider first the assessment of behavioural skills.

A number of experimental studies have compared the micro-level behavioural skills of schizophrenic and non-schizophrenic patients. Some studies suggested that schizophrenics display abnormally low levels of gaze in conversations (Lefcourt *et al.*, 1967; Riemer, 1949, 1955; Rutter and Stephenson, 1972a, b). However, Rutter (1973) questioned the methodology of these studies and in a later series of experiments (Rutter, 1976, 1978) found no differences in gaze patterning between schizophrenics and non-schizophrenics. The crucial variable was the topic of conversation: with personal matters schizophrenic performance was impaired, with non-personal matters the difference disappeared. Rutter (1977a, b) found a similar pattern of results for the skill of "turn-taking" in conversation. Conversely, Lindsay (1984) reported less skilled performance from schizophrenic patients, compared with non-schizophrenic controls, on specific items of social interaction such as speech volume, tone, and clarity, amount spoken, facial expression, eye contact, and posture. Similarly Argyle, Alkema and Gilmour (1971) and Newman (1977) reported that schizophrenics are less sensitive than non-schizophrenics to nonverbal stimuli in social interaction.

The failure to find consistent behavioural differences between patient and non-patient groups is consistent with the failure to find clear behavioural differences between other socially skilled and unskilled individuals (Arkowitz et al., 1975; Glasgow and Arkowitz, 1975). There are often differences in *global* ratings of behavioural skills, but these are not necessarily reflected in differences between individual, "micro-level", behavioural elements. As Curran (1979) has put it rather dryly, "everyone seems to know what good and poor social skills are, but no one can define them adequately" (p. 321).

A possible explanation of this failure to find consistent behavioural differences between skilled and unskilled individuals is that social competence depends upon much more subtle parameters of interactional style such as the placement and timing of responses, rather than their absolute frequency (Fischetti, Curran and Wessberg, 1977; Peterson et al., 1981). Alternatively, it may depend upon a truly *interactive* skill e.g. the ability to respond to changes in the behaviour of the other person (Trower, 1980). In support of this Bryant et al. (1976) found that the strongest behavioural correlates with independently judged social skills in a sample of outpatients with neurotic problems were complex multi-behavioural constructs which they labelled "rewardingness" and "control". These involved "meshing" skills such as encouraging, reinforcing the other, showing interest and controlling the interaction in a flexible and sensitive way.

A second possible kind of explanation is that the relationship between behavioural skills and general social performance only applies at the extremes of the distributions, i.e. it is moderated by level. Thus, if a person makes no eye contact, or says nothing, then they will have predictable difficulties in social interaction. However, if they possess a minimum level of behavioural competence then there is no correlation — in the sense of a continuous relationship — between levels of behavioural skills and social success. It is not surprising then that several investigators have identified extreme behavioural skills deficits in clinical populations, particularly in terms of lack of speech (Gillingham, Griffiths and Care, 1977; Marzillier, 1975; Trower, 1980). But this does not imply that such deficits are characteristic across the *range* of social competence. Identifying "norms" of social behaviour may therefore be helpful in focusing attention on gross deficits (Lindsay, 1982; Minkin et al., 1976), but detailed quantification may be of doubtful value. This is certainly the case in schizophrenia where gross behavioural deficits may be apparent, but it is less clear just how useful a very detailed analysis would prove to be.

With regard to specific methodologies, role-play simulations have remained the dominant paradigm in clinical, as in non-clinical, samples (Bellack, 1983). This is despite the fact that considerable doubts have been expressed regarding the external validity of such assessments. Certainly, as Kern (1982) and others have shown, the more role-play assessments can approximate to the conditions of "free" social behaviour the greater their generality is likely to be. Unfortunately, we can then encounter problems of increasing validity, but decreasing reliability. The more the behaviour is free and uncontrolled, the more difficult it is to assess reliably. Shepherd (1977, 1978) attempted to develop a measure which could be used to assess behaviour in free social situations in and around a day hospital. Staff made the ratings retrospectively on the basis of the patients' performance in the previous week. This measure had the added advantage of being able to be used "non-reactively", i.e. without the subject's awareness. It possessed good reliability on total score, but the reliability of individual items was variable, dependent upon both specific item content and the raters used (Shepherd, 1984a). This suggests that for clinical purposes a two-stage assessment process may be necessary. First, a general screening procedure aimed at identifying specific behavioural problems through observations across a wide range of social situations. This might be achieved with a simple inventory or checklist with good content validity, but not necessarily high reliability. The second stage would then be to take the specific problems so identified and construct detailed measures for each of them, paying particular attention to inter-observer reliability. A form of target problem rating scales might be used. Such a strategy has been used in single case studies with clinical populations (Shepherd, 1984a) and seems to be feasible. Of course, it is a strategy which is more oriented towards the identification and monitoring of behavioural problems in individuals, rather than comparisons between groups.

Next, we can consider the assessment of cognitions in schizophrenia, e.g. beliefs, feelings, expectations, predictions about self and other's behaviour. As we have seen earlier, these occupy a central place in the phenomenology of the disorder, but their assessment poses particular problems. Firstly, their very uniqueness means that they are unlikely to be adequately covered by standard social anxiety questionnaires such as Watson and Friend's (1969) "Social Anxiety and Distress" scale, or Goldsmith and McFall's (1975) "Interpersonal Situation Inventory". There are obvious problems with regard to their content validity. Secondly, even if standard questionnaires did possess satisfactory content validity, they would still demand a considerable amount of sustained concentration and co-operation on the part of the respondent and this is unlikely to be

forthcoming from most schizophrenic patients. Thirdly, standard questionnaires may have inherent psychometric limitations. For example, they may
make assumptions about a "standard" interpretation of item content, the
equivalence of scaling between items, or the homogeneity of scaling
intervals. They may fail to control adequately for responses and position
bias, or achieve high test-retest reliability at the expense of low sensitivity
to change. These problems are well known and have been thoroughly
discussed by others (Bellack, 1983; Kendall, 1983). They lead one back to
some form of structured interview as the basis for gathering initial data,
followed by specific measures for particular cognitions or beliefs which are
then identified.

Richardson and Tasto's (1976) factor analytic study of standard
questionnaires, desensitisation hierarchies and therapists' reports provides
a useful summary of the seven major dimensions of common social fears
(criticism, assertiveness, confrontation, heterosexual closeness, intimacy,
conflict with parents, and interpersonal loss) which could form the basis of
such a structured interview. It could then be supplemented by additional
questions aimed at identifying other potentially important cognitive
dimensions, e.g. general attributional style (Rotter, 1966), social perception skills (Forgas, 1983), self-efficacy expectations (Moe and Zeiss, 1982)
and frequency of positive and negative self-statements (Glass *et al.*, 1982).
As Bernard (1981) has pointed out, clients — particularly schizophrenic
clients — may need considerable help in identifying and articulating the
sorts of cognitions that seem to be important in monitoring and controlling
their behaviour. Assessment of such cognitions may therefore require a
more active, actually *interactive*, method. This raises interesting questions
concerning the "reactivity" of such a procedure. Will it succeed in changing
the very cognitions it is attempting to assess? Only careful process studies
will provide an answer.

This still leaves the problem of how to quantify the specific cognitions
identified in the initial interview. Shepherd (1984b) has reviewed a number
of individually centred assessment techniques and recommends a Personal
Questionnaire (PQ) method after Shapiro (1961, 1970, 1975). The
advantage of PQ methods is that they provide an individually-centred
approach where the item content is formulated in the subjects' own words.
The internal reliability (consistency) of each item can also be checked at
the time it is administered. We can therefore be sure that the person is at
least communicating with the assessor in a logical and internally consistent
manner, although what they are communicating about may sometimes
remain difficult to understand. Phillips (1977) has shown that a whole
variety of Personal Questionnaires are possible with differing degrees of
complexity depending on the underlying scaling of the items, and Mulhall
(1976) has produced a rapid, easy-to-use booklet to guide in adminis-

tration. PQ methods therefore seem highly suitable for assessing the unique cognitions and beliefs of individual schizophrenic patients.

We also noted earlier how difficulties in overall social functioning are a common feature of schizophrenia and how these are important prognostically. Studies of schizophrenics' social networks both in hospital and in the community suggest that they tend to have a smaller range of contacts compared with non-schizophrenics, particularly in terms of the number and proportion of non-kin connections (Pattison, de Francisio and Wood, 1975; Sokolovsky, Cohen, Berger and Geiger, 1978; Tolsdorf, 1976). However, the research on the relationship between social support and symptomatic relapse in schizophrenia points increasingly towards the importance of *qualitative* aspects of the social network, as well as simple *quantitative* features. Hence, the studies mentioned earlier, demonstrating the part that over-involved and critical family interactions play in symptomatic relapse. Similarly, the work of Goldstein and Caton (1983) showing that levels of supportive understanding, and the frequency and intensity of interpersonal conflicts, predicted clinical functioning and rehospitalisation rates among schizophrenics discharged to the community much more strongly than the type of living arrangement (e.g. nuclear family vs. living in hotel), or its physical characteristics (e.g. overcrowding, adequacy of housing). Assessment of the social networks of schizophrenics must therefore include not only the number and range of their social contacts, but also their nature and quality. Standardised instruments such as those developed by Henderson and his colleagues (Henderson, Byrne and Duncan-Jones, 1981) may therefore be useful. Also, shortened versions of the Camberwell Family Interview designed to assess levels of expressed criticism and over-involvement (Vaughn and Leff, 1976b). This kind of data can only really be collected by careful interviewing of the patient and their relatives. One then needs to consider the network characteristics carefully before going on to decide whether qualitative or quantitative changes might be the most important targets for treatment.

Treatment Approaches

The heterogeneity of possible social difficulties in schizophrenic patients should now be clear and the individual pattern of possible behavioural, cognitive and performance difficulties is therefore diverse and various. As a direct example, Curran *et al.* (1980) surveyed a general psychiatric population, around a quarter of whom were schizophrenic, and showed that those labelled by therapists as "socially inadequate" differed considerably amongst themselves. Some showed flat affect, others were characterised by violent mood swings. Some were socially anxious, others were markedly over-assertive. One of the few characteristics they had in common was a poorer outcome in the two months following discharge. All this suggests that when attempting to treat social difficulties in clinical populations it may be necessary to tailor treatment interventions specifically to the needs of the individual patients concerned (Marzillier and Winter, 1978). A careful consideration of the pattern of behavioural, cognitive and performance difficulties may then lead to strikingly different treatment plans.

For example, the traditional kind of SST package (modelling, instructions, role-play, feedback, etc.) will be appropriate if there are clear "micro-level", behavioural deficits. Similarly, cognitively-oriented interventions may take priority if it is thought that the problems are not due to a lack of behavioural skills, but rather to cognitive distortions. Finally, if the problem is simply a restricted range of social contacts the client can be made aware of what opportunities already exist in their local community — e.g. clubs, churches, societies — and then be encouraged to use these through goal-setting or by using peer group support. Old friendships which have lapsed may thus be revived. On the other hand, if the problems are more to do with the quality of social support available, then this can be analysed and an intervention designed accordingly, e.g. to reduce areas of critical comment by relatives. At this stage the basis for deciding which kind of problem to tackle and what effects different interventions might have is bound to be largely intuitive. In practice, many of these decisions will be taken on purely pragmatic grounds. A problem will be selected for treatment simply because it is felt that it is likely to respond within a reasonable time period. This is not a bad criterion, but an analysis of the decision-making process in treatment and a clearer understanding of how problems relate to one another at different levels would certainly make the design of treatment programmes very much easier.

Are special modifications in technique necessary when dealing with schizophrenic patients? In the first place, their special learning difficulties must be acknowledged. It was noted earlier that the studies on information processing in schizophrenia tend to suggest the breakdown of normal mechanisms which control stimulus filtering and selective attention. This has led writers like Hemsley (1977, 1978) to stress the importance of slowing the rate of presentation of new information as much as possible and attempting to enhance the distinctiveness of both stimulus and response cues by labelling them clearly and repeatedly. It is also necessary to "chain" new skills slowly and use "overlearning" trials to strengthen the responses and retard extinction (Goldstein, Lopez and Greenleaf, 1979). Short training sessions with fairly brief inter-session intervals therefore seem generally more appropriate than longer sessions spaced widely apart. Durham (1983) recommends sessions of not longer than forty-five minutes and not less than once per week. With regard to the effectiveness of particular techniques, there is some evidence that modelling may be particularly useful with chronic patients (Eisler *et al.*, 1978) and that tangible rewards such as tokens are helpful in promoting generalisation (Lindsay, 1980). However, in general, an additive principle seems to operate: the more techniques that are used, the greater the effect is likely to be. Whether this stems from increased effectiveness, enhanced expectations of therapeutic gain, or simply more fortuitous matches between individuals and techniques is not clear.

With regard to the application of cognitive approaches, a different set of problems arise. The effectiveness of cognitive therapy approaches with clinical populations is still controversial and their application to problems of social functioning is even more uncertain. Recent studies with non-clinical samples have found no, or only very slight, evidence for a significant increment in effectiveness following the addition of a cognitive element to traditional, behaviourally-oriented skills training packages (Hammen *et al.*, 1980; Hatzenbuehler and Schroeder, 1982; Jacobs and Cochran, 1982; Kaplan, 1982). There are no similar studies available with schizophrenic samples. We are therefore faced with a dilemma: cognitive factors seem crucial to an understanding of how social difficulties arise, but as yet we have little evidence that we can do much to directly affect them. What does this imply about the status of cognitive versus behavioural treatments? Which kind of approach should we choose? Which will be most effective?

These kinds of questions rest on what is probably a spurious distinction between "cognitive" therapies on the one hand and "behavioural" therapies on the other. Both theoretically and practically this does not seem to be a very valid or useful distinction to draw. Cognitions cannot be changed directly, they can only be changed through behaviour. Therapists cannot, as Coyne (1982) has pointed out, "replace faulty self-statements in the same way a mechanic replaces old spark-plugs in an automobile" (p. 6). Nearly all treatments, including cognitive treatments, contain a mixture of both cognitive and behavioural elements. What is distinctive about cognitive therapies is their emphasis on the subjective interpretation and evaluation of behavioural change. Techniques such as those described by Bandura (1977) and Beck *et al.* (1979) therefore depend upon a gradual assimilation by underlying cognitive structures of carefully planned behavioural "tests". Hence, they are based on an assumption of *reciprocal* causality between cognitions and behaviour, rather than a simple, linear relationship. Now, whether such approaches will be effective in schizophrenia is another matter. Schizophrenic cognitions are, almost by definition, not likely to be amenable to reality testing procedures. Nevertheless, there is some preliminary evidence which suggests that cognitive-behavioural techniques may be effective for certain kinds of problems (Shepherd, 1984b) and it seems a reasonable line to pursue. Detailed studies of the rate and pattern of change in cognitive and behavioural variables during the process of treatment may then help to elucidate these mechanisms more clearly. For the moment, we can attempt to incorporate cognitive ideas into our treatment interventions on the basis that they might add to its effectiveness (on the "additive principle") and that they are unlikely to do much harm.

So, to a consideration of the attempts to change social performance directly. As indicated earlier, there have been relatively few examples of this approach. Most studies attempt to change behavioural skills and assume that improvements at this level will somehow "generalise" to improvements in actual social performance. These assumptions are maintained despite the fact that we know very clearly that the possession of behavioural skills is no guarantee that successful role performance will actually occur. Clients may have the skills, but successful role functioning depends upon the ability to use them according to the demands of a *specific* role situation (Kelvin, 1970). Since no two specific sets of role expectations are ever strictly identical — no two friends, lovers, parents or employers have exactly the same expectations — it will never be possible to equip a client with exactly the right combination of skills *a priori*. The best one can do is to provide what might be relevant role skills and then hope that the client can adapt them accordingly. Or, alternatively, provide them with access to the specific role setting first and then concentrate on helping them develop the skills that are required. It should not be surprising then that there is little empirical evidence that improving micro-level skills alone will affect clinically meaningful outcomes (Bellack, 1979). It is not a problem of generalisation across responses; it is a problem of quite separate treatment targets.

One of the few examples of attempts to change social performance directly in schizophrenia has been reported by Liberman *et al.* (1978). They used multiple baseline designs to evaluate the effectiveness of SST with three schizophrenic patients in day settings and in the community. Clients received thirty hours per week of training, with almost daily sessions. Outcome was evaluated using homework assignments based on specific interactions with care staff, relatives and the completion of a number of social and vocational tasks. Their results suggest that completion of homework assignments did not change until training was applied to that specific problem and that training was therefore the effective element in the increase in the rate of completed assignments. It is disappointing that not more studies have attempted to change "micro-level" social perform-ance directly in this way. This is an issue we will return to again later. For the moment let us now turn to the question of outcome.

The Outcome Evidence

There have been a number of reviews of the outcome of SST with psychiatric patients, including schizophrenics. Hersen and Bellack (1976) in an early paper concluded that skills training seemed "useful" in promoting improvements in interpersonal functioning. They noted that it had been applied to a variety of out-patient and in-patient psychiatric populations with positive results and that these studies included some psychotic patients whose florid symptomatology was controlled by medication. They also noted some evidence of response generalisation, with improvements in the target behaviours apparently leading to general reductions in psychopathology, e.g. anxiety, somatic preoccupations and self-concept. However, they considered these results as "preliminary findings" and argued for further controlled research to corroborate and extend them. They also noted the rather limited evidence then available for stimulus generalisation of treatment effects and the lack of demonstrable durability of behaviour change.

Marzillier (1978) concluded there was strong evidence that social skills training could improve behavioural skills in both in-patient (i.e. mainly psychotic) and out-patient (i.e. mainly neurotic) samples. However, the evidence for the differential effectiveness of skills training compared with control procedures was stronger for the in-patient studies. He suggests that this might be due to the fact that more of the out-patient studies used active alternative treatments (e.g. desensitisation, group psychotherapy) thus attenuating the differences.

There seemed to be some evidence of stimulus generalisation and durability of treatment effects, particularly in the out-patient studies. The failure to find strong evidence for generalisation and durability with the in-patient samples he attributes to a number of factors including: (i) brevity of training; (ii) artificiality of training settings; (iii) lack of opportunity for "real-life" practice; and (iv) an overly narrow model of social skills and its treatment. He also concedes that the evidence for generalisation in some of the out-patient studies was essentially based upon uncorroborated self-reports and might therefore be subject to bias. Finally, he notes some evidence of response generalisation to other clinical improvements, e.g. reductions in social anxiety. Again, these were only demonstrated in the out-patient studies and they were also evident in the control treatments suggesting non-specific effects.

Hersen (1979) begins his review of the modification of social skills deficits in psychiatric patients by noting the very strong relationship between premorbid social competence and outcome irrespective of diagnosis or the nature of intervening treatments. He goes on to discuss the assessment and treatment methods that have usually been employed and concludes that both the group and individual outcome studies show clear evidence of significant pre–post treatment effects. However, in his view, the maintenance of gains and generalisation to extrahospital settings is still "another question". He also notes a number of problems in the outcome literature including: (i) differences in the nature of the treatment interventions deployed; (ii) over-reliance on laboratory-based outcome measures, i.e. role-play tests; (iii) failure to programme or adequately evaluate generalisation and maintenance; and (iv) failure to consider questions of cost effectiveness.

Wallace *et al.*'s (1980) review is specifically concerned with social skills training with schizophrenic patients, although they note at the outset that due to weak diagnostic practices they cannot be sure that all the subjects involved were actually schizophrenic. However, they excluded non-psychiatric samples and those clearly diagnosed as non-schizophrenic, e.g. depressives, neurotics and personality disorders. Their review is also solely concerned with studies aimed at improving clinically relevant goals and they do not consider those which focused upon discrete behaviours or very limited classes of responses. They begin by examining the problems of defining social skills, the composition of treatment packages and the methods used to evaluate outcome and they suggest that concepts of social skills have tended to over-emphasise behaviour at the expense of cognitions. They also argue that treatment packages have tended to focus upon improving behavioural skills and that the techniques used and the outcome measures neglect the importance of subjects' internal states (thoughts, feelings, etc.). With regard to outcome, they conclude that the single-case studies show clear evidence for the effectiveness of training in changing the topographical elements of social skills. They also found some evidence of stimulus generalisation. As far as the group-based outcome data are concerned, again there was clear evidence of changes in the topographical features of social skills and self-reported reductions in social anxiety. However, when the effects of training were evaluated in situations dissimilar from the training sessions the results were "not particularly promising". They also note the difficulty of drawing inductive conclusions from studies with highly dissimilar treatment methods and outcome measures and list a number of other methodological shortcomings which include the lack of standardised diagnostic criteria and the failure to control for medication effects. They end by arguing for an expanded definition of social skills which includes a greater emphasis on cognitive components and on clinically meaningful outcomes.

The most comprehensive reviews of SST with adult psychiatric patients have been reported by Shepherd (1983b, 1984a). He examined a total of 52 studies which appeared between 1970 and 1980. Although nearly 1200 subjects were involved, he notes a general failure to describe sample characteristics adequately. There was very little information regarding subjects' premorbid social competence and their history of previous social adaptation (e.g. occupational record, history of social contacts, etc.). In terms of experimental design, the group-based studies, which constituted about two-thirds of the total, tended to use no-treatment controls, weak "placebos", or simply modified versions of skills training itself (e.g. instructions alone). Thus, there was very little evidence for the effectiveness of skills training compared with active and credible alternative treatments. Regarding the single-case studies, there seemed to be a preponderance of multiple-baseline designs with the inherent difficulties of identifying specific treatment effects. There also seemed a marked tendency for very short periods of baseline observation. The treatment packages themselves contained similar elements (modelling, instructions, role-play, and homework) however there was enormous variability in the number, organisation and spacing of sessions. Outcome measures were dominated by behavioural role-play tests and there was extensive use of various standard self-report questionnaires. When an attempt was made to assess stimulus generalisation this usually involved relatively weak measures, e.g. the transfer from trained to untrained scenes. In only about a quarter of the studies was there a genuine attempt to assess outcome by observing social behaviour in some free setting independent of treatment. In terms of outcome, the group-based studies showed that SST was nearly always superior to no-treatment or a placebo control. However, in the small number of studies where it was compared with active non-behavioural treatments, e.g. psychotherapy, a mixed picture emerged. Shepherd concludes that the evidence for the differential effectiveness of skills training against plausible alternative treatment approaches is weak. The data also showed some evidence for the influence of individual differences (e.g. anxiety) on outcome and strong evidence for an "additive" effect, e.g. the more treatment components the intervention contained, the greater its effect was likely to be. Although the methods for assessing stimulus generalisation were rather weak, where it was sought positive evidence was usually found. Follow-up data were provided in roughly half the studies and, although again the lengths of follow-up were highly variable, and there was a considerable amount of missing information, nevertheless the results tended to confirm that treatment effects were maintained. However, there was a strong tendency for differences between treatments to attenuate. The outcome evidence therefore seemed equivocal. SST did seem capable of producing changes in behaviour which would not otherwise have occurred. However many important unanswered questions remain.

Over the past few years these kinds of outcome studies with clinical samples have become much less common. Instead, attention has been switched to more detailed studies of the *nature* of social difficulties, with particular reference to the role of cognitive factors. Also, there has been the very strong upsurge of interest in evaluating the effects of cognitively-oriented treatment interventions which was noted earlier (see above).

Nevertheless, from these reviews a number of general points emerge. Firstly, a clear and detailed description of the subjects sampled is vital. We have already noted the possibility of cross-cultural differences with regard to diagnostic practices and obviously if the term "schizophrenia" is interpreted differently by different researchers then the external validity of any set of findings becomes questionable and reviews based upon an inductive appraisal of the evidence are frankly impossible. Of course, by itself, a diagnostic label actually conveys very little information regarding subject characteristics and again we have stressed repeatedly the heterogeneity of social difficulties that may be found in schizophrenic patients. Since these factors have considerable prognostic significance, in order to evaluate the impact of skills training, some attempt must be made to take account of them. Matching with regard to all aspects of previous social history is obviously not practical, but a simple description of the level of social adaptation (e.g. history of independent living, employment record, number of non kin friends seen in last month) would at least help researchers make more informed comparisons between their samples and might also permit some *post hoc* investigation of the relationship between such social background factors and treatment outcome.

Secondly, the problem of outcome measures remains unresolved. SST has clinical appeal not because it holds the promise of improving "topographical features of social skills" but because it holds the promise of improving fundamental aspects of social adjustment. Thus, outcome measures must begin to reflect a concern with social performance data, rather than simply with micro-level, behavioural skills. Valid assessments of behavioural skills (and cognitive ones) are not unimportant, but they should be seen as the means to an end, not the end in itself. In the future, we might hope to see more studies using the completion of "real life" homework assignments as the dependent measure. Also, studies aimed at assessing the effects of training on "real" social adaptation (e.g. the ability to initiate and sustain relationships, occupy some kind of work role, etc.). These might be evaluated by using social diary measures (Marzillier, Lambert and Kellet, 1976) or the social network assessments mentioned earlier.

A shift in the nature of outcome measurement also implies changes in the design of treatment interventions. Skills training approaches with schizophrenics have generally conformed to the traditional random controlled trial with pre–post assessment and a short-term treatment intervention. This paradigm may be suitable for the laboratory-based investigations, but clinical problems in clinical settings may require a different kind of design. For example, we know very little about the natural variability of social performance and repeated pre-test observations during an extended baseline period might yield some very interesting results. This applies particularly to single-case investigation, but might also be employed in non-equivalent control group designs as described by Cook and Campbell (1980). It is also clear that we know very little about the relative effectiveness of SST compared with other active treatments, behavioural or otherwise. What evidence is available suggests that at least with clinical populations, the difference between SST and other therapeutic alternatives may not be all that great (Shepherd, 1983b). Certainly, SST *per se* may add little to the effectiveness of an already active social milieu (Jackson and Marzillier, 1982; Marzillier and Jackson, 1983).

In addition to a better understanding of its comparative effectiveness (against alternative treatments or no treatment at all) we also need to examine much more carefully the organisation of interventions, their length, frequency, duration of sessions, etc. There is such variability in these basic parameters that it is often very difficult to compare results between studies. While it is not desirable to prevent therapists from applying their techniques in a flexible manner so as to suit the needs of individual clients, such basic questions of treatment delivery surely merit further investigation. "A little and often" seems most effective, but this has yet to be formally evaluated. With regard to the techniques themselves, if the emphasis is to be upon social performance in the "real" world then treatment techniques must reflect this by employing much more *in vivo* training. Scott, Himadi and Keane (1983) suggest from their review that conducting a significant proportion of treatment interventions in natural social settings was a major factor in contributing to successful stimulus generalisation. This shift in techniques would mean that formal training sessions might constitute only a relatively minor part of the overall intervention. They would simply serve to prepare and support the *in vivo* practice. This is a rather different perspective from the traditional therapeutic model.

A final area which the outcome literature highlights is that of the importance of therapist variables. Marholin and Touchette (1979) and Scott, Himadi and Keane (1983) both argue that to improve stimulus generalisation we should consider not only varying the *settings* of treatment, but also the *persons*. Establishing a good therapeutic relationship is still a prerequisite for effective treatment, but it can also be a handicap if the treatment effects become too bound up with one specific individual. Thus, in addition to shortening the length and increasing the frequency of formal treatment sessions, it is desirable to involve a wider range of therapists in addition to the regular team (e.g. students, para-professionals, volunteers, etc.). This is particularly important in relation to SST with schizophrenics since a knowledge of subcultural social norms is essential and most professional therapists come from very different social and cultural backgrounds from that of their clients.

With regard to the problems of generalisation, we have already argued that stimulus generalisation can only be improved by including as many stimulus elements as possible from everyday life into the treatment programme. Similarly, response generalisation may best be seen not as a problem of generalisation within a single response class, but as a problem of devising a number of treatments for a number of different treatment targets. Whether such individually centred packages will prove significantly more effective awaits further evaluation.

This still leaves us with the problem of maintenance. In general, treatment effects have been found to hold up reasonably well over time. However, once again our traditional ideas about outcome evaluation may need some modification. Thus, if a longer-term perspective and an emphasis on social performance are accepted, then the traditional "pre–post assessment and follow-up" design may not hold so much relevance. If we believe that social functioning is maintained by an adaptation of the person to their social environment, then what is the point of mounting a treatment intervention, stopping it, and returning some months later to "follow-up" its effects? This is simply an A–B–A design. A failure to find that treatment effects have been maintained would therefore be predicted: if they were maintained it would be more surprising. Of course, an underlying cognitive change might occur and this could support the behavioural change. This is a possibility, but as yet there have been few demonstrations that durable changes in underlying cognitions are easy to achieve. Alternatively, there may be environmental changes, perhaps in terms of the client's access to social settings and the responses of significant others encountered there. This seems a more likely alternative and suggests a rather different set of treatment goals and different methods of evaluation. If social functioning is a dynamic adaptation between the individual and their social context, then outcome research should stress the active long-term management of social disabilities, rather than its short-term treatment followed by "no-treatment" follow-up.

Future Directions

Finally, we may turn our attention to some of the broad directions that SST approaches may take with schizophrenic patients in the future. Firstly, it is clear that the theoretical and technical developments that are taking place elsewhere in the field are also likely to have an impact with this client group. Thus, the continued elaboration of cognitive perspectives (Trower,

1984) is bound to have considerable influence upon both theory and practice. However, it is important to remember Hugdahl's (1981) warning that cognitive perspectives will only yield more effective treatments if cognitive techniques can be found which are differentially more effective than the behavioural approaches they seek to replace. As we have seen, as far as schizophrenia is concerned, this does not yet seem the case. Our ability to theorise about the cognitive distortions underlying social difficulties in schizophrenia thus continues to outstrip our ability to change them. For the future, a combination of cognitive and behavioural techniques therefore seems likely to hold sway. Changes in social performance remain the primary focus, but an understanding of the possible influence of underlying cognitions may help inform the process of feedback and interpretation of these behavioural changes to the individual client.

At a technical level, we have hopefully made clear a wish to see a move away from the ubiquitous role-play test towards more naturalistic measures and measures which aim to tap social functioning in terms of everyday social performance. Regarding treatment methods, since we actually have very little evidence that SST is significantly superior to a number of plausible alternatives, the therapeutic potential of a wide range of treatment techniques might be explored, e.g. psychodrama and gestalt. Some purists may recoil from this kind of eclecticism, but it is worth remembering that what is novel in the social skills approach is not the methods themselves — they were well established in psychiatry fifty years ago — it is the emphasis on theory, research and evaluation. This can continue whatever the technical content of the methods. A technique which already looks promising is an adaptation of the "problem-solving" model (D'Zurilla and Goldfried, 1971; Platt and Spivack, 1972). Spratt (1984) has developed a variant of this approach specifically for use with long-term psychiatric patients and the preliminary results seem encouraging.

One of the most important developments for the future of SST approaches with schizophrenic patients is undoubtedly work with the patients' families. This is important not only as a way of circumventing some of the problems of generalisation but also because of the very direct effects that family interactions have been shown to have on schizophrenic symptomatology and functioning. There have already been four major studies in this area. Goldstein *et al.* (1978) used a brief, six-week, crisis-oriented family intervention and compared it with standard aftercare for a group of recently discharged first-admission schizophrenics. They also evaluated the effects of high- and low-dosage maintenance phenothiazine medication. During the treatment period, significantly fewer of the experimental group required admission and there was a marked effect of the intervention on reducing symptom ratings of social withdrawal. After six months the differences between experimental and control groups were much attenuated, but still favoured the experimental group. The results also confirmed the importance of premorbid social functioning in predicting outcome and showed an interaction between sex and premorbid status. The authors concluded that a combination of family therapy and medication was most effective.

Anderson, Hogarty and Reiss (1980) developed an elaborate "psychoeducational approach" which involved giving the families information, teaching them appropriate coping strategies, attempting to resolve chronic stresses and enhancing their social networks. A preliminary evaluation indicated that patients returning to families treated in this way showed a significant reduction in relapse rates compared with medication alone over a one year period, although there were still considerable residual social difficulties in many patients (Anderson, Hogarty and Reiss, 1981). Leff *et al.* (1982) reported on a family intervention designed specifically for schizophrenics being discharged to high expressed-emotion (EE) homes. This consisted of an educational programme, depot medication, a relatives' support group and individual family sessions. Over a nine-month period, none of the patients whose families had been included in the intervention relapsed, compared with half of the control who received depot medication only and routine out-patient care. There was a significant reduction in relatives' critical comments in three-quarters of the experimental group and a similar proportion showed a reduction in hours of face-to-face contact to below thirty-five hours per week. The same pattern of changes was not seen in the control group and in both groups expressed over-involvement proved difficult to change. The specificity of these results and the clear association between family functioning and the likelihood of relapse lead the authors to conclude that there is unequivocal support both for the effectiveness of the intervention and for the causal significance of high EE and face-to-face contact in determining levels of schizophrenic symptomatology.

The work of Falloon *et al.* (1982) is probably the most closely related to a social skills approach. They used medication together with information and a behavioural problem-solving approach to treat a group of schizophrenics mainly living in high EE homes. After nine months the experimental group showed significantly lower levels of symptomatology and significantly fewer relapses and less time in hospital compared with the control group who received only medication and individual counselling. A more detailed presentation of the results reveals that these improvements in symptomatic functioning apparently facilitated small improvements in participation in work and educational programmes, household tasks, and social performance outside the home (Falloon, Boyd and McGill, 1984). However, the authors also note that considerable residual deficits in social functioning still persisted in many patients and that this was associated with a general dearth of suitable rehabilitation facilities. Despite only slight gains in social performance, the relatives in the family intervention group reported substantially less distress concerning the patients' social deficits and both patients and families reported higher levels of overall satisfaction with the programme. The family intervention programme was also considerably cheaper than traditional individual care, mainly because it reduced the length of hospital admissions. The authors conclude that behavioural family therapy, combined with medication and effective case management, appears to represent a major advance in the community care of schizophrenia.

These studies suggest very strongly that it is possible to intervene effectively with the families of schizophrenic patients and that this can have very considerable benefits in terms of postponing, or even preventing, symptomatic relapse. However, a number of important points also emerge. Firstly, all these studies indicate that a combination of medication and a family intervention is likely to be the most successful. A family intervention is not likely to be effective on its own. Secondly, despite the effectiveness of these interventions with regard to improvements in symptomatology, considerable social deficits still persist in many patients and their successful long-term management depends upon what other social opportunities are available. Thirdly, although most of these interventions contain similar elements — medication, information, social problem-solving, case management — it is by no means clear which of these ingredients are the crucial ones. For example, how important is improved family problem-solving compared with reducing hours of face-to-face contact? Finally, all these studies underline the importance of an extended treatment intervention and the necessity of periodic "booster" sessions, perhaps with an indefinite time limit in some cases, to maintain functioning. This may be contrasted with the "hit-and-run" model which characterises many other treatment interventions.

The final area where ideas and techniques from SST may be applied in the care of schizophrenic patients lies in the design of services. This follows on from the family therapy approaches described above, since it is clear that the social difficulties of schizophrenics are often pervasive and often long-standing. It is also commonly the case that whatever improvements can be achieved through treatment itself are limited and may require considerable effort just to be maintained. Irrespective of whether the individual is cared for in hospital or in the community, SST principles may be used to help construct sheltered social environments which will promote and maintain positive functioning. Shepherd (1984c) has discussed this concept in terms of "Quality of Care" offered by long-term institutional settings. He argues that this is a complex construct which can be analysed at a number of different levels; physical facilities, resources, staff–client interaction, and organisation and management practices, etc. If a good quality of care is to be maintained then an understanding of how these different levels interact is necessary. For example, what are the minimum staffing levels necessary to provide individually-centred treatment plans? What kinds of organisation and management practices are likely to support (or inhibit) high levels of staff–client interaction? What factors affect staff morale and the maintenance of individually-centred programmes and staff–resident interaction? These are difficult questions, but an understanding of the organisational context of treatment interventions is a prerequisite for maintaining effective treatment interventions. It may then be possible to design sheltered environments such as hostels, workshops, day centres, which will maintain a permanent state of "treatment" and will continually promote, or at least maintain, adaptive behaviour. This may seem like a remote possibility, but if schizophrenics are to be managed more effectively in the community services than they were in the custodial institutions of the past, then these problems will have to be solved.

An alternative to the deployment of formal therapeutic techniques in long-term care settings is to build the services themselves around the principle of access to positively valued social roles. This principle is sometimes known as "normalisation" (Wolfensberger, 1972) and has already been highly influential in the development of services for mentally handicapped people (O'Brien and Tyne, 1981). For schizophrenics, it means attempting to ensure that they have opportunities to function in as normal a social context as possible. This means not restricting them in institutions unless absolutely necessary, but also providing a range of sheltered and open social opportunities in the community. We saw earlier how the long-term outcome of schizophrenia was dependent upon the "normalising" opportunities offered by different cultures. We have seen too that social skills have been plagued by the gap between skills and performance and that there is a sense in which skills training can *never* prepare an individual to deal with the specific demands of a particular role situation. So, perhaps we should simply concentrate upon giving clients access to specific social role opportunities, e.g. as a friend, a worker, a family member, and then help them identify and develop those skills that are necessary to cope with that particular situation. Instead of starting with the skills and somehow hoping that the client will be able to "generalise" them, perhaps we should start with the role setting and then work out which skills, and in which combination, might be important. This is like turning the social skills model upside-down. However by trying to start from the place where we hope to end up, eventually we might achieve more significant improvements in "real" social adaptation. The nature and availability of social roles for chronic patients would then become a central concern of social therapists and not just a peripheral interest. It is interesting to speculate what effects this kind of change might have.

These sorts of developments are very much in the future. For the present it is clear that SST is a useful and effective approach for dealing with some of the long-standing social difficulties associated with schizophrenia. The "social skills" approach also highlights the limitations of a "treatment" model. It gives us a clearer idea of what treatment can and can not be expected to achieve. This is important, since those problems that cannot be treated still have to be managed and lived with. SST also gives us some clues as to how this might be done — perhaps these are the most important findings of all.

References

Anderson, C. M., Hogarty, G. E. and Reiss, D. J. (1980) Family treatment of adult schizophrenic patients: A psychoeducational approach. *Schizophrenia Bulletin*, **6**, 490–505.

Anderson, C. M., Hogarty, G. E. and Reiss, D. J. (1981) The psychoeducational family treatment of schizophrenia. In: M. J. Goldstein (Ed.), *New developments in interventions with families of schizophrenics*. San Francisco: Jossey-Bass.

Argyle, M., Alkema, F. and Gilmour, R. (1971) The communication of friendly and hostile attitudes. *British Journal of Social and Clinical Psychology*, **10**, 386–401.

Arkowitz, H., Lichtenstein, E., McGovern, K. and Hines, P. (1975) The behavioral assessment of social competence in males. *Behavior Therapy*, **6**, 3–13.

Bandura, A. (1977) Self-efficacy: Toward a unifying theory of behavioral change. *Psychological Review*, **84**, 191–215.

Beck, A. T., Rush, A. J., Shaw, B. F. and Emery, G. (1979) *Cognitive therapy of depression*. New York: Guilford Press.

Bellack, A. S. (1979) Behavioral assessment of social skills. In: A. S. Bellack and M. Hersen (Eds.), *Research and practice in social skills training*. New York: Plenum Press.

Bellack, A. S. (1983) Recurrent problems in the behavioural assessment of social skill. *Behaviour Research and Therapy*, **21**, 29–41.

Bernard, M. E. (1981) Private thought in rational emotive psychotherapy. *Cognitive Therapy and Research*, **5**, 125–142.

Brown, G. W. and Birley, J. L. T. (1968) Crises and life changes and the onset of schizophrenia. *Journal of Health and Social Behaviour*, **9**, 203–214.

Brown, G. W., Birley, J. L. T. and Wing, J. K. (1972) Influence of family life on the course of schizophrenic disorders: A replication. *British Journal of Psychiatry*, **121**, 241–258.

Brown, G. W., Monck, E. M., Carstairs, G. M. and Wing, G. K. (1962) The influence of family life on the course of schizophrenic illness. *British Journal of Preventive and Social Medicine*, **16**, 55–68.

Bryant, B., Trower, P., Yardley, K., Urbieta, H. and Letemendia, F. J. J. (1976) A survey of social inadequacy among psychiatric out-patients. *Psychological Medicine*, **6**, 101–112.

Cook, T. D. and Campbell, D. T. (1980) *Quasi-experimentation — design & analysis issues for field settings*. Chicago: Rand McNally.

Cooper, J. E., Kendell, R. E., Gurland, B. J., Sharpe, L., Copeland, J. R. M. and Simon, R. (1972) *Psychiatric diagnosis in New York and London. Maudsley Monographs Number 20*. London: Oxford University Press.

Cooper, J. and Sartorius, N. (1977) Cultural and temporal variations in schizophrenia: A speculation on the importance of industrialization. *British Journal of Psychiatry*, **130**, 50–55.

Coyne, J. C. (1982) A critique of cognitions as causal entities with particular reference to depression. *Cognitive Therapy and Research*, **6**, 3–13.

Curran, J. (1979) Social skills: Methodological issues and future directions. In: A. S. Bellack and M. Hersen (Eds.), *Research and practice in social skills training*. New York: Plenum Press.

Curran, J. P., Miller, I. W., Zwick, W. R., Monti, P. M. and Stout, R. L. (1980) The socially inadequate patient: Incidence rate, demographical and clinical features, hospital and post-hospital functioning. *Journal of Consulting and Clinical Psychology*, **48**, 375–382.

Durham, R. C. (1983) Long-stay psychiatric patients in hospital. In: S. Spence and G. Shepherd (Eds.), *Developments in social skills training*. London: Academic Press.

D'Zurilla, T. J. and Goldfried, M. R. (1971) Problem solving and behavior modification. *Journal of Abnormal Psychology*, **78**, 107–126.

Eisler, R. M., Blanchard, E. B., Fitts, H. and Williams, J. G. (1978) Social skills training with and without modeling for schizophrenic and non-psychotic hospitalized psychiatric patients. *Behavior Modification*, **2**, 147–171.

Falloon, I. R. H., Boyd, J. L. and McGill, C. W. (1984) *Family care of schizophrenia*. New York: Guilford Press.

Falloon, I. R. H., Boyd, J. L., McGill, C. W., Razani, J., Moss, H. B. and Gilderman, A. M. (1982) Family management in the prevention of exacerbations of schizophrenia. *New England Journal of Medicine*, **306**, 1437–1440.

Fischetti, M., Curran, J. P. and Wessberg, H. W. (1977) Sense of timing: A skill deficit in heterosexual socially anxious males. *Behavior Modification*, **1**, 179–194.

Forgas, J. P. (1983) Social skills and the perception of interaction episodes. *British Journal of Clinical Psychology*, **22**, 195–207.

Glasgow, R. E. and Arkowitz, H. (1975) The behavioral assessment of male and female social competence in dyadic heterosexual interactions. *Behaviour Therapy*, **6**, 488–498.

Glass, C. R., Merluzzi, T. V., Biever, J. L. and Larsen, K. H. (1982) Cognitive assessment of social anxiety: Development and validation of a self-statement questionnaire. *Cognitive Therapy and Research*, **6**, 37–55.

Gibbons, J. S., Horn, S. H., Powell, J. M. and Gibbons, J. L. (1984) Schizophrenic patients and their families: A survey in a psychiatric service based on a DGH unit. *British Journal of Psychiatry*, **144**, 70–77.

Gillingham, P. R., Griffiths, R. D. P. and Care, D. (1977) Direct assessment of social behaviour from videotape recordings. *British Journal of Social and Clinical Psychology*, **16**, 181–187.

Goldsmith, J. B. and McFall, R. M. (1975) Development and evaluation of an interpersonal skill — training program for psychiatric in-patients. *Journal of Abnormal Psychology*, **84**, 51–58.

Goldstein, A. P., Lopez, M. and Greenleaf, D. O. (1979) Introduction. In: A. P. Goldstein and F. H. Kanfer (Eds.), *Maximising treatment gains*. New York: Academic Press.

Goldstein, A. P., Sprafkin, R. P. and Gershaw, N. J. (1976) *Skill training for community living: Applying structural learning therapy*. New York: Pergamon Press.

Goldstein, J. M. and Caton, C. L. M. (1983) The effects of the community environment on chronic psychiatric patients. *Psychological Medicine*, **13**, 193–199.

Goldstein, M. J., Rodnick, E. H., Evans, J. R., May, P. R. A. and Steinberg, M. R. (1978) Drug and family therapy in the aftercare of acute schizophrenics. *Archives of General Psychiatry*, **35**, 1169–1177.

Hammen, C. L., Jacobs, M., Mayol, A.. and Cochran, S. D. (1980) Dysfunctional cognitions and the effectiveness of skills and cognitive-behavioural assertion training. *Journal of Consulting and Clinical Psychology*, **48**, 685–695.

Hatzenbuehler, L. and Schroeder, H. E. (1982) Assertiveness training with outpatients: The effectiveness of skill and cognitive procedures. *Behavioural Psychotherapy*, **10**, 234–252.

Hemsley, D. R. (1977) What have cognitive deficits to do with schizophrenic symptoms? *British Journal of Psychiatry*, **130**, 167–173.

Hemsley, D. R. (1978) Limitations of operant procedures in the modification of schizophrenic functioning: The possible relevance of studies of cognitive disturbance. *Behaviour Analysis and Modification*, **2**, 165–173.

Henderson, S., Byrne, D. G. and Duncan-Jones, P. (1981) *Neurosis and the social environment*. Sydney: Academic Press.

Hersen, M. (1979) Modification of skill deficits in psychiatric patients. In: A. S. Bellack and M. Hersen (Eds.), *Research and practice in social skills training*. New York: Plenum Press.

Hersen, M. and Bellack, A. S. (1976) Social skills training for chronic psychiatric patients: Rationale, research findings and future directions. *Comprehensive Psychiatry*, **17**, 559–580.

Hugdahl, K. (1981) The Three-Systems-Model of fear and emotion — a critical examination. *Behaviour Research and Therapy*, **19**, 75–85.

Jackson, M. F. and Marzillier, J. S. (1982) The Youth Club Project: A community-based intervention for shy adolescents. *Behavioural Psychotherapy*, **10**, 87–100.

Jacobs, M. K. and Cochran, S. D. (1982) The effects of cognitive restructuring on assertive behaviour. *Cognitive Therapy and Research*, **6**, 63–76.

Kaplan, D. A. (1982) Behavioral, cognitive, and behavioral-cognitive approaches to group assertion training. *Cognitive Therapy and Research*, **6**, 301–314.

Kelvin, P. (1970) *The bases of social behaviour*. London: Holt, Rinehart & Winston.

Kendall, P. C. (1983) Methodology and cognitive-behavioural assessment. *Behavioural Psychotherapy*, **11**, 285–301.

Kern, J. M. (1982) The comparative external and concurrent validity of three role-plays for assessing heterosocial performance. *Behavior Therapy*, **13**, 666–680.

Lamb, H. R. and Goertzel, V. (1971) Discharged mental patients — are they really in the community? *Archives of General Psychiatry*, **24**, 29–34.

Lefcourt, H. M., Rotenberg, F., Buckspan, B. and Skefly, R. A. (1967) Visual interaction and performance of process and reactive schizophrenics as a function of examiner's sex. *Journal of Personality*, **35**, 535–546.

Leff, J. (1982) Chronic syndromes of schizophrenia. In: J. K. Wing and L. Wing (Eds.), *Handbook of psychiatry: Vol. 3. Psychoses of uncertain aetiology*. Cambridge: Cambridge University Press.

Leff, J., Kuipers, L., Berkowitz, R., Eberlein-Vries, R. and Sturgeon, D. (1982) A controlled trial of social intervention in the families of schizophrenic patients. *British Journal of Psychiatry*, **141**, 121–134.

Liberman, R. P., Lillie, F., Falloon, I. R. H., Vaughn, C. E., Harpin, E., Leff, J., Hutchinson, W., Ryan, P. and Stoute, M. (1978) *Social skills training for schizophrenic patients and their families*. Unpublished manuscript, Clinical Research Center, Box A, Camarillo, California.

Lindsay, W. R. (1980) The training and generalisation of conversation behaviours in psychiatric in-patients: A controlled study employing multiple measures across settings. *British Journal of Social and Clinical Psychology*, **19**, 85–98.

Lindsay, W. R. (1982) Some normative goals for conversation training. *Behavioural Psychotherapy*, **10**, 253–272.

Lindsay, W. R. (1984) A comparison between schizophrenic patients and non-patient matched controls on several aspects of social skill under three conditions of labelling. *American Journal of Psychiatry*, **142**, 1233–1235.

Marholin, D. and Touchette, P. E. (1979) The role of stimulus control and response consequences. In: A. P. Goldstein and F. H. Kanfer (Eds.), *Maximising treatment gains*. New York: Academic Press.

Marzillier, J. S. (1975) *Systematic desensitisation and social skills training in the treatment of social inadequacy*. Unpublished doctoral dissertation. London University: Institute of Psychiatry.

Marzillier, J. (1978) Outcome studies of skill training: A Review. In: P. Trower, B. Bryant and M. Argyle (Eds.), *Social skills and mental health*. London: Methuen.

Marzillier, J. S. and Jackson, M. F. (1983) An investigation of the treatment of adolescent social difficulty in a community-based setting. *Behavioural Psychotherapy*, **11**, 302–319.

Marzillier, J. S., Lambert, J. C. and Kellett, J. (1976) A controlled evaluation of systematic desensitisation and social skills training for chronically inadequate psychiatric patients. *Behaviour Research and Therapy*, **14**, 225–239.

Marzillier, J. S. and Winter, K. (1978) Success and failure in social skills training: Individual differences. *Behaviour Research and Therapy*, **16**, 67–84.

McGhie, A. and Chapman, J. (1961) Disorders of attention and perception in early schizophrenia. *British Journal of Medical Psychology*, **84**, 103–116.

Minkin, N., Braukman, C. J., Minkin, B. L., Timbers, G. D., Timbers, B. J., Fixsen, D. L., Phillips, E. L. and Wolf, M. M. (1976) The social validation and training of conversational skills. *Journal of Behavior Analysis*, **9**, 127–139.

Mischel, W. (1968) *Personality and assessment.* New York: Wiley.

Moe, K. O. and Zeiss, A. M. (1982) Measuring self-efficacy expectations for social skills: A methodological inquiry. *Cognitive Therapy & Research*, **6**, 191–205.

Mulhall, D. J. (1976) Systematic self-assessment by P.Q.R.S.T. (Personal Questionnaire Rapid Scaling Technique). *Psychological Medicine*, **6**, 591–597.

Neale, J. M. and Oltmanns, T. F. (1980) *Schizophrenia.* New York: Wiley.

Newman E. H. (1977) Resolution of inconsistent attitude communications in normal and schizophrenic subjects. *Journal of Abnormal Psychology*, **86**, 41–46.

O'Brien, J. and Tyne, A. (1981) *The principle of normalisation: A foundation for effective services.* London: Campaign for Mental Health.

Oltmanns, T. F. and Neale, J. M. (1982) Psychological deficits in schizophrenia. In: J. K. Wing and L. Wing (Eds.), *Handbook of psychiatry: Vol. 3. Psychoses of uncertain aetiology.* Cambridge: Cambridge University Press.

Pattison, E. M., de Francisio, D. and Wood, P. A. (1975) A psychological kinship model for family therapy. *American Journal of Psychiatry*, **32**, 1246–1251.

Paul, G. L. (1969) Chronic mental patient: Current status — future directions. *Psychological Bulletin*, **71**, 81–94.

Peterson, J., Fischetti, M., Curran, J. P. and Arland, S. (1981) Sense of timing: A skill deficit in heterosocially anxious women. *Behavior Therapy*, 12, 195–201.

Phillips, J. P. N. (1977) Generalised personal questionnaire techniques. In: P. Slater (Ed.), *The measurement of intrapersonal space by grid techniques, Volume II.* Chichester: Wiley.

Platt, J. J. and Spivack, G. (1972) Problem-solving thinking of psychiatric patients. *Journal of Consulting and Clinical Psychology*, **39**, 148–151.

Rainer, J. D. (1982) Genetics of schizophrenia. In: J. K. Wing and L. Wing (Eds.), *Handbook of psychiatry: Volume 3. Psychoses of uncertain aetiology.* Cambridge: Cambridge University Press.

Riemer, M. D. (1949) The averted gaze. *Psychiatry Quarterly*, **23**, 108–115.

Riemer, M. D. (1955) Abnormalities of gaze — a classification. *Psychiatry Quarterly*, **29**, 659–672.

Richardson, P. C. and Tasto, D. L. (1976) Development and factor analysis of a social anxiety inventory. *Behavior Therapy*, **7**, 453–462.

Rodnight, R. (1982) Biochemistry and pathology of schizophrenia. In: J. K. Wing and L. Wing (Eds.), *Handbook of psychiatry: Volume 3. Psychoses of uncertain aetiology.* Cambridge: Cambridge University Press.

Rotter, J. B. (1966) Generalised expectancies for internal vs. external control of reinforcement. *Psychological Monographs*, **80**, Whole No. 609.

Rutter, D. R. (1973) Visual interaction in psychiatric patients: A review. *British Journal of Psychiatry*, **123**, 193–202.

Rutter, D. R. (1976) Visual interaction in recently admitted and chronic long-stay schizophrenic patients. *British Journal of Social and Clinical Psychology*, **15**, 295–303.

Rutter, D. R. (1977a) Speech patterning in recently admitted and chronic long-stay schizophrenic patients. *British Journal of Social and Clinical Psychology*, **16**, 47–55.

Rutter, D. R. (1977b) Visual interaction and speech patterning in remitted and acute schizophrenic patients. *British Journal of Social and Clinical Psychology*, **16**, 357–361.

Rutter, D. R. (1978) Visual interaction in schizophrenic patients: The timing of looks. *British Journal of Social and Clinical Psychology*, **17**, 281–282.

Rutter, D. R. and Stephenson, G. M. (1972a) Visual interaction in a group of schizophrenic and depressive patients. *British Journal of Social and Clinical Psychology*, **11**, 57–65.

Rutter, D. R. and Stephenson, G. M. (1972b) Visual interaction in a group of schizophrenic and depressive patients: A follow-up study. *British Journal of Social and Clinical Psychology*, **11**, 410–411.

Ryan, P. (1979) Residential care for the mentally disabled. In: J. K. Wing and R. Olsen (Eds.), *Community care for the mentally disabled*. Oxford: Oxford University Press.

Scott, R. R., Himadi, W. and Keane, T. M. (1983) A review of generalisation in social skills training: Suggestions for future research. In: M. Hersen, R. M. Eisler and P. M. Miller (Eds.), *Progress in behaviour modification: Volume 15*. New York: Academic Press.

Shapiro, M. B. (1961) The single case in fundamental research. *British Journal of Medical Psychology*, **34**, 285–298.

Shapiro, M. B. (1970) Intensive assessment of the single case. In: P. Mittler (Ed.), *The psychological assessment of mental and physical handicaps*. London: Methuen.

Shapiro, M. B. (1975) *The assessment of self-reported dysfunctions: A manual with its rationale and applications. Parts I & II*. Unpublished manuscript. London University: Institute of Psychiatry.

Shepherd, G. (1977) Social skills training: The generalisation problem. *Behavior Therapy*, **8**, 1008–1009.

Shepherd, G. (1978) Social skills training: The generalisation problem — some further data. *Behaviour Research and Therapy*, **16**, 287–288.

Shepherd, G. (1983a) Introduction. In: S. Spence and G. Shepherd (Eds.), *Developments in social skills training*. London: Academic Press.

Shepherd, G. (1983b) Social skills training with adults. In: S. Spence and G. Shepherd (Eds.), *Developments in social skills training*. London: Academic Press.

Shepherd, G. (1984a) *Studies in the assessment and treatment of social difficulties in long-term psychiatric patients*. Unpublished doctoral dissertation. London University: Institute of Psychiatry.

Shepherd, G. (1984b) Assessment of cognitions in social skills training. In: P. Trower (Ed.), *Radical approaches to social skills training*, London: Croom Helm.

Shepherd, G. (1984c) *Institutional care and rehabilitation*. London: Longmans.

Sokolovsky, J., Cohen, C., Berger, D. and Geiger, J. (1978) Personal networks of ex-mental patients in a Manhattan SRO Hotel. *Human Organisations*, **37**, 5–18.

Spratt, G. (1984) *A skills training approach to facilitate social behaviours in long-term psychiatric patients: Models, principles and techniques*. Unpublished manuscript. Prestwich Hospital, Manchester, England.

Strauss, J. S. and Carpenter, W. T. (1972) The prediction of outcome in schizophrenia: I. Characteristics of outcome. *Archives of General Psychiatry*, **27**, 739–746.

Strauss, J. S. and Carpenter, W. T. (1974) The prediction of outcome in schizophrenia: II. Relationships between predictor and outcome variables. *Archives of General Psychiatry*, **31**, 37–42.

Strauss, J. S. and Carpenter, W. T. (1977) Prediction of outcome in schizophrenia: III. Five-year outcome and its predictors. *Archives of General Psychiatry*, **34**, 159–163.

Strauss, J. S., Klorman, R. and Kokes, R. F. (1977) Premorbid adjustment in schizophrenia: Part V: The implications of findings for understanding research and application. *Schizophrenia Bulletin*, **3**, 240–244.

Tolsdorf, C. C. (1976) Social networks, support and coping: An exploratory study. *Family Processes*, **15**, 407–418.

Trower, P. (1980) Situational analysis of the components and processes of the behavior of socially skilled and unskilled patients. *Journal of Consulting and Clinical Psychology*, **48**, 327–339.

Trower, P. (Ed.) (1984) *Radical approaches to social skills training*. London: Croom Helm.

Van Putten, T. and May, P. R. A. (1976) Milieu therapy of the schizophrenias. In: L. J. West and D. E. Flinn (Eds.), *Treatment of schizophrenia: Progress and prospects*. New York: Grune & Stratton.

Vaughn, C. E. and Leff, J. P. (1976a) The influence of family and social factors on the course of psychiatric illness. *British Journal of Psychiatry*, **129**, 125–138.

Vaughn, C. E. and Leff, J. P. (1976b) The measurement of expressed emotion in families of psychiatric patients. *British Journal of Social and Clinical Psychology*, **15**, 157–165.

Wallace, C. J., Nelson, C. J., Liberman, R. P., Aitchison, R. A., Lukoff, D., Elder, J. P. and

Ferris, C. (1980) A review and critique of social skills training with schizophrenic patients. *Schizophrenia Bulletin*, **6**, 42–62.

Watson, D. and Friend, R. (1969) Measurement of social-evaluative anxiety. *Journal of Consulting and Clinical Psychology*, **33**, 663–670.

Watt, D. C., Katz, K. and Shepherd, M. (1983) The natural history of schizophrenia: A five-year prospective follow-up of a representative sample of schizophrenics by means of a standardised clinical and social assessment. *Psychological Medicine*, **13**, 663–670.

Wing, J. K. (1982a) Psychosocial factors influencing the onset and course of schizophrenia. In: J. K. Wing and L. Wing (Eds.), *Handbook of Psychiatry: Volume 3. Psychoses of uncertain aetiology*. Cambridge: Cambridge University Press.

Wing, J. K. (1982b) Course and prognosis of schizophrenia. In: J. K. Wing and L. Wing (Eds.), *Handbook of Psychiatry: Volume 3. Psychoses of uncertain aetiology*. Cambridge: Cambridge University Press.

Wing, J. K. and Brown, G. W. (1970) *Institutionalism and schizophrenia: A comparative study of three mental hospitals, 1960–1968*. Cambridge: Cambridge University Press.

Wolfensberger, W. (1972) *The principle of normalisation in human services*. Toronto: National Institute on Mental Retardation.

World Health Organisation (1979) *Schizophrenia: An international follow-up study*. Chichester: Wiley.

2

Social Skills Training and Social Anxiety

PETER TROWER

Introduction

Social anxiety is something of an enigma among psychological problems. Firstly, in the clinical literature it constitutes a tiny proportion of psychiatric problems, yet other research shows it to be a problem of endemic proportions (Pilkonis and Zimbardo, 1979). Secondly, it is one of the least researched of the phobic disorders (Barlow and Wolfe, 1981; Emmelkamp, 1982) yet social anxiety is a commonly researched variable in more mainstream, particularly social, psychology (e.g. Schlenker and Leary, 1982). Thirdly, there is considerable uncertainty as to the definition of social anxiety, unless one takes a somewhat arbitrary "clinical" definition, which excludes much of the essential phenomena.

At the present time, social psychology has as much, if not more, to offer than the clinical literature, given these and many other considerations. Firstly, social psychology is principally concerned with social behaviour, with problems which characterise all forms of social anxiety by definition. Secondly, social psychology has provided some of the most influential models of social skills in general (e.g. Argyle and Kendon, 1967) and SST in particular (Trower, Bryant and Argyle, 1978) and continues to provide advanced models which give a lead to future developments (Carver and Scheier, 1984; Lazarus and Folkman, 1984; Schlenker and Leary, 1982). For these and other reasons, this review of social anxiety — its definition, assessment, characteristics and treatment — will draw upon a wide literature, in particular social, as well as clinical and behavioural, literature and use a broad concept of social anxiety, given the state of the art. The review will also draw upon the assertiveness literature, in view of the importance of social anxiety in inhibiting assertive behaviour (e.g. Alden and Safran, 1978).

Definition of Social Anxiety

We are immediately confronted with a lack of agreement about the

39

definition of the problem. Reference is made to social anxiety, shyness, dating anxiety, heterosexual-social anxiety, stage fright, speech anxiety, communication apprehension, reticence, and embarrassment (Schlenker and Leary, 1982). However, researchers might do well to be wary of embracing the apparent simplicity of a clinical definition as in DSM III, (American Psychiatric Association, 1980), given the present lack of understanding of the problem.

A first step is to decide what components to include under the definition of social anxiety. Most definitions of anxiety-based problems include not only the subjective experience of anxiety, but also cognitive, physiological and behavioural components — hence the 3-systems model (Rachman, 1978). This is no less true of social anxiety, although we may make a simpler two-fold distinction into internal components (cognitions, the fear experience, and physiological arousal) and external (behavioural and situational variables), bearing in mind that these are not independent but integrally related.

A second step is to decide upon the essential characteristics of social anxiety. The principal commonality among the terms listed above involves the perception, evaluation and performance of social behaviour. A possible loose definition might be: fear of negative evaluation of social performance in real or imagined social situations.

A third step is to decide upon the principal subtypes of social anxiety. There is some consensus in the literature that the term "social anxiety" itself be used as a generic term and not as one of the subtypes.

What are the principal subtypes of social anxiety? Clinical definitions tend to refer to specific social fears, and specific fears are traditionally termed phobias. The term "social phobia" then might be defined as the fear of performing a specific, "unskilled" behaviour, such as shaking, blushing, fainting, or urinating, in a public place (Shaw 1976), the emphasis here being on the specificity of the skill deficit, though specific situations are also implied (Trower, in press).

If social phobia refers to specific social fear, and the clinical i.e. more severe, end of the spectrum, we also need a term to refer to more diffuse forms of social anxiety, of the type more common in nonclinical populations. The term "shyness" has now become commonly used in research into this broader spectrum of social fears. Jones and Briggs (1984) suggest that the experience of "shyness" involves attention to the self in social situations and results in timid, inappropriate, overt behaviours (i.e. poor skills) and internal distress (e.g. anxiety, self-deprecating thoughts etc.). Jones, Briggs and Smith (1985) find no evidence for justifying different subtypes of shyness, though Crozier (1982) reasonably argues that this is open to further empirical question, and offers, as likely candidates, shyness, shame and embarrassment.

There are other important distinctions to be made which complicate the picture still further. The dimensions of anxiety and social skill interact to give us two subtypes: high anxious/high skill, and high anxious/low skill (Curran, 1977); and anxiety can be further subdivided, on a repression-sensitization dimension, to give us high anxiety/high repression versus high anxiety/low repression (Asendorpf and Scherer, in press), giving us a two-dimensional matrix and four subtypes (see Fig. 1). These distinctions cut across the social phobia *and* shyness subtypes, and may be functionally more useful, as research reviewed below shows.

S K I L L

	HIGH	LOW
HIGH	High skill High repression	Low skill High repression
LOW	High skill Low repression	Low skill Low repression

(left vertical label: R E P R E S S I O N)

FIG. 1. Four Sub-types of Social Anxiety.

Demographic and General Characteristics

Demographic information on clinical samples remains scanty. In an early study, Marks (1969), reporting on clinical social phobics, found that they constituted only 8% of the total monosymptomatic phobics referred in a decade. In stark contrast, Pilkonis and Zimbardo (1979), reporting on nonclinical shyness, found in several large-scale surveys that over 40% described themselves as shy and the majority reported this to be a major problem for them. Bryant and Trower (1974) found that 9% of a random sample of students reported great difficulty in, or tried to avoid, six common social situations. Preliminary findings in our current research suggests English students are if anything more shy than American students.

Research by Shaw (1976) shows social phobia to be a male problem, as is "social inadequacy" (Bryant *et al.*, 1976). In a social phobia group, 61% were male compared to only 13% in agoraphobia. Shaw also found social phobia has a particularly early onset — 60% had developed the problem by age twenty. Social phobics rated their parents as less caring and more over-protective than matched controls. Parents who are socially withdrawn and anxious tend to rear children who are similarly withdrawn and anxious (Filsinger and Lamke, 1983). Personal characteristics of the socially anxious are reported later.

A related body of research on "loneliness" shows this problem to be widespread and serious. Rook's (1984) review showed that lonely students had difficulty introducing themselves, participating in groups, enjoying themselves at parties, asserting themselves and taking social risks. These lonely people approached social encounters with cynicism and, mistrust, rated others negatively and expressed little desire for continued contact. They evaluated themselves negatively and expected others to reject them, and they were characteristically self-conscious.

Theories and Models of Social Anxiety

A broad distinction has been made between high anxiety/high skill and high anxiety/low skill. In the first case anxiety may be regarded as primary, causing disruption to social skills, whereas in the second, lack of skill is primary, giving rise to anxiety (Argyle, Trower and Bryant, 1974; Trower *et al.*, 1978). A number of models have evolved out of this distinction (Crozier, 1982; Curran, 1977; Schlenker and Leary, 1982).

The model in which lack of skill is primary is called the *skills deficit model*. It assumes that anxiety experienced in social situations is due to an inadequate or inappropriate repertoire of social skills. Behaviour of this kind produces negative social consequences, giving rise to present and anticipatory anxiety.

There are two models in which anxiety is primary. First is the *cognitive self-evaluation model*: this states that social anxiety results not from an objective skills deficit *per se*, but from *perceived* deficits which may or may not actually exist. Second is the *classical conditioning model*: this assumes that anxiety is conditioned when neutral stimuli become paired with aversive social consequences. A third model which embraces both anxiety and skills deficiency is the *personality trait approach*: here shyness is a trait distinguishable from all other traits.

These well-known models have been criticised and further conceptualisations offered. Probably the most comprehensive model of social anxiety from the social-psychological perspective is the *self-presentation approach* of Schlenker and Leary (1982). They argue that the four models described above can be reconceptualised as converging on the notion that social anxiety is generated when people are motivated to impress others but hold low impression-relevant outcome expectancies, i.e. they anticipate they will fail in effective self-presentation. In this cognitive model, anxiety is produced by the expectation that one will not accomplish one's self-presentational goal of impressing real or imagined audiences, and implies that skills deficits will only affect social anxiety to the extent that they lower the individual's expectations of success. In a series of propositions, Schlenker and Leary state that anxiety results from the interplay of a number of factors, including the discrepancy between audience reaction and personal standard, the importance of the standard, and whether or not individuals label themselves as "socially anxious".

These authors and others (Crozier, 1982; Trower, 1982) explain the process of social anxiety by drawing upon Carver's (1979) cybernetic model of self-attention processes. In brief, this describes a "matching-to-standard" process in which an individual assesses a deficient performance, makes a judgement that he or she cannot produce an adequate performance, and so withdraws. If withdrawal is impossible, the individual continuously re-examines and replays the problems, which in turn leads to various behavioural and cognitive strategies in an attempt to deal with it.

Similar processes are incorporated in Trower and Turland's (1984) feedback model, which proposes two linked systems — an appraisal system and a coping system — in either of which problems may occur which give rise to anxiety. Both Hartman (1983) and Crozier (1982) offer models which are essentially similar. Hartman describes the socially anxious as caught in a closed loop of self-centred "meta-cognition" — excessive self-attention. When self-awareness or "editing" becomes recursive in an interpersonal context, the individual is removed from the interactive process, resulting in anxiety and impaired social performance.

Assessment

There are literally dozens of assessment devices in the field of social skills/social anxiety, but quantity has outstripped quality in terms of reliability and validity as recent reviews have shown (Bellack, 1983; Trower, 1982). The importance of valid measures cannot be overestimated, since without them experimental evaluations of SST would be meaningless. No attempt will be made here to review comprehensively all the measures. The revision will be divided according to two main measures — self-report and behavioural.

Self-Report

Social anxiety questionnaires. Hersen and Bellack (1977) reviewed eight measures: *Social Avoidance and Distress Scale* and *Fear of Negative Evaluation Scale* (Watson and Friend, 1969), *S-R Inventory of Anxiousness* (Arkowitz *et al.*, 1975), the *Fear Survey Schedule* (Curran, 1975), the *Survey of Heterosexual Interactions* (Twentyman and McFall, 1975), the *Self Rating Form* (McGovern, Arkowitz and Gilmore, 1975), and various anxiety and skill thermometers. The majority of the measures had less than satisfactory psychometric properties (Bellack, 1979). The exceptions included the Fear of Negative Evaluation scale (FNE) and Social Avoidance and Distress scale (SAD) — two of the most widely used questionnaires. They were developed in parallel because, Watson and Friend argue, social anxiety consists of two components: (1) negative affect and discomfort in social situations (SAD), and (2) fear of receiving negative evaluations from others (FNE). Leary (1983a) points out that the SAD consists of two further dimensions — anxiety (subjectively experienced distress) and avoidance-sociability. Both scales have good psychometric properties. They both demonstrate high inter-item reliability (KR-20 = .94) and moderate test-retest reliability (r = .6 to .7 range). Evidence of validity, particularly external validity, is strong. The two scales have some common variance (.51).

Shyness questionnaires. More recently, Jones, Briggs and Smith (1985) assessed five "shyness" measures, including the SAD, and their own *Social Reticence Scale*. They gave the questionnaires to a sample of 1200 students and produced a comprehensive analysis of their norms and psychometric properties, including those shown in Table 1.

They found all the measures were highly intercorrelated (.70 to .86) but showed much lower correlations with other measures of social ability and social anxiety. In summary they reported measures to be valid, reliable and largely interchangeable.

Leary (1983b) provides a useful review of other shyness/social anxious-

TABLE 1. *Psychometric Properties of Five Shyness Questionnaires*

	Items	Mean	s.d.	Alpha
SRS	20	47.2	13.5	.92
MS	14	45.4	13.0	.87
SAD	28	6.6	5.8	.90
SS	11	25.9	7.7	.82
IA	15	39.1	10.6	.88

Note: SRS = Social Reticence Scale II (Jones, Briggs and Smith, 1985); MS = Morris Shyness Scale (Morris, 1984); SAD = Social Avoidance and Distress Scale (Watson and Friend, 1969); SS = Shyness Scale (Cheek and Buss, 1981); IA = Interpersonal Anxiousness Scale (Leary, 1983a).

ness questionnaires which are popular and have potential for future research.

Situation-specific questionnaires. A criticism of the above types of scales is that they are too global, and a host of scales have been developed which focus more on specific situations. Levenson and Gottman (1978) reported the development of a scale assessing the degree of discomfort and expected incompetence in two types of social situations (dating and assertive situations). The scale was found to have good test-retest reliability and internal consistency, was able to discriminate between client and normal populations, and reflected differential improvement following treatment intervention.

Bryant and Trower (1974) developed the *Social Situations Questionnaire*, consisting of 30 common social situations rated for social difficulty. The scale was found to have two main factors — "social difficulty" and "casual-intimate". In subsequent research the scale was found to have discriminant validity, reliability (Alpha = .82) and norms for psychiatric, as well as student samples were obtained (Trower, in press).

Richardson and Tasto (1976) developed a social anxiety scale, the *Social Anxiety Inventory* (SAI), which was designed to be both general and specific. Using factor analysis of a large item pool, they clustered situations into the following seven subtypes: (1) Disapproval or criticism; (2) Social assertiveness and visibility; (3) Confrontation and anger expression; (4) Heterosocial contact; (5) Intimacy and interpersonal warmth; (6) Conflict with or rejection by parents; (7) Interpersonal loss. The scale was tested and reported to be reliable and valid on various criteria and has proved popular in subsequent research.

Heimberg *et al.* (1980) tested the *Situation Questionnaire* (Rehm and Marston, 1968). They provide data showing good reliability, concurrent validity and external validity with a role-play test.

Assertiveness questionnaires. Beck and Heimberg (1983) provide a useful review of the norms, reliability and validity of nine commonly used assertiveness questionnaires. To summarise their findings briefly, they report that the following questionnaires had "not been exposed to sufficient validation efforts": *Wolpe–Lazarus Assertiveness Schedule* (Wolpe and Lazarus, 1966), the *Wolpe–Lazarus Schedule* (revised) (Hersen *et al.*, 1979), the *Assertion Questionnaire* (Callner and Ross, 1976), the *Adult Self-Expression Scale* (Gay, Hollandsworth and Galassi, 1975), and the *Assertion Inventory* (Gambrill and Richey, 1975). In contrast the *Conflict Resolution Inventory* (McFall and Lillesand, 1971), *College Self-Expression Scale* (Galassi, Galassi and Litz, 1974), and *Rathus Assertiveness Schedule* (Rathus, 1973) have received much more attention and "a base of validity information has been generated" (p. 472). The Conflict Resolution Inventory seems to fare best in all areas.

However, with the exception of the Rathus Assertiveness Schedule, the above self-report scales lack an adequate foundation of reliability data. According to Beck and Heimberg, there is an absence of extended test-retest and internal consistency information. Also, much more normative information is needed for all the scales.

Social skill questionnaires. Just as there was a move to make self-report questionnaires more specifically situational, so there have been other attempts to develop more behavioural self-report measures. One of the best known of these is the *Social Performance Survey Schedule* (Lowe and Cautela, 1978). It contains 50 positive and 50 negative descriptions of social behaviours whose frequency can be rated on a five-point Likert scale. Reported reliability tests are in the .8 to .9 range but the only test of validity reported by the authors is a modest correlation with the Social Avoidance and Distress Scale.

Cognitive questionnaires. Despite its neglect until relatively recently (Bellack, 1979) cognitive assessment is already a large and growing subject and beyond the scope of the present chapter. An excellent review is provided in Glass and Merluzzi (1981). Current opinion is that cognitive assessment is now an essential component in further research and practice, given the role of expectancies in social anxiety and social performance (e.g. Fiedler and Beach, 1978).

Combined questionnaires. Attempts have been made to combine some of the above components in a single measure. For example, Curran *et al.* (1980) report an instrument, based on Richardson and Tasto's Social Anxiety Inventory, which measures both skill and anxiety. Reliability was acceptable and factor structure promising, but at the time of reporting the instrument required validation.

In summary, there are encouraging improvements in the psychometric properties of questionnaires. It should be pointed out that high reliability of such tests is by no means necessary or even desirable in outcome studies, where change is the main focus of interest (Nicewander and Price, 1983).

Behavioural Assessment of Skill and Anxiety

A large proportion of existing behavioural assessment methods were originally developed for and on socially anxious and unassertive subjects, and then modified for other populations. However it has recently become clear that social-behavioural assessment is even more fraught with problems than questionnaire measurement (see Herbert, Volume 1). A selection of behavioural tests will be described and then some of these problems reviewed.

One type of role-play test which became the standard in American research may be termed *brief role-play*, mainly single-response, format (Kern, 1982). A prototype is the *Behavioral Role Playing Test* (McFall and Marston, 1970). Eighty scenes are presented with narration, in sequential order, a confederate gives a "prompt" and the subject expected to respond, the response being subsequently rated by blind raters for its skill or assertiveness. More popular and influential have been the *Behavioral Assertiveness Test* (BAT) (Eisler, Miller and Hersen, 1973) and the *Behavioral Assertiveness Test-Revised* (BAT-R) (Eisler *et al.*, 1975) which were similar in format, but controlled for various variables, such as sex of role model, familiarity of the protagonist and so on. In the BAT R subjects were rated on 12 verbal and nonverbal measures and reliability was in the .9s. The *Interpersonal Behavior Role-playing Test* (Goldsmith and McFall, 1975) required patients to give role-played responses to 25 interpersonal situations. Blind raters achieved 95% agreement on total scores of all responses.

Perhaps one of the most rigorous examples of this type of procedure is the *Simulated Social Interaction Test* (Curran *et al.*, 1980). Responding to the poor psychometric foundation of the earlier procedures, Curran *et al.* obtained role-played responses in eight simulations, each rated for anxiety and skill. Using generalisability theory procedures, Curran *et al.* found ratings had good generalisability across judges, good agreement between judges with respect to absolute magnitude of scores, and good discriminant validity between skill and anxiety. Another methodological rigorous test is the *Heterosocial Adequacy Test* (Perri and Richards, 1979). Construction and evaluation of the test were carried out following the five-stage test development strategy of Goldfried and D'Zurilla (1969). Perri and Richards reported good inter-rater reliability and criterion-related validity.

A second type of role-play test may be termed *extended role-play*, typically using more global rating scales of skill and social anxiety. One of these, the *Social Interaction Test*, required patients to converse with two strangers for twelve minutes, and were rated both on global scales and molecular measures of verbal and nonverbal behaviour (Trower *et al.*, 1978). Rater reliability was .7–.8 for global measures and in excess of .9 for most molecular measures.

A third type of role-play test used commonly in ordinary clinical settings may be termed *replication role-play* (Kern, 1982) in which the client attempts to replicate a previously encountered situation. This is the most promising of the role-play tests (see below) though so far little used in research.

Despite the efforts of many investigators there are still serious problems with the behavioural assessment of skill and anxiety (Bellack, 1979, 1983; Trower, 1982). Two of these will be briefly reviewed here — the role-plays and the behavioural measures.

Validity of Role-Play

The ideal behavioural assessment of skills and anxiety would entail direct observation of the subject in the natural environment, but the difficulty of doing this has inevitably meant the use of role-play simulation, as we have seen. However, recent research has revealed major worries about the "ecological" validity of role-play enactments, i.e. skills and anxiety levels are by no means isomorphic between real and role-played simulations of situations. It may be useful to summarise Bellack's (1983) review of these problems.

Instructions to subjects before role-plays have a major impact on performance, yet instructions vary widely between studies. Subjects under high demand to perform well may indeed appear skilful in the role-play but not in the real situation. It is essential for subjects to "get into" role but this requirement is often not met. Subjects are exposed to a shot-gun type of experience, with a rapid-fire series of scenes or a stilted encounter with a stranger, and are probably anxious and confused. Information normally available in real life is usually not provided, particularly about the consequences of different responses, i.e. the risks involved. Background information, and the behaviour of the confederate, can elicit vastly different responses. All these problems are compounded by lack of realism, which often seems to be deliberately minimised for the sake of standardisation, e.g. the BAT-R. Related to this is the difficulty of raters making sound judgements. Bellack asserts the single prompt role-play yields extremely limited and stilted responses and *is no longer justified*, nor are the use of taped role-play tests.

Recent research substantiates much of Bellack's critique. Kern (1982) assessed the external validity of brief, extended and replication role-plays, and found the brief role-play was relatively invalid and elicited *greater* increases in heart rate than real situations. The replication role-play provided a moderately to highly valid representation of more naturalistic behaviour. In a further study, Kern, Miller and Eggers (1983) distinguished between *typical* role-play (as used in standardised tests described earlier), *replication* (described above) and *specification* (subjects told to replicate specific behaviours) role-plays. Results showed specification role-plays were most valid, followed by replication role-plays. Kern *et al.* suggest "the field should move towards the adoption of such methodologies" (p. 489).

A number of studies have shown that merely instructing subjects to be more assertive in role-play, and giving them information on what the rater would be looking for, results in increased assertiveness. In one of these studies, Higgins, Frisch and Smith (1983) found that role-play instructions diminished subjects' concerns about the appropriateness or riskiness of being assertive.

Validity of Behavioural Measures

If role-play is one side of the behavioural assessment coin, measurement is the other, and is equally problematic. This field of enquiry is complex and again an exhaustive treatment of it is beyond space limitations. In summary, definitions and rating or scoring of behavioural elements are somewhat arbitrary and vary widely. Adherence to behavioural goals of objectivity and operationalism has resulted in simple, clear-cut measures, but ones with major shortcomings when it comes to assessing critical features of social performance (Bellack, 1983). Molecular and molar measurement have both been attacked for quite the wrong reasons (Curran, Farrell and Grunberger, 1984; Trower, 1982) and there is good reason to doubt the appropriateness of means-comparison based forms of statistical analysis when dealing with the relatively neglected sequential and interactional nature of social behaviour (Gottman, 1979; Thomas, Bull and Roger, 1982). Yet another area concerns the reliability and validity of raters' judgements, and the related problems of good and poor observation skills, well reviewed by Boice (1983). All of these and the foregoing problems, mean that much of the accepted findings on assessment and training in the social skills/social anxiety literature — partly reviewed below — must surely now be re-evaluated.

Characteristics of the Socially Anxious

Social anxiety can for convenience be divided into the external factors of behaviour and situations, and the internal factors of thinking, emotional experience and physiological arousal. We shall consider these in turn, and how they interact.

Behavioural Characteristics

Some socially anxious people may be highly skilled but negatively misperceive their abilities. Other anxious individuals exhibit actual skill deficits either because their performances are disrupted by anxiety or may be anxious because their skills are deficient (see above). Whatever the case, we need to know the skill profiles of these socially anxious subgroups and the profiles of comparison groups who are non-anxious and "ordinary".

Skill differences between high- and low-anxious individuals. There are *general* findings that socially anxious people are seen as less skilled than low-anxious individuals (e.g. Halford and Foddy, 1982) and indeed this seems to be the consensus in the literature (Leary, 1983b). However at the level of *specific* behavioural differences the picture is mixed. Firstly we'll consider encoded or "sent" behaviour. There is substantial evidence that the principal difference is that the anxious speak less — they initiate fewer conversations, speak less often, talk a lower percentage of the time, take longer to respond to others, allow more silences to develop and are less likely to break conversational silences (Cheek and Buss, 1981; Conger and Farrell, 1981; Marzillier and Lambert, 1976; Zimbardo, 1977). The second most prominent difference is that the anxious look less (Cheek and Buss, 1981; Conger and Farrell, 1981; Pilkonis, 1977). There are other nonverbal differences — less smiling, few facial expressions, speech dysfluencies, fidgeting movements etc. (e.g. Jones and Briggs, 1984; Marzillier and Lambert, 1976). The third main difference is that the socially anxious are more avoidant — they leave encounters sooner, date less, choose remoter living accommodation and sit and interact at greater distances (see Leary, 1983b). More recent studies tend to confirm these findings. Kern (1982) found anxious low daters emitted fewer "you" statements, were less skilful in taking the initiative and used less open-ended questions. Other studies have shown few or no behavioural differences between high- and low-anxious individuals (Arkowitz, 1977). This points to the importance of differentiating subtypes — there is little dispute now that there are high-skilled and low-skilled socially anxious people. Trower (1980) found significant differences between high- and low-skill rated socially anxious patients in amounts of speech, looking, smiling and gesturing and posture. The unskilled group also showed less variability in response to situation changes.

Another group of findings concerns the decoding or "reception" of behaviours. Whether certain behaviours are skilled or not is partly dependent on how they are perceived by others, an important topic still under-researched. Kupke, Hobbs and Cheney (1979) found one particular behaviour — personal attention (which involved "you" statements or questions) significantly predicted increased female attraction. Men trained in this skill were judged more attractive by women peers. Muehlenhard and McFall (1981) looked at what skills a woman needed to date a man and found that most men preferred a woman to take the *initiative* (contrary to common belief), but only if they already liked her, and if they did not, no skill — asking, hinting or waiting — would work. They also unravelled some of the *cues* to male interest. The best were "frequently watches her and talks to her about impersonal matters" and the worst were "frequently ignores her or treats her like one of the guys" (Muehlenhard and McFall, p. 690).

A number of studies have looked at more general aspects of the communication of warmth and liking. Bayes (1972) found warmth ratings were related to increased speech rate, smile frequency, body and head movements and hand movements. Argyle (1975), Trower (1979), Heslin and Patterson (1982), and others have reviewed a number of such cues.

Recently Shrout and Fiske (1981) confirmed that the more active the target was, the more likely they would be positively perceived. Number of smiles, filled pause rate, nod rate, gaze number and short vocal back-channel rate were the key elements contributing to the impression. Scott and Edelstein (1981) found two interaction strategies significantly and equally related to attraction. These were *other-enhancement* (asks many questions, follow-up questions, positive feedback, encourages others to talk), and *positive self-presentation* (talks about self interests in positive terms, expresses favourable opinions, does not encourage others to talk). Badly rated was the *incompetent presentation* (few questions, no follow-up, lapses into silence, looks bored).

Research has also recently turned to examining the effect of assertion. One problem especially for shy people is that any kind of *negative assertion* is likely to be perceived negatively and punished, while remaining unassertive is viewed more positively and rewarded. A number of studies have shown this. For example, Kelly *et al.* (1982) found that assertive subjects were viewed as skilled and able but much *less* friendly than unassertive subjects. Lewis and Gallois (1984) found judges rated expression of negative feeling as aggressive, but such findings varied depending on whether the sender was known or a stranger. Schroeder *et al.* (1983) found expressing positive feelings, initiating interactions, and making behaviour change requests achieved the most favourable evaluation. Heisler and McCormack (1982) showed that being assertive was better received than being passive with familiar others, but best of all if preceded by warm and empathic comments.

McFall *et al.* (1982) found that nonverbal was more important than verbal behaviour in communicating assertiveness, especially in males. Judges' evaluation of assertiveness was influenced by controlled, smooth, steady and purposive movement, as opposed to shifting, shaky, fidgeting activity.

Situations and Social Anxiety

Though socially anxious people may exhibit characteristic skill profiles across situations, it is equally to be expected that situations will vary in their anxiety- and behaviour-eliciting characteristics. Trower (in press) reviewed several studies and found that a wide range of people — including students, nurses and patients — reported the same kinds of situations as the most anxiety-provoking. These were approaching others for the first time, going into a room full of people, taking the initiative in conversation, going to dances and meeting strangers. Speculating on the dimensions which make such situations difficult, Trower suggested the following: they were unscripted (lack of explicit rules, roles, goals etc. for guiding appropriate behaviour — see Argyle, this volume), carried heavier sanctions for rule deviation, were more demanding of complex skill repertoires, were unfamiliar situations and involved appearing in public, and provoked self-consciousness (Buss, 1980) (i.e. involved self-presentation and role-responsibility).

Buss (1980) suggested that shyness was elicited by three factors — physical, social and role novelty, the presence of others when involving formality, high status or conspicuousness, and the actions of others, particularly excessive or insufficient attention or intrusiveness. Some confirmation of these and the above speculations was provided by Pilkonis (1977), Russell, Cutrona and Jones (in press), and Zimbardo (1977). Russell *et al.*, for example, reported that meeting strangers and authority figures were by far the most difficult, followed by public performances, introductions, embarrassments and heterosexual risks.

In an innovative approach, Rudy, Merluzzi and Henahan (1982) used multidimensional scaling techniques to show that low-assertive people and clients construe complex assertion situations in characteristic ways which may pepetuate social skill deficits. For example, low-assertive, compared to high-assertive people, do not place importance on more subtle dimensions, for example on "social intelligence", and are more prone to use the dimensions reflecting anxiety and arousal constructs. This seems a very promising line for future research.

Cognitive Characteristics of Socially Anxious Individuals

There are now an overwhelming number of studies implicating the role of negative cognitions in social anxiety and disrupted social performance (e.g. Halford and Foddy, 1981; Leary, 1983a; Schlenker and Leary, 1982). The author has fully reviewed this important topic elsewhere (Trower and Turland, 1984) so will only briefly discuss it here.

A pioneering study by Schwartz and Gottman (1976) was one of the first to reveal that unassertive subjects were distinguished by a pattern of negative self-statements. Clark and Arkowitz (1975) similarly found their anxious subjects overestimated negative outcomes and underestimated positive outcomes. Further research has begun to identify types of negative cognitions. Fiedler and Beach (1978) found that unassertive subjects had unrealistically high expectations of bad consequences occurring if they behaved assertively. Other findings are that the socially anxious evaluate themselves negatively (Alden and Cappe, 1981), endorse irrational beliefs (Goldfried and Sobocinski, 1975) and apply perfectionistic standards to themselves (Alden and Safran, 1978; Goldfried and Sobocinski, 1975). In similar vein, Sutton-Simon and Goldfried (1981) found socially anxious subjects exhibited the above patterns and were more likely to attribute social failure to themselves and less likely to attribute social success to themselves. I would argue that one of the main implications of these studies is that anxious people *choose* to behave in a socially "deficient" way, at least with regard to assertiveness, as a result of their cognitive evaluations (Alden and Cappe, 1981).

Social Skills Training

Rationale and Procedures

The original — and still valid — rationale for SST was that unskilled subjects would become less anxious as a result of positive rather than negative responses from others following more skilful performances. SST also helps skilled phobics since it provides a form of exposure *in vivo* and may also help improve self-efficacy beliefs (see below). An alternative rationale for SST has been presented by Hartman (1983): the clients have to escape from their meta-cognitive self-preoccupation, and are therefore taught to be other-centred by means of SST.

The technology of skill acquisition has now become a standard package of procedures in most studies. These are briefly as follows: *Instruction* — A skill and its function is described, and analysed into its behavioural elements, so the client can see exactly what has to be done. *Modelling* — Learning by observing others is a very efficient way of acquiring complex new skills, since the trainee can see the entire sequence carried out as a whole and can judge for her or himself its effectiveness. *Rehearsal* — After instruction and modelling, the client can try the new skill in role-play with a role partner, and practise until a desired standard is reached. *Coaching, feedback and reinforcement* — During rehearsal, the client gets guidance and feedback on his performance. Video feedback is a popular mode. Properly handled, feedback can be reinforcing in itself, but is supplemented with praise and other rewards. *Homework* — The new skills are practised in real situations between training sessions. Homework is widely regarded as essential for transfer of training.

Outcome Studies

Since SST research began in the late 1960s, there have been numerous reviews, let alone studies, and the reviews themselves have been frequently referred to. In this section, some of the reviews will be summarised, and some of the more recent outcome studies evaluated.

The reviews. A number of reviews appeared in the late 1970s (e.g. Arkowitz, 1977; Curran, 1977; Hersen, 1979; Marzillier, 1978; Twentyman and Zimering, 1979) which on the whole were rather sceptical about the efficacy of SST for socially anxious and other clients, or at least agnostic about outcome because of the methodological weakness of so many of the studies. More recent reviews (e.g. Emmelkamp, 1982; Shepherd, 1983; Stravinsky and Shahar, 1983) are more mixed, and on the whole more optimistic about SST effects and about some aspects of methodology. There are also quite clear disagreements about the importance and effectiveness of cognitive therapy as an adjunct to SST.

In a foresightful review, Curran (1977) concluded that in the area of heterosocial anxiety, the majority of studies demonstrated therapeutic effects with regard to increased social skills and a reduction of anxiety at post-treatment as measured by both self-report and behavioural indices. However this optimism was undermined by his other conclusion — that every single one of the studies adopting a response acquisition approach was marred by one or more methodological flaws. He listed these and made recommendations for future research, concerning subject selection and screening, inadequate and invalid assessment procedures, lack of transfer and follow-up measurement, and inattention to the interaction between treatment procedures and subject characteristics.

In a comprehensive review of a broader literature — both psychiatric patients and volunteer subjects — Marzillier (1978) reached a number of conclusions, including: (1) SST can produce positive changes in the short term; (2) Most of this evidence came from studies of assertive training, but the evidence failed to show that improvements were maintained, or that they helped individuals cope with real-life situations; (3) SST with outpatients showed only limited effects but did show some evidence of generalisation and maintenance; (4) Components of SST had not been clearly established; (5) Too many studies were marred by methodological problems.

Twentyman and Zimering (1979) undertook a wide-ranging review of a number of factors, culled from 150 studies. First they looked at the treatment components. Evidence for effectiveness of *rehearsal* when used alone was equivocal. When used with other components it produced changes, as did cognitive rehearsal and *in vivo* rehearsal. Similarly, *modelling* alone was by no means consistently effective but was better used in conjunction with other components. The clinical use of modelling should encompass a wide range of target behaviours to facilitate generalisation. Models portrayed in differing social situations may promote transfer and appeared to be effective in this regard. *Coaching* appeared to be effective in delineating what constitutes successful responding. To enhance change the content of coaching must be empirically validated.

With regard to the effectiveness of *response feedback*, studies specifically designed to test this produced mixed results. However studies using feedback in conjunction with other components found positive results. The authors warned that anxious subjects needed special preparation for feedback. *Reinforcement* was found most effective when designed for use outside a laboratory setting — hence transfer was more likely with "environmental reinforcement". *Homework* also appeared to be a most promising method for producing transfer.

Twentyman and Zimering also looked at two, more cognitive, methods of training. One of these, *projected consequences* was an expanded modelling condition in which subjects were presented the probable consequences of the modelled behaviour. Studies suggested that projected consequences were effective when employed with cognitive modification training. They facilitated a positive set, and may enhance transfer effects. Finally cognitive modification (teaching clients to modify self statements) seemed to be at least as effective as standard training programmes.

Judging the overall efficacy of SST, Twentyman and Zimering's conclusions were not promising. When compared to waiting list or no-treatment control groups, SST was clearly superior in teaching new social behaviours, but differences between therapies were small or non-existent when SST was compared with traditional psychotherapy or treatments which provide subjects with information about handling problem situations. Both SST and systematic desensitisation (SD) produced equally effective results with anxious clients, but neither was superior to the other. "Thus it cannot be concluded that behavioral training is the treatment of choice for clients with interpersonal skill deficits until more convincing evidence is adduced" (Twentyman and Zimering, 1979, p. 390). They also concluded that evidence in support of the generalisation of treatment effects had to be considered tentative.

In one of the more recent reviews, Emmelkamp (1982) pointed out that comparatively few studies had been carried out on psychiatric patients. The picture here was clearly different from that described by Twentyman and Zimering (who had included patients and volunteer subjects from studies completed some years earlier). Comparison of SST and SD for socially anxious clients produced mixed results, with some studies showing the former superior for some kinds of clients. He concluded that SST *and* cognitive restructuring produced the most promising results for socially anxious clients, and he pointed out that *both* treatments involved exposure *in vivo*, which may also be an essential component in effective treatment.

Stravynski and Shahar (1983) also took studies based on psychiatric patients who in the main were diagnosed personality disorders, social phobia and neurosis (unspecified). They carried out a selective review, including only those studies which satisfied certain minimal methodological criteria, including random assignment, multiple-measurement of change, control for concurrent treatment, minimal treatment length, minimal sample size and minimal follow-up. These criteria left a mere nine studies which could be included.

Stravynski and Shahar concluded from their review that SST was superior to no-treatment controls. Moreover, with the possible exception of SD, SST appeared to be a more potent approach to the treatment of social dysfunction than contrasting methods such as short-term psychotherapy, group discussion, sensitivity training, and bibliotherapy. Therapeutic gains were produced in an average of 12 sessions (range 6–20 sessions) and had mostly maintained for an average of eight months (range six–sixteen months). Further improvement was noted during follow-up in some studies. Evidence for transfer to real life, however, was still scarce.

The best combination of components appeared to be instructions, modelling, role rehearsal, feedback and homework. Homework was an especially potent ingredient. The addition of an anxiolytic in one study or cognitive modification in one study had not enhanced outcome.

Shepherd (1983) reviewed 52 studies on social skills and assertive training conducted with psychiatric patients between 1970 and 1980. Group-based studies nearly all found SST superior to no treatment and rather weak placebo controls. The full package of components was most effective but modelling seemed the most powerful component. Evidence comparing SST with active non-behavioural treatments tended to produce rather mixed results. Evidence on generalisation remained weak. Results tended to maintain but there was a strong tendency for differences between treatments to attenuate. Even these weak results for SST had to be treated with considerable caution due to the continued methodological weaknesses of studies (e.g. reliance on role-play tests criticised earlier). Shepherd concluded — interested, but sceptical.

There have been comparatively few reviews of the effects of cognitive-change techniques as an adjunct to SST. Goldfried (1979) concluded his review by stating that social anxiety can be effectively reduced by a procedure that trains clients to re-evaluate realistically their behaviour in social situations. This was more effective than SD and at times just as effective as SST, though a combination of both procedures was most beneficial.

Many of the above studies treated socially anxious subjects as a homogeneous group. Future work will undoubtedly have to heed the various subgroups referred to earlier, and separate specific effects for specific problems. Some studies have already looked at this question. Ost, Jerremalm and Johansson (1981) found "behavioural responders" did best with SST while "physiological responders" did best with applied relaxation. Marshall, Keltner and Marshall (1981) found assertive training led to increased assertion but did not decrease social fear, while an anxiety reduction procedure achieved the reverse result. Safran, Alden and

Davidson (1980) found that SST improved behaviour and cognitive restructuring improved cognitions in socially anxious subjects — a specific effect. (Other studies fail to support this specific effects hypothesis.)

Trower and Turland (1984) divided studies and reviews into those that seemed to be based on skilled social phobics versus those based on unskilled phobics. Skilled phobics should benefit from exposure *in vivo* with cognitive restructuring as perhaps the necessary and sufficient conditions for change, while unskilled phobics would also need skills acquisition to produce change. Emmelkamp (1979) in his review found support for SST in both cases because it was probably acting as an exposure *in vivo* procedure as well as a skills acquisition technique. Studies also supported cognitive methods, and he concluded a combination of the two would probably be the treatment of choice. There is now good evidence for the effectiveness of exposure *in vivo*. In a well-designed study Butler *et al*. (1984) found that social phobics did well with straight exposure *in vivo*, but a second group did better when anxiety management was added. Although not explicitly stated, it appears these patients were reasonably skilled. Alstrom *et al*. (1984) also found their social phobics did best with exposure *in vivo* but no combined cognitive treatment was tested. In a methodologically exemplary study Kazdin and Mascitelli (1982) found a combined behavioural form of SST and a cognitive method were considerably superior to either one alone with their unassertive subjects. The authors concluded the two methods were complementary in their effect, such that the one enhanced the other. However Frisch *et al*. (1982) found their combined SST and cognitive treatment added nothing to SST identification of subject groups, e.g. skilled and unskilled phobics are likely to respond differently. Trower *et al*. (1978) found their skilled phobics did as well with SD and SST while their unskilled anxious patients responded only to SST.

The Generalisation Problem

The ultimate validity of SST with socially anxious people is whether in the long-term it improves their social skills in their everyday lives *and* reduces their anxiety. What do the reviews have to say about the problems of generalisation and maintenance? The evidence of the earlier reviews was emphatically that SST could produce change in the short-term — in role-play type behavioural tests and self-report questionnaires — but that the evidence on generalisation was either lacking entirely (usually because not measured) or very weak (usually because not sought). When the effects *were* evaluated in situations dissimilar from the training sessions, the results were not encouraging. Twentyman and Zimering (1979) concluded that there was considerable evidence that SST was effective in producing transfer effects in the laboratory but fewer studies had demonstrated consistent effects outside the laboratory. The later reviews reported better methodological studies, but the conclusions were not substantially changed. For example Stravynski and Shahar (1983) thought that the continued paucity of findings on the issue of generalisation reflected the methodological and logistical difficulties of assessment in a natural environment.

How can SST be improved to ensure generalisation, and what methodological improvements can be made to ensure such changes can be assessed?

In a foresightful book, Kazdin (1975) suggested several ways to improve generalisation and maintenance of newly learned behaviour — suggestions which are still highly relevant a decade later. (1) Rewards which normally occur in the environment should be used in training, so that new behaviour will have the same reinforcing consequences outside the training situation. (2) Individuals in the patient's environment, such as parents and other significant others can be trained to reward him or her in appropriate ways. (3) When new skills are established, training sessions and therapist support can be gradually rather than abruptly discontinued. (4) Reward schedules can be made more intermittent. (5) New behaviour can be developed in a variety of situations and with a variety of individuals. (6) Patients can be taught to evaluate their own behaviour and set their own criteria for rewarding themselves.

One of the most important developments in improving the generalisation of SST lies in "homework" — i.e. actually carrying out social skills tasks, if necessary under supervision, in the environment. The promising studies on exposure *in vivo* described previously demonstrate the effectiveness of confronting real situations and carrying out social interactions. A recent review by Martin and Worthington (1982) contains many useful methods for ensuring graded homework assignments are carried out. For example they emphasise the importance of carefully designing the homework, so that the tasks are manageable, specific, and consistent with the client's abilities and needs. Two other stages in their homework model are presenting the assignment and monitoring performance.

It is undoubtedly the view of a number of the authors and reviewers discussed that one of the keys to improved generalisation, in addition to the more "behavioural" kinds summarised by Kazdin, is in the realm of changing dysfunctional cognitions. If clients believe they "cannot" change, are intrinsically inadequate, are helpless and hopeless etc., it is unlikely they will carry out the new responses *in vivo* — i.e. the homework described above — which is vital to generalisation (Dryden, 1984; Trower, O'Mahoney and Dryden, 1982). In a review of self-statement modification,

Dush, Hirt and Schroeder (1983), showed that unassertive and socially anxious people, among others, responded well to self-statement modification.

Most SST studies focus on the components of training — the actual behavioural elements — and one problem in this area is the lack of norms to ensure that the elements trained are the appropriate ones and the ones most likely to be reinforced. Few studies have paid attention to the *process* of skill learning (Trower, 1980), i.e. the perception and discrimination of cues, the monitoring of feedback and continuous modification of responses in the light of feedback. Training of these process skills offers great promise in the area of generalisation, since such skills teach the patient how to *generate* appropriate responses in new situations as they are needed. Trower (1980) showed that unskilled, anxious clients were indeed lacking in these skills.

In this vein, a few studies have focused on training social sensitivity. Azrin and Hayes (1984) suggest that social sensitivity is a matter of cue control and timing of responses, and that generalisation is more likely to occur if subjects can discriminate potential rewards and behave accordingly. The authors trained their male subjects to discriminate female interest and found it generalised to new females, and led to an improvement in actual skills.

What methodological changes can be made to test generalisation effects? Most SST outcome studies have inferred efficacy on the basis of statistical comparisons between two or more conditions. But they are based on the average improvement score and thus provide no information on the effects of therapy for individual clients. They also rely on the "significance test" which often has little *clinical* significance (Kazdin, 1977). Without some information regarding variability of outcome, we have no way of determining the proportion of clients who make genuine improvements. New standards and conventions are needed to serve as criteria for classifying subjects into "improved", "unimproved" and "deteriorated", based on response to treatment. Jacobson, Follette and Revenstorf (1984) offered a two-fold criterion for determining improvement, based on both statistical reliability and clinical significance. They also suggested statistical procedures for determining whether the criteria have been met.

A great deal more work needs to be done on specifying subgroups of socially anxious subjects, types and components of SST, and training processes and the contexts in which the problems occur. This degree of specificity and precision requires more work based on single case methodology. Additionally, Barrios (1984) points out that we still do not know what the joint effects of treatment components are, and he offers a methodology for testing these. The measurement of generalisation and maintenance will undoubtedly benefit from this kind of precision. One of the most powerful demonstrations of this is the study of Kazdin and Mascitelli (1982) described earlier in which combined covert *and* overt rehearsal and homework practice produced enduring (eight-month) improvements and generalisation to novel situations — an effect not produced by either treatment alone.

Conclusion

This chapter has tried to take a bird's eye view of an extremely diverse field which has generated a wealth of rather unfocused research. It is becoming clear that the problem of social anxiety is highly important (Rook, 1984), complex (Schlenker and Leary, 1982), and the role of skills deficiency difficult to assess (Bellack, 1983) and treat (Trower and Turland, 1984). A decade and a half of outcome research has probably done little more than encourage us in the pursuit of an SST approach, and map more clearly the difficulties we face in such an approach. These difficulties will force investigators to re-think their assessment, training and methodologies. The important changes needed are discussed in the concluding chapter of this volume. Regarding social anxiety in particular, the following seem most pertinent. (1) Greater specification of client problems, skill norms, and situational contexts where problems arise. (2) Greater use of single case methodology to reflect this, and use of forms of analysis which take account of the sequential and interactional nature of social behaviour. (3) Changing the emphasis of training from initiating social contact and assertion to the skills involved in greater intimacy (Rook, 1984) and establishing longer-term relationships (Duck and Gilmour, 1981). (4) Changing the emphasis from teaching component skills to process skills, to help clients generate their own skills appropriately in novel situations as they arise (Trower, 1982).

References

Alden, L. and Cappe, R. (1981) Nonassertiveness: Skill deficit or selective self-evaluation. *Behavior Therapy*, **12**, 107–114.
Alden, L. and Safran, J. (1978) Irrational beliefs and nonassertive behavior. *Cognitive Therapy and Research*, **2**, 357–364.
Alstrom, J. E., Nordlund, C. L., Persson, G., Harding, M. and Ljungqvist, C. (1984) Effects of four treatment methods on social phobic patients not suitable for insight-oriented psychotherapy. *Acta Psychiatrica Scandinavica*, **70**, 97–110.
American Psychiatric Association (1980) *Diagnostic and statistical manual of mental disorders* (3rd ed.). Washington, DC: Author.
Arygle, M. (1975) *Bodily communication*. London: Methuen.
Arygle, M. and Kendon, H. (1967) The experimental analysis of social performance. In: L. Berkowitz (Ed.), *Advances in experimental social psychology Vol. 3*. New York: Academic Press.

Argyle, M., Trower, P. E. and Bryant, B. M. (1974) Explorations in the treatment of personality disorders and neuroses by social skills training. *British Journal of Medical Psychology*, **47**, 63–72.

Arkowitz, H. (1977) Measurement and modification of minimal dating behavior. In: M. Hersen, R. Eisler and P. M. Miller (Eds.), *Progress in behavior modification Vol. 5*. New York: Academic Press.

Arkowitz, H., Lichtenstein, B., McGovern, K. and Hines, P. (1975) The behavioral assessment of social competence in males. *Behavior Therapy*, **6**, 3–13.

Asendorpf, J. B. and Scherer, K. R. (in press) The discrepant repressor: Differentiation between low anxiety, high anxiety, and repression of anxiety by autonomic–facial–verbal patterns of behaviour. *Journal of Personality and Social Psychology*.

Azrin, R. D. and Hayes, S. C. (1984) The discrimination of interest within a heterosexual interaction: Training, generalization, and effects on social skills. *Behavior Therapy*, **15**, 173–184.

Barlow, D. H. and Wolfe, B. E. (1981) Behavioral approaches to anxiety disorders: A report on the NIMH-SUNY, Albany Research Conference. *Journal of Consulting and Clinical Psychology*, **49**, 448–454.

Barrios, B. A. (1984) Single-subject strategies for examining joint effects: A critical evaluation. *Behavioral Assessment*, **6**, 103–120.

Bayes, M. A. (1972) Behavioral cues of interpersonal warmth. *Journal of Consulting and Clinical Psychology*, **9**, 222–231.

Beck, J. G. and Heimberg, R. G. (1983) Self-report assessment of assertive behavior. *Behavior Modification*, **7**, 451–487.

Bellack, A. S. (1979) A critical appraisal of strategies for assessing social skill. *Behavioral Assessment*, **1**, 157–176.

Bellack, A. S. (1983) Recurrent problems in the behavioral assessment of social skill. *Behaviour Research and Therapy*, **21**, 29–42.

Bolce, R. (1983) Observational skills. *Psychological Bulletin*, **93**, 3–29.

Bryant, B. M. and Trower, P. E. (1974) Social difficulty in a student sample. *British Journal of Educational Psychology*, **44**, 13–21.

Bryant, B. M., Trower, P. E., Yardley, K., Urbieta, H. and Letemendia, F. J. J. (1976) A survey of social inadequacy among psychiatric outpatients. *Psychological Medicine*, **6**, 101–112.

Buss, A. H. (1980) *Self-consciousness and social anxiety*. San Francisco: Freeman.

Butler, G., Cullington, A., Munby, M., Amies, P. and Gelder, M. (1984) Exposure and anxiety management in the treatment of social phobia. *Journal of Consulting and Clinical Psychology*, **52**, 642–650.

Callner, D. A. and Ross, S. M. (1976) The reliability of three measures of assertion in a drug addiction population. *Behavior Therapy*, **7**, 659–667.

Carver, C. S. (1979) A cybernetic model of self-attention processes. *Journal of Personality and Social Psychology*, **37**, 1251–1281.

Carver, C. S. and Scheier, M. F. (1984) A control-theory approach to behaviour, and some implications for social skills training. In: P. Trower (Ed.), *Radical approaches to social skills training*. London: Croom Helm.

Cheek, J. M. and Buss, A. H. (1981) Shyness and sociability. *Journal of Personality and Social Psychology*, **41**, 330–339.

Clark, J. V. and Arkowitz, H. (1975) Social anxiety and self-evaluation of interpersonal performance. *Psychological Reports*, **36**, 211–221.

Conger, J. C. and Farrell, A. D. (1981) Behavioral components of heterosocial skills. *Behavior Therapy*, **12**, 41–55.

Crozier, W. R. (1982) Explanations of social shyness. *Current Psychological Reviews*, **2**, 47–60.

Curran, J. P. (1975) Social skills training and systematic desensitization in reducing dating anxiety. *Behavior Research and Therapy*, **13**, 65–68.

Curran, J. P. (1977) Skills training as an approach to the treatment of heterosexual-social anxiety: A review. *Psychological Bulletin*, **84**, 140–157.

Curran, J. P., Corriveau, D. P., Monti, P. M. and Hagerman, S. B. (1980) Social skill and social anxiety: Self-report measurement in a psychiatric population. *Behavior Modification*, **4**, 493–512.

Curran, J. P., Farrell, A. D. and Grunberger, A. J. (1984) Social skills training: A critique and a rapprochement. In: P. Trower (Ed.), *Radical approaches to social skills training*. London: Croom Helm.

Curran, J. P., Monti, P. M., Corriveau, D. P., Hay, L. R., Hagerman, S., Zwick, W. R. and Farrell, A. D. (1980) The generalizability of a procedure for assessing social skills and social anxiety in a psychiatric population. *Behavioral Assessment*, **2**, 389–402.

Duck, S. W. and Gilmour, R. (1981) *Personal relationships 2: Developing personal relationships*. London: Academic Press.

Dush, D. M., Hirt, M. L. and Schroeder, H. (1983) Self-statement modification with adults: A meta-analysis. *Psychological Bulletin*, **94**, 408–422.

Dryden, W. (1984) Social skills assessment and training from a rational-emotive perspective. In: P. Trower (Ed.), *Radical approaches to social skills training*. London: Croom Helm.

Eisler, R. M., Hersen, M., Miller, P. M. and Blanchard, E. B. (1975) Situational determinants of assertive behaviors. *Journal of Consulting and Clinical Psychology*, **43**, 330–340.

Eisler, R. M., Miller, P. M. and Hersen, M. (1973) Components of assertive behavior. *Journal of Clinical Psychology*, **29**, 295–299.

Emmelkamp, P. M. G. (1979) The behavioral study of clinical phobias. In: M. Hersen, R. M. Eisler and P. M. Miller (Eds.), *Progress in behavior modification Vol. 7*. New York: Academic Press.

Emmelkamp, P. M. G. (1982) *Obsessions and phobias*. New York: Plenum.

Fiedler, D. and Beach, L. R. (1978) On the decision to be assertive. *Journal of Consulting and Clinical Psychology*, **46**, 537–546.

Filsinger, E. E. and Lamke, L. K. (1983) The lineage transmission of interpersonal competence. *Journal of Marriage and the Family*, **45**, 75–80.

Frisch, M. B., Elliott, C. H., Atsaides, J. P., Salva, D. M. and Denney, D. R. (1982) Social skills and stress management training to enhance patients' interpersonal competencies. *Psychotherapy: Theory, Research and Practice*, **19**, 349–357.

Galassi, J. P., Galassi, M. D. and Litz, M. C. (1974) Assertive training in groups using video feedback. *Journal of Counseling Psychology*, **21**, 390–394.

Gambrill, E. D. and Richey, C. A. (1975) An assertion inventory for use in assessment and research. *Behavior Therapy*, **6**, 550–561.

Gay, M. L., Hollandsworth, J. G. and Galassi, J. P. (1975) An assertiveness inventory for adults. *Journal of Counseling Psychology*, **22**, 340–344.

Glass, C. R. and Merluzzi, T. V. (1981) Cognitive assessment of social-evaluative anxiety. In: T. V. Merluzzi, C. R. Glass and M. Genest (Eds.), *Cognitive assessment*. New York: Guilford Press.

Goldfried, M. R. (1979) Anxiety reduction through cognitive-behavioral intervention. In: P. C. Kendall and S. D. Hollon (Eds.), *Cognitive-behavioral interventions: Theory, research, and procedures*. New York: Academic Press.

Goldfried, R. and D'Zurilla, R. J. (1969) A behavioral-analytic model for assessing competence. In: C. D. Spielberger (Ed.), *Current topics in clinical and community psychology*. New York: Academic Press.

Goldfried, M. R. and Sobocinski, D. (1975) Effect of irrational beliefs on emotional arousal. *Journal of Consulting and Clinical Psychology*, **43**, 504–510.

Goldsmith, J. B. and McFall, R. M. (1975) Development and evaluation of an interpersonal skill-training program for psychiatric inpatients. *Journal of Abnormal Psychology*, **84**, 51–58.

Gottman, J. M. (1979) Detecting cyclicity in social interaction. *Psychological Bulletin*, **86**, 338–348.

Halford, K. and Foddy, M. (1982) Cognitive and social skills correlates of social anxiety. *British Journal of Clinical Psychology*, **21**, 17–28.

Hartman, L. M. (1983) A metacognitive model of social anxiety: Implications for treatment. *Clinical Psychology Review*, **3**, 435–456.

Heimberg, R. G., Harrison, D. F., Montgomery, D., Madsen, C. H. and Sherfey, J. A.

(1980) Psychometric and behavioral analysis of a social anxiety inventory: The Situation Questionnaire. *Behavioral Assessment*, **2**, 403–416.

Heisler, G. A. and McCormack, J. (1982) Situational and personality influences on the reception of provocative responses. *Behavior Therapy*, **13**, 743–750.

Hersen, M. (1979) Modification of skill deficits in psychiatric patients. In: A. S. Bellack and M. Hersen (Eds.), *Research and practice in social skills training*. New York: Plenum.

Hersen, M. and Bellack, A. S. (1977) Assessment of social skills. In: A. R. Ciminero, K. S. Calhoun and N. E. Adams (Eds.), *Handbook for behavioral assessment*. New York: Wiley.

Hersen, M., Bellack, A. S., Turner, S. M., Williams, M. T., Harper, K. and Watts, J. G. (1979) Psychometric properties of the Wolpe–Lazarus Assertiveness Scale. *Behaviour Research and Therapy*, **17**, 63–69.

Heslin, R. and Patterson, M. L. (1982) *Nonverbal behavior and social psychology*. New York: Plenum.

Higgins, R. L., Frisch, M. B. and Smith, D. (1983) A comparison of role-played and natural responses to identical circumstances. *Behavioral Therapy*, **14**, 158–169.

Jacobson, N. S., Follette, W. C. and Revenstorf, D. (1984) Psychotherapy outcome research: Methods for reporting variability and evaluating clinical significance. *Behavior Therapy*, **15**, 336–352.

Jones, W. H. and Briggs, S. R. (1984) The self–other discrepancy in social shyness. In: R. Schwarzer (Ed.), *The self in anxiety, stress and depression*. Amsterdam: North Holland.

Jones, W. H., Briggs, S. R. and Smith, T. G. (1985) *Shyness: Conceptualization and measurement*. Unpublished MS., University of Tulsa.

Kazdin, A. E. (1975) *Behavior modification in applied settings*. Homewood, Illinois: Dorsey Press.

Kazdin, A. E. (1977) Assessing the clinical or applied importance of behavior change through social validation. *Behavior Modification*, **1**, 427–452.

Kazdin, A. E. and Mascitelli, S. (1982) Covert and overt rehearsal and homework practice in developing assertiveness. *Journal of Consulting and Clinical Psychology*, **50**, 250–258.

Kelly, J. A., St. Lawrence, J. S., Bradlyn, A. S., Himadi, W. G., Graves, K. A. and Keane, T. M. (1982) Interpersonal reactions to assertive and unassertive styles when handling social conflict situations. *Journal of Behavior Therapy and Experimental Psychiatry*, **13**, 33–40.

Kern, J. M. (1982) The comparative external and concurrent validity of three role-plays for assessing heterosocial performance. *Behavior Therapy*, **13**, 666–680.

Kern, J. M., Miller, C. and Eggers, J. (1983) Enhancing the validity of role-play tests: A comparison of three role-play methodologies. *Behavior Therapy*, **14**, 482–492.

Kupke, T. E., Hobbs, S. A. and Cheney, T. H. (1979) Selection of heterosocial skills I. Criterion-related validity. *Behavior Therapy*, **10**, 327–335.

Lazarus, R. S. and Folkman, S. (1984) *Stress, appraisal, and coping*. New York: Springer.

Leary, M. R. (1983a) Social anxiousness: The construct and its measurement. *Journal of Personality Assessment*, **47**, 66–75.

Leary, M. R. (1983b) *Understanding social anxiety*. Beverly Hills: Sage.

Levenson, R. W. and Gottman, J. M. (1978) Toward the assessment of social competence. *Journal of Consulting and Clinical Psychology*, **46**, 453–462.

Lewis, P. N. and Gallois, C. (1984) Disagreements, refusals, or negative feelings: Perception of negatively assertive messages from friends and strangers. *Behavior Therapy*, **15**, 353–368.

Lowe, M. R. and Cautela, J. R. (1978) A self-report measure of social skill. *Behavior Therapy*, **9**, 535–544.

McFall, M. E., Winnett, R. L., Bordewick, M. C. and Bornstein, P. H. (1982) Nonverbal components in the communication of assertiveness. *Behavior Modification*, **6**, 121–140.

McFall, R. M. and Lillesand, D. B. (1971) Behavioral rehearsal with modeling and coaching in assertion training. *Journal of Abnormal Psychology*, **81**, 199–218.

McFall, R. M. and Marston, A. R. (1970) An experimental investigation of behavior rehearsal in assertive training. *Journal of Abnormal Psychology*, **76**, 295–303.

McGovern, K. B., Arkowitz, H. and Gilmore, S. K. (1975) Evaluation of social skills training programs for college dating inhibitions. *Journal of Counseling Psychology*, 22, 505–512.

Marks, I. M. (1969) *Fears and phobias*. London: Heinemann.

Marshall, P. G., Keltner, A. A. and Marshall, W. L. (1981) Anxiety reduction, assertive training, and enactment of consequences. *Behavior Modification*, 5, 85–102.

Martin, G. A. and Worthington, E. L. (1982) Behavioral homework. In: M. Hersen, R. M. Eisler and P. M. Miller (Eds.), *Progress in behavior modification Vol. 13*. New York: Academic Press.

Marzillier, J. S. (1978) Outcome studies of skills training: A review. In: P. Trower, B. M. Bryant and M. Argyle (Eds.), *Social skills and mental health*. London: Methuen.

Marzillier, J. S. and Lambert, C. (1976) *The components of conversational skills: Talking to a stranger*. Unpublished MS., Birmingham University.

Morris, C. G. (1984) *Assessment of shyness*. Unpublished MS., University of Michigan.

Muehlenhard, C. L. and McFall, R. M. (1981) Dating initiating from a woman's perspective. *Behavior Therapy*, 12, 682–691.

Nicewander, W. A. and Price, J. M. (1983) Reliability of measurement and the power of statistical tests: Some new results. *Psychological Bulletin*, 94, 524–533.

Ost, L. G., Jerremalm, A. and Johansson, J. (1981) Individual response patterns and the effects of different behavioural methods in the treatment of social phobia. *Behaviour Research and Therapy*, 19, 1–16.

Perri, M. G. and Richards, C. S. (1979) Assessment of heterosocial skills in male college students: Empirical development of a behavioral role-playing test. *Behavior Modification*, 3, 337–354.

Pilkonis, P. A. (1977) The behavioral consequences of shyness. *Journal of Personality*, 45, 596–611.

Pilkonis, P. A. and Zimbardo, P. G. (1979) The personal and social dynamics of shyness. In: C. E. Izard (Ed.), *Emotions in personality and psychopathology*. New York: Plenum.

Rachman, S. J. (1978) *Fear and courage*. San Francisco: Freeman.

Rathus, S. A. (1973) A 30-item schedule for assessing assertive behavior. *Behavior Therapy*, 4, 398–406.

Rehm, L. P. and Marston, A. R. (1968) Reduction of social anxiety through modification of self-reinforcement: An instigation therapy technique. *Journal of Consulting and Clinical Psychology*, 32, 565–574.

Richardson, F. C. and Tasto, D. (1976) Development and factor analysis of a social anxiety inventory. *Behavior Therapy*, 7, 453–462.

Rook, K. S. (1984) Promoting social bonding. *American Psychologist*, 39, 1389–1407.

Rudy, T. E., Merluzzi, T. V. and Henahan, P. T. (1982) Construal of complex assertion situations: A multidimensional analysis. *Journal of Consulting and Clinical Psychology*, 50, 125–137.

Russell, D., Cutrona, C. and Jones, W. H. (in press) A trait-situational analysis of shyness. In: W. H. Jones, J. M. Cheek and S. R. Briggs (Eds.), *A sourcebook on shyness: Research and treatment*. New York: Plenum.

Safran, J. D., Alden, L. E. and Davidson, P. O. (1980) Client anxiety level as a moderator variable in assertion training. *Cognitive Research and Therapy*, 4, 189–200.

Schlenker, B. R. and Leary, M. R. (1982) Social anxiety and self-presentation: A conceptualization and model. *Psychological Bulletin*, 92, 641–669.

Schroeder, H. E., Rakos, R. F. and Moe, J. (1983) The social perception of assertive behavior as a function of response class and gender. *Behavior Therapy*, 14, 534–544.

Schwartz, R. M. and Gottman, J. M. (1976) Toward a task analysis of assertive behavior. *Journal of Consulting and Clinical Psychology*, 48, 478–490.

Scott, W. O. N. and Edelstein, B. A. (1981) The social competence of two interaction strategies: An analog evaluation. *Behavior Therapy*, 12, 482–492.

Shaw, P. M. (1976, April) *The nature of social phobia*. Paper delivered at the Annual Conference of the British Psychological Society, York.

Shepherd, G. (1983) Social skills training with adults. In: S. Spence and G. Shepherd (Eds.), *Developments in social skills training*. London: Academic Press.

Shrout, P. E. and Fiske, D. W. (1981) Nonverbal behaviors and social evaluation. *Journal of Personality*, **49**, 115–128.

Stravynski, A. and Shahar, A. (1983) The treatment of social dysfunction in non-psychotic psychiatric outpatients: A review. *Journal of Nervous and Mental Diseases*, **171**, 721–728.

Sutton-Simon, K. and Goldfried, M. R. (1981) *A task analysis of cognitive processes in social anxiety*. Unpublished MS., Oberlin College.

Thomas, A., Bull, P. and Roger, D. (1982) Conversational exchange analysis. *Journal of Language and Social Psychology*, **1**, 141–155.

Trower, P. (1979) Fundamentals of interpersonal behavior. In: A. S. Bellack and M. Hersen (Eds.), *Research and practice in social skills training*. New York: Plenum.

Trower, P. (1980) Situational analysis of the components and processes of behavior of socially skilled and unskilled patients. *Journal of Consulting and Clinical Psychology*, **30**, 526–537.

Trower, P. (1982) Towards a generative model of social skills: A critique and synthesis. In: J. P. Curran and P. M. Monti (Eds.), *Social skills training: A practical handbook for assessment and treatment*. New York: Guilford.

Trower, P. (in press) Social fit and misfit: An interactional account of social difficulty. In: A. Furnham (Ed.), *Social behaviour and context*. Chicago: Allyn and Bacon.

Trower, P., Bryant, B. M. and Argyle, M. (1978) *Social skills and mental health*. London: Methuen.

Trower, P., O'Mahony, J. M. and Dryden, W. (1982) Cognitive aspects of social failure: Some implications for social skills training. *British Journal of Guidance and Counselling*, **10**, 176–184.

Trower, P. and Turland, D. (1984) Social phobia. In: S. M. Turner (Ed.), *Behavioral theories and treatment of anxiety*. New York: Plenum.

Trower, P., Yardley, K., Bryant, B. M. and Shaw, P. (1978) The treatment of social failure: A comparison of anxiety reduction and skills acquisition procedures on two social problems. *Behavior Modification*, **2**, 41–60.

Twentyman, G. T. and McFall, R. M. (1975) Behavioral training of social skills in shy males. *Journal of Consulting and Clinical Psychology*, **43**, 384–395.

Twentyman, C. T. and Zimering, R. T. (1979) Behavioral training of social skills: A critical review. In: M. Hersen, R. M. Eisler, and P. M. Miller (Eds.), *Progress in behavior modification Vol. 7*. New York: Academic Press.

Watson, D. and Friend, R. (1969) Measurement of social-evaluative anxiety. *Journal of Consulting and Clinical Psychology*, **33**, 448–457.

Wolpe, J. and Lazarus, A. A. (1966) *Behavior therapy techniques: A guide to the treatment of neuroses*. Oxford: Pergamon.

Zimbardo, P. G. (1977) *Shyness: What it is and what to do about it*. New York: Jove.

3

Social Skills Training and Mental Handicap and Organic Impairment

JOHNNY L. MATSON and THOMAS M. DiLORENZO

Client Population

The mentally handicapped and organically impaired constitute a heterogeneous group with relatively distinct parameters compared to many clinical populations. These individuals have been defined as exhibiting marked impairment in cognitive ability as measured by IQ and adaptive behaviour scales. Scores on standardised tests which are two or more standard deviations below the mean define mental handicap (Matson and Mulick, 1983). This definition of mental handicap and the instruments that have been employed to measure it are generally well accepted within the fields of mental health and education. The effects of organic impairments and the developmental disabilities of the mentally handicapped are similar (e.g., poor memory, conceptual and psychomotor skills). The primary differentiating criteria between these two conditions are age of onset and the factors that may result in such conditions (Matson and LaGrow, 1983).

Most definitions of mental handicap or mental retardation require the individual to manifest symptoms of the disorder before age 18. Also, contributing genetic (e.g., Down's Syndrome), biochemical (e.g., phenyl-ketonuria or PKU), and environmental influences (e.g., poor nutrition and lack of cognitive and psychosocial stimulation) are present. Finally, traumatic events (e.g., head contusions) or medical difficulties (e.g., a cut-off of oxygen at birth) can contribute to the mental impairments observed with this disorder (Matson and Mulick, 1983).

Mental handicap as defined and used in this chapter follows the American Association on Mental Deficiency (AAMD) criteria (i.e., below average intellectual functioning and deficits in adaptive behaviour). Intellectual functioning is assessed with a standardised intelligence test, usually the Stanford-Binet or one of the Wechsler scales. As noted, IQ score for a person must be two or more standard deviations below the mean. While adaptive behaviour is also used to assess the condition, cut-off from normal to mentally handicapped has tended to be much more subjective. More than 100 adaptive behaviour scales have been constructed (Meyers, Nihira and Zetlin, 1979) although the most widely used is the Adaptive Behavior Scale developed by the AAMD. The AAMD also divided mental retardation into four levels. These are mild, moderate, severe and profound mental retardation. These levels are roughly based on standard deviations of an IQ test and range from two to five standard deviations below the mean. Many individuals in the profound range of mental retardation are functioning at such a low level that they are virtually untestable; and many have no verbal and few gross and fine psychomotor skills. It should be noted also that while adaptive behaviour and IQ are conceptually distinct, they do correlate highly with each other. However, using both criteria provides a safeguard for a person with very poor academic and conceptual skills who may be very competent in skills of daily living or vice versa.

Organic impairments are often associated with diseases typical of older age (e.g., Alzheimer disease) as well as brain damage due to heart attack, stroke, and other similar conditions. Car accidents, falls, excessive use of some medications including illicit drugs or long-term use of major tranquillisers and other prescription drugs may produce substantial brain damage and related CNS difficulties in some patients. Also, severe isolation that accompanies many forms of psychopathology (e.g., severe depression) may produce deterioration in intellectual functioning. Similarly, specific organic conditions such as seizures, minimal brain dysfunction, hyperactivity and dyslexia are conditions which may result in organic impairment (Lubar and Deering, 1981).

Theoretical/Empirical Grounds for Training

Behaviour therapy has expanded into areas previously considered the exclusive domain of physicians (Melin, Sjoden and James, 1983), and organic impairment and mental retardation are prime examples of this expansion. Both of these conditions certainly have a component of organicity or physically/medically related impairment. However, psychological interventions have been successfully applied to these disorders as well as other physically based problem areas including chronic pain (Sanders, 1979), stroke (Lutzker and Martin, 1981), hypertension and Raynaud's disease (Kallman and Gilmore, 1981).

Behavioural interventions have been applied to persons with mental retardation and organic impairment mostly in the areas of ameliorating maladaptive behaviour patterns resulting from the specific disorder. For example, one of the criteria noted earlier which defines the mental retardation diagnosis is deficits in adaptive behaviour. These deficits are established by comparing an individual's specific adaptive behaviours (or lack thereof) to normal age peers and cultural group. For example, Wetherby and Baumeister (1981) note that specific behaviours are considered adaptive and typical for early childhood (i.e., sensorimotor function, communication, and self-help skills), early adolescence (i.e., school-related behaviours), and late adolescence and adulthood (i.e., vocational performance). They go on to state that stress is placed on appropriate social responding in all cases. Therefore, when severe deficits are observed in these age-appropriate behaviours, including adaptive social responding in all individuals, behavioural interventions, and explicitly, social skills training, are implicated.

Individuals with organic impairment evince similar maladaptive behaviour patterns as these just noted. Therefore, these individuals would benefit from similar interventions. Behavioural programmes would be designed to retrain deficits which were a result of the physical insult or disease process. The most common form of treatment for deficits in behaviour patterns with this population is some form of behaviour modification through teaching (Wetherby and Baumeister, 1981). This chapter outlines assessment and treatment procedures designed to ameliorate social skill deficits with a mentally handicapped or organically impaired population within the behavioural treatment tradition.

Assessment

Clinical methods of evaluating social skills deficits with mentally retarded and organically impaired persons have closely paralleled the efforts made with other populations (Andrasik and Matson, 1984). The primary methods of assessment have included direct observations (which have been by far the most frequently employed method), rating scales, sociometric ratings, and social validation procedures. These assessment methods have typically been used both for selecting target behaviours for treatment and as a method of evaluating outcome (Matson, DiLorenzo and Andrasik, 1982). These procedures have been referred to throughout both volumes of this Handbook. While many similarities exist with respect to the application of these methods to all persons with social problems, there are also special problems and difficulties that may arise respective to the mentally handicapped and organically impaired.

The major mitigating factor with the population discussed here is the limited repertoire of responses due to mental and physical disabilities. This problem is particularly pronounced with respect to deficiencies in verbal behaviour, personal hygiene skills, and self-help skills (Matson, 1982a; Matson, DiLorenzo and Esveldt-Dawson, 1981; Matson, Ollendick and Adkins, 1980). In addition, this group often exhibits severely disruptive behaviours such as self-injury (Schroeder et al., 1981).

The range of positive responses defined primarily as social in nature is as broad as the identified deficits. They include answering a telephone in an acceptable fashion (Matson, 1982a), physical gestures, facial mannerisms, eye contact, number of words spoken, voice intonation, verbal content of speech, overall social skills (Matson, Kazdin and Esveldt-Dawson, 1980; Senatore, Matson and Kazdin, 1982), subject changes, discussion of past problems, using words appropriately, and duration of speech (Stephens, Matson, Westmoreland and Kulpa, 1981).

Direct observation

Most of the behaviours noted above have been evaluated via direct observation through role-played interactions. This assessment procedure is modelled after similar procedures developed for other populations (Bellack, Hersen and Turner, 1976; Eisler *et al.*, 1975). The focus of both assessment and training revolve around a series of scenes involving interpersonal interactions in which the individuals role-play their responses. In the instance of research with the mentally retarded, the content of the scenes differ considerably from those developed for persons of normal intelligence such as the Behavioral Assertiveness Test (Eisler *et al.*, 1975). Scenes are generally developed based on descriptions provided by ward staff relative to various problem situations. Scenes are presented one at a time with two therapists and one patient. A typical scene used in this type of research is described below (Matson and Senatore, 1981).

Narrator:	You are at the workshop and have just received your paycheck for this month. You had missed several days of work last week. Therefore your paycheck was much smaller than usual. Instead of receiving $8.00, you received $4.00. You are mad because you need the money.
Role model prompt:	Well, how do you like your paycheck?
Narrator:	(to client) You say . . .
Client:	(client response)

The number of scenes assessed per baseline and/or training sessions varies from 6 to 10. These are audiotaped (or videotaped if nonverbal behaviours were being trained) and the clients' responses recorded. The method of recording varies depending on the behaviour rated: response length is timed, words counted, and appropriate intonation rated on a Likert scale where 1 = very poor and 5 = very good. Recordings would be completed for each session and agreement between raters compared.

A second type of direct observation method pertains to observations made in the natural environment. In one study of this type, Matson and Andrasik (1982) attempted to establish appropriate social interactions while decreasing inappropriate social interactions of eight mentally retarded institutionalised adults. Observations were made by staff during leisure time in a lounge area. This technique was used as a method of assessing generalisation of training effects from the therapy room.

Rating scales

A second type of assessment procedure, typically used as an adjunct measure of generalisation in social skills training is the rating scale. The NOSIE-30 (Honigfeld, Gillis and Klett, 1966), a frequently used scale for assessing chronic psychiatric populations (Paul and Lentz, 1978), and the Social Skills Performance Survey (SSPS) (Lowe and Cautela, 1978) have been adapted for use with a mentally retarded population (Matson et al., 1983). The NOSIE consists of 30 items, each of which is rated on a 5-point scale from never to always. Typical items from the scale include: is sloppy; cries; is messy in his eating habits; keeps himself clean; is slow-moving or sluggish; sleeps unless directed into activity; laughs or smiles at funny comments or events; and starts a conversation with others. The scale has a positive and negative factor. As can be readily ascertained from above, the items are designed to reflect one or the other of these two directions.

The SPSS is a 57-item 5-point Likert scale although a previous 100-item version has also been used in some studies (Matson and Senatore, 1981). The scale, which has proven to be a sensitive measure of social functioning with mentally retarded persons, has well established reliability and validity data. It has also been factor analysed on a diverse group of patients from Illinois and Pennsylvania who fall in the mild to moderate ranges of mental retardation. Typical items include: has eye contact when speaking, shows enthusiasm for others' good fortunes, demonstrates concern for others' rights, seeks others out too often, gives unsolicited advice, makes embarrassing comments, puts himself/herself down, complains, takes advantage of others, and deceives others for personal gain. In their factor analytic study, Matson et al. (1983) established four factors called appropriate social skill, poor communication skills, inappropriate assertion, and sociopathic behaviour.

A measure of childhood social skills has also been developed recently which may prove to be of some value. The Matson Evaluation of Social Skills with Youngsters (MESSY) is a scale with both self- and teacher-report versions. Norms for the self-report scale were derived from 322 children and the teacher report was completed on a sample of 422. The scales have 62 and 64 items respectively. Items are rated on a 5-point Likert scale with anchors for each of the points including not at all (1), a little (2), some (3), much of the time (4), and very much (5). In addition to obtaining reliability data, both versions of the scale were factor analysed.

The self-report scale had factors entitled appropriate social skill, inappropriate assertiveness, impulsive/recalcitrant, overconfident, and jealousy/withdrawal. The teacher report had two factors called inappropriate assertiveness/impulsivity and appropriate social skills.

To date, use of checklists and rating scales have been used infrequently in the social skills literature with mentally handicapped and organically impaired persons. However, the multimethod approach to assessment in social skills treatment and research has been stressed recently (Senatore *et al.*, 1982). These methods are likely to provide a much more valid and reliable picture of treatment effects. It should be pointed out, however, that a number of scales have been developed that may be of value indirectly in assessing mental retardation and/or organic impairment and some aspects of social behaviour. Examples of these include the Vineland Social Maturity Scale (Doll, 1953, 1965), American Association on Mental Deficiency Adaptive Behavior Scale (Lambert *et al.*, 1975; Nihira *et al.*, 1974, 1975), Balthazar Scale of Adaptive Behavior (Balthazar, 1971, 1973), Fairview Self-Help Scale (Ross, 1969, 1970), Fairview Social Skills Scale (Giampiccolo, 1974; Ross and Giampiccolo, 1972), Cain–Levine Social Competency Scale (Cain, Levine and Elzey, 1963; Levine, Elzey and Lewis, 1969), Social Prevocational Information Battery (Halpern *et al.*, 1975), and Adaptive Behavior Inventory (Mercer and Lewis, 1978). The reader should be warned however that even though these measures refer to social behaviour, they are most often referring to self-help behaviour such as toileting or dressing and aggression to others or themselves (self-injury). These measures are however primarily geared toward the mentally retarded. Measures of self-care and independent living skills (some of which may relate to social skills) have also been developed for the organically impaired. They include the PULSES Profile (Moskowitz and McCann, 1957), the Barthal Index (Mahoney and Barthel, 1965), the Kenny Self-Care Evaluation (Schoening *et al.*, 1965), the Katz Index (Katz *et al.*, 1963), and the level of Rehabilitation Scale (Carey and Posavac, 1978).

Sociometric ratings

A third assessment approach employed in clinical research with mentally handicapped and organically impaired persons is sociometric ratings. This procedure has received only brief attention with the population reviewed in our present chapter (Hops and Greenwood, 1981). Sociometric ratings constitute aggregate evaluations by a group of persons. Typically, individuals are rated on a particular characteristic such as "most popular". The two common groups of raters include familiar adults (Mueller, 1972; Mueller and Brenner, 1977), and peers (Asher *et al.*, 1979; Ballard *et al.*, 1977).

The major advantage of this approach is the good reliability and validity of the measure. However, while sociometric ratings can be used to help pick out children at risk, they do not provide data on particular deficiencies or strengths. (See Connolly (1983) for a more detailed review of this topic.)

Social validation

A final type of assessment is social validation. This procedure initially was described by Wolf (1978) and Kazdin (1977). This approach is a systematic way of assessing the perceptions of others regarding the acceptability of specific target behaviours for treatment and for establishing the clinical significance of treatment effects. The two approaches developed to evaluate the selection of dependent variables and treatment outcome are called social comparison and subjective evaluation (Kazdin and Matson, 1981).

Social comparison involves the evaluation of a patient's performance relative to a peer comparison group. Matson et al. (1980) have used this approach experimentally with two moderately mentally retarded children, age 11 and 12 years. The children were hospitalised on a psychiatric unit because of conduct disorders and problems in interacting with others. They were trained individually in several social skills including appropriate facial expression, voice intonation, motor movements, eye contact, and verbal content of responses to the therapist. Two "normal" children were matched on age and sex with each of the patients: all the children were matched on age and sex with each of the patients, and were evaluated under identical conditions on the target responses. The level of responding for the comparison children was used to define the optimal point of performance on various target behaviours. Walker and Hops (1976) have used a similar strategy for mainstreaming developmentally disabled children into normal classrooms. Deficiencies in following directions and related classroom behaviours were evident in their population. These handicapped children were compared to the normal group prior to and following intervention as a means of evaluating progress.

The second form of social validation, subjective evaluation, involves individuals not involved in a particular treatment programme giving their opinion about behaviours for treatment or the effects of the treatment. These evaluations have generally been of a global nature and are used to assess how well the patient is functioning, while providing an overall appraisal of performance. These evaluations are typically made after independent evidence has established that behaviours among the patients have actually changed after the treatment.

An example of subjective evaluation is provided by Bornstein et al. (1980). They treated six mild to moderately mentally retarded persons for poor posture, enunciation problems, inappropriate speech content, loudness, inappropriate hand movements, intonation, eye contact, and rate of speech.

A number of videotaped sessions were mixed in a random fashion and shown to a group of three volunteer raters who had agreed to judge general social competency. These data were used along with frequency counts and ratings of discrete responses made by trained observers for the target behaviours noted above. Similar methods with mentally retarded adults have been used to evaluate social behaviours that characterise depression (Matson, 1982b) and with obsessive-compulsive behaviour (Matson, 1982c).

Work performance has also been an issue for study with the subjective evaluation method of social validation. Subjects were employed in one of five cafeterias at the University of Illinois at Champaign-Urbana. Participants included five managers, five shift supervisors, seven non-handicapped workers, and 10 mentally handicapped workers. These individuals were to rate 26 items that reflected job skills and work quality, level of responsibility, relationship to supervisors and co-workers, and ability to manage time. The purpose of this study was not to use social validation to evaluate a particular treatment. Rather, a closer evaluation of aspects of social validation as an assessment strategy was being made. Co-workers and the mentally retarded persons rated social and vocational responses differently than supervisors. It was concluded that more empirical attention should be given to the role of co-workers in consensual validation.

Effects of assessment conditions

We have reviewed the major forms of assessment. There are also a number of studies, recently conducted, that put into question some findings pertaining to social skills assessments. These studies argue for making a conservative evaluation of data taken in brief analogue settings and suggest that several variables need to be considered when evaluating data. The studies to be reviewed were conducted with children including those of normal intelligence, children with learning disabilities, and mentally retarded persons. These data are also likely to have important implications for adults as well, though this is yet to be confirmed.

Kazdin *et al.* (1981) conducted a study to determine if children could alter their performance on tests commonly used to assess appropriate social skills, namely role-play tests. Sixty children between 6 and 12 years of age were assessed. Half were children with mixed diagnosis, selected from a psychiatric inpatient unit. The other half of the subjects were from a university laboratory school matched on age, gender, and race with the psychiatric population. It was found that performance of social skills during overt role-play assessment was influenced by the incentives such as praise, feedback and stars. Incentives were equally effective for normal and inpatient children and resulted in statistically significant improvements in performance on post-tests and the performance of children who had not been reinforced.

In a second related study, 32 children between 7 and 12 years of age were evaluated (Kazdin, Esveldt-Dawson and Matson, 1982). All of the children in this study were inpatients from the programme described above. Role-play scenes were similar to those used in the Kazdin *et al.* (1981) study. In addition, raters scored elements of social skill such as eye contact and facial expression, and overall social skills. A final assessment consisted of a self-confidence measure. It was found that performance on post-assessment conditions were significantly influenced by experiences prior to the post-test. Children who received a positive-induction task improved more on both specific behaviours and global measures.

The data from these studies show that performance on different social skills assessments can be varied due to testing conditions. It can be concluded that careful attention to a number of factors should be taken into account and that a variety of measures over time should be employed.

Assessment in the social skills area has not received nearly the attention that is characteristic of the treatment literature but some major advances have been made. Direct observational methods have been researched more than other methods. It is likely that some of the other areas of assessment will catch up to some degree with this former method of assessment in the next few years. For example, social validation is beginning to receive more attention in the literature. Similarly, checklists such as the MESSY and SSPS are likely to be used more frequently in future research as the emphasis of training shifts from the demonstration of skills training in analogue situations to naturalistic settings.

Treatment

A large number of behaviourally based treatment procedures have been employed to train social skills in mentally handicapped and organically impaired persons, with adults in the former group receiving the most attention. Several strategies have been employed to treat social skills deficits in this population including simple contingencies, the SST package, social skills games, and the social skills curriculum. Studies will be grouped and reviewed based on the treatment strategy used. Most of the studies reviewed will be based on the available research literature. However, brief mention will also be made of some of the numerous and rapidly proliferating training kits for social skills.

Simple contingencies

As noted previously, a number of studies have been conducted which are primarily operant in nature, emphasising overt reinforcement and punishment without the use of modelling, verbal feedback, and related strategies.

The earliest published study of this type which seemed to relate to social skills was conducted by Brodsky (1967). Two mentally handicapped females aged 17 and 25 years were trained for lack of social responding to others, despite having considerable verbal fluency. Behaviours were assessed in a naturalistic setting (social area on the ward) and during structured social activities. For one patient, tokens were used to reinforce social statements during the interview. This procedure was rapidly and dramatically effective. However, very little generalisation outside the analogue setting occurred. The second patient was provided with reinforcement for social behaviour emitted in the structured social setting. This procedure not only led to significant in-session increases in appropriate social behaviour, but also to generalisation both in the playground and interview situations. Other studies with similar methodologies also have proven effective (Deutsch and Parks, 1978; Wehman, Karan and Retif, 1976).

In addition to studies with adults, several operant experiments to enhance social skills with children have also been conducted. Stokes, Baer and Jackson (1974) treated four severely to profoundly mentally handicapped children between 10 and 13 years of age. Handwaving was selected as a positive social greeting and was scored if the child's hand was empty, raised above elbow level, and with at least two back-and-forth motions. Treatment effects were assessed in a multiple-baseline design and training was conducted by the senior author. Each subject was approached at times when they were standing or sitting. Therapist contact lasted for ten seconds, or until a greeting response from the subject was given. Approximately 20 contacts daily in the child's natural environment were made. A spontaneous wave by a child resulted in delivery of a tangible reinforcer (e.g. potato chips). Social reinforcers included a smile or hello by the trainer along with a nonverbal contact such as a pat on the shoulder. The greeting response was trained very rapidly with dramatic improvements over baseline for all subjects.

In addition to these studies, there are a number of other experiments which have produced similar findings (Braam and Poling, 1983; Jackson and Wallace, 1974; McClure, 1968; Paloutzian et al., 1971; Peterson, Robinson and Littman, 1983; Twardosz and Baer, 1973; Whitman, Burish and Collins, 1972). These studies suggest that very rudimentary skills can be trained to mentally handicapped children and adults. Later studies were to demonstrate that more complex training strategies and more extensive and complicated interpersonal behaviours could also be enhanced. (See Singh and Winton (1983) for a more detailed review of this topic.)

Social skills package

The majority of studies on social skills have involved a standard social skills package described and used for college students (McFall and Lillesand, 1971; McFall and Marston, 1970) and chronic schizophrenics (Hersen, Eisler and Miller, 1973, 1974). The basic package includes a number of component techniques. First, *instructions* are presented detailing how the child or adult should behave in the role-play setting. Second, *modelling* may be provided by one of the trainers as to how the particular social skill is to be performed. Third, and perhaps in addition to or in place of modelling, *role-playing* is used. This procedure consists of rehearsal of both verbal and nonverbal behaviours that may constitute appropriate social responding. A fourth procedure is *performance* feedback and consists of specific comments on the appropriate performance of target behaviours just demonstrated by the trainee. Fifth, the trainee is provided *social reinforcement* consisting of praise, smiles, pats on the back and related interpersonal behaviours. Finally, the individual may be asked to exhibit particular *target behaviours* in the natural environment. A more detailed explanation of these procedures is provided elsewhere (e.g., Kelly, 1982; Matson, 1984; Matson *et al.*, 1982). These techniques could be conceptualised as following social learning theory. In addition, the behaviours treated have tended to constitute a much more complex grouping than the one or two behaviours typically treated in most of the contingency programmes noted previously.

The first SST study labelled as such with the mentally retarded and using the social skills package was described by Matson and Stephens (1978). Subjects were four male mentally handicapped chronic schizophrenics. They ranged in age from 28 to 38 years and they all had been hospitalised for several years. Ten scenes were developed based on situations in which the patients had been involved in an argument or fight. Typical situations involved patients begging for money or cigarettes, making insulting or derogatory comments, or verbally threatening others. The behaviours targeted for training included frequency of looking, inappropriate requests, inappropriate laughing, making irrelevant comments, interrupting others while they were speaking, making appropriate statements, being appropriately assertive, looking neat, having good posture, displaying appropriate affect, and using acceptable facial mannerisms. Treatment proved effective for the patients on these target behaviours as measured using analogue clinical research methodology. In addition, the frequency of arguing and fighting dramatically decreased during treatment. However, these gains were not maintained during follow-up.

A second study conducted on the same ward of this inpatient hospital was conducted using a group training procedure (Matson and Zeiss, 1978). In this study, 12 women were trained on the following behaviours: appropriate affect, appropriate tone of voice, physical gestures, appropriate content of speech, overall assertiveness, personal appearance, co-operation, requests for attention, and content of speech. The treatment was provided in groups of three and comparisons were made using a multiple-baseline design. Training proved effective for all the target behaviours. Arguing and fighting which were assessed on the ward decreased for 11 of the 12 trainees. Effects at follow-up showed that gains were maintained better for behaviours trained in the analogue setting when compared to generalisation of training to the ward. Other researchers have verified that mentally handicapped adults can be trained to exhibit more proficient social skills (Bornstein *et al.*, 1980; Stacy, Doleys and Malcolm, 1979).

The SST package proven so successful with mentally retarded adults has also been demonstrated as effective with children (Matson *et al.*, 1980). These investigators treated two black males of 11 and 12 years of age and in the moderate range of mental handicap. One child had been diagnosed as anxiety disordered while the second was designated as conduct disordered. Two normal children were matched on age and sex with each subject and tested on the same target behaviours with the same role-play scenes. Their performance was used as a clinical criterion of success. Target behaviours included physical gestures, facial mannerisms, eye contact, number of words spoken, verbal content, and a rating of overall social performance. Behaviours were treated in a multiple-baseline fashion and treatment proved to be highly effective.

A second social skills study was conducted by Nelson, Gibson and Cutting (1973). They treated a 7-year-old mildly mentally handicapped boy in three deficit areas, including difficulty in asking grammatically correct questions, infrequent smiling, and poor content of speech. Training included having the child observe two normal 7-year-olds performing the target responses correctly, providing instructions plus social reinforcement for correct responses, and these two treatments combined. Effects of these methods were evaluated in a multiple-baseline design. The various training procedures all proved effective in increasing positive behaviours. The study was not designed in such a way as to make comparisons of treatment effectiveness.

A final study evaluated the training of 10 mild to moderately mentally handicapped adolescents (Kelly *et al.*, 1979). Behaviours on which these youths were deficient included eliciting information about oneself, and reinforcing or complimenting others. Training followed the standard skills training package and was conducted in groups. Training effects were assessed by observing each subject's participation in a conversation with one other peer. Treatment sessions were held three times weekly for four weeks. Generalisation of treatment effects was evaluated by having the target child talk with an unfamiliar nonretarded peer. Effects of training were marked and generalised to the unfamiliar peer.

Another area beginning to receive attention in the social skills literature and also utilising a package of procedures is job interviewing skills. Kelly, Wildman and Berler (1980) have published a study which is representative of the research in this area. They trained four mildly mentally retarded adolescent males who were enrolled in a short-term residential treatment programme. To assess the job interviewing skills of the patients, several personnel managers were asked to provide feedback on the relevance of an initial pool of potential interview questions. Ten standard interview questions were developed including: "Can you tell me something about your work experience?"; "How do you think you'll be able to handle both school and job?"; and "Do you have any questions for me?". These questions were developed into role-play situations similar to those described in the assessment section of this chapter. Each participant responded to the questions as though applying for a job that they would be interested in, such as a gas station helper, a supermarket clerk, or a baker's helper. Four types of behaviour were scored and trained. These were positive information about job-related past experience and training, positive information about oneself, questions directed to the interviewer, and verbal expressions of enthusiasm and interest. Patients were trained in a group with two or three therapists. Each session began with a brief introduction of the skill (one of the four noted above) to be trained that day. One of three modelling tapes showing a socially skilled individual in a job interview was then shown to the group for approximately ten minutes. The modelling tapes were presented in a random order with the limitation that the same tape not be shown for two consecutive training sessions. On the tapes, the models were of similar age and sex as the trainees to help them further identify how to perform in the most socially desirable manner. While the trainees were observing the videotapes, the therapists pointed out statements that the interviewee made that illustrated the particular response being trained during that session. Following the tape presentation, the experiments provided a rationale for the importance of the target behaviour in a job interview and gave further examples. Patients then practised and were reinforced for making the appropriate target responses. In a period of 5 to 16 training sessions, marked improvements on all the target behaviours were found. A more detailed review of job interviewing with mentally handicapped persons following these basic strategies can be found elsewhere (Kelly and Christoff, 1983).

Social skills games

Foxx, McMorrow and Schloss (1983) used a procedure somewhat different to that reported in previous sections of this chapter for training social skills. They suggest that the games method is superior, although there are no data to support this contention. The rationale for this claim is that the procedures do not require a trained therapist and that the training method would be more easily replicated. Six patients from a referral group of 10 with social skill deficits were selected for training because they were familiar with the board game which was to be used in training. Social skills that were trained were rudimentary ones such as learning to say "please" and "thank you".

Trainees were mentally retarded adults, with some having dual diagnoses. Training was provided in groups of two men and a woman, with ages ranging from 20–47 years. In playing the board game, the number of spaces a trainee could move depended on their response to a social situation which was incorporated into the game. Skills to be trained were determined by reviewing the literature, consulting with unit staff, and observing players' general levels of social competence in specific situations. Behaviours selected for treatment included compliments, social interactions, politeness, criticism, social confrontation, and questions/answers.

As the game proceeded, the therapist would read to the trainee the social situation from the card they had selected, and then patients had ten seconds to provide a response. Specific verbal feedback was then given to the trainee on the appropriateness of their response. The method was successful in enhancing social skill levels of the trainees.

Social skill curriculum

A number of professionals have begun developing materials on SST for a rapidly expanding market. In our view there are a number of problems with this approach to SST. Typically, there are no empirical data to support the efficacy of these approaches and often they do not closely adhere to well-established guidelines for the administration of training. However, in some instances they are the only materials written in such a way as to provide readily applicable information for teachers and other direct care staff. One manual of this type is a programme called *Social Skills for Severely Retarded Adults* (McClennen, Hoekstra and Bryan, 1980). Their programme is of interest since it provides a teaching curriculum for severe and profoundly mentally handicapped persons, whereas most of the research to date has been conducted with those able to function at a higher level.

Their programme is broken down into a number of objectives including appropriate physical interactions, touching/manipulating objects, responding to their name, smiling, making eye contact, interacting with a trainer, travelling with a trainer, waiting, developing leisure skills, and engaging in group interactions. The programme is developed for use by paraprofessionals and is complete with data sheets, suggestions about reinforcers that can be used, evaluating progress, definitions of target behaviours, and examples of appropriate responses. The authors claim success through a controlled study which is briefly described at the beginning of the manual. Unfortunately, the information provided is not sufficient for an outside evaluator to accept or refute these claims. Additionally, the data they report have not been published elsewhere. The manual would likely serve as a useful adjunct if appropriate supervision by an experienced psychologist were available.

Strain (1983) has conducted an empirical study that attempted to define behaviours which should be included in a social skills curriculum. He studied the social interactions of 80 children with 20 in each of four groups. The four groups were composed of nonhandicapped 3- to 5-year-olds who received high sociometric ratings from class peers; severely handicapped 3- to 5-year-olds who received relatively higher sociometric ratings compared to their handicapped class peers; nonhandicapped 3- to 5-year-olds who received lower sociometric ratings from class peers; and severely handicapped 3- to 5-year-olds who received lower sociometric ratings than their handicapped class peers. Children were recruited from 10 mainstreamed classrooms. Continuous observations of specific social initiations and responses to those initiations were made. Each child was evaluated for a total of 210 minutes. The purpose of the study was to generate a set of social interaction data on both severely handicapped and nonhandicapped children that could be used to construct a hierarchy of context-specific social skills. It was found that nonhandicapped children seemed not to have been affected adversely by exposure to handicapped peers, and normal subjects regulated the complexity of their social initiations to match the developmental level of handicapped interactants. Additionally, negative social initiations emerged as a behaviour pattern that influenced children's negative evaluations of others and specific approach behaviours such as play organisers, shares, affection and assistance were displayed more frequently by higher regarded handicapped children. The author concludes that these data have several implications for social skills curricula. First, it was concluded that high rates of positive and negative social behaviours are likely to occur simultaneously. Thus, it is suggested that negative behaviours should be eliminated. In addition, the positive behaviours noted above are considered particularly important for targeting in a social skills curriculum. These data provide some demographic guidelines for curriculum development. Unlike the materials mentioned above, they do not provide specific guidelines for training. Further research is needed before widespread implementation of tested procedures can occur.

Head trauma victims

Very little research currently exists that involves patients that have major cognitive handicaps that are not due to mental handicap. Two notable exceptions are described by a research team at Pennsylvania State University. In one of these studies (Schloss *et al.*, 1984), two young adults who had been brain-damaged in automobile accidents were treated. One subject, a 20-year-old male, had been hospitalised for five months and had been in a coma for the first month. He experienced severe retrograde amnesia for six months and milder amnesia for an additional four months, and exhibited dense right side hemiplegia and limited expressive speech. The second male, aged 21 years, had a subdural haematoma and dense right side hemiplegia, and had been hospitalised for three months following the accident. He had also received multiple facial fractures and loss of his right eye. Both patients were near recovery, with permanent brain damage.

Patients self-monitored three heterosexual conversational skills including complimenting others, asking others about themselves, and telling others about themselves during thirty-minute recording sessions. Training included providing the response definition used in the training phase, providing examples, soliciting examples from the patients, playing an audiotape of a typical conversation between two people, and asking the patients to tally each time the target behaviour was used in the conversation. Feedback was provided when the patients' record of target behaviour was different from the actual responses on the tape. Finally, patients were asked to practise monitoring the target behaviour in one conversation following the session. Training proved effective and the responses generalised to other sessions where training was not provided. Additionally, social validation data, modelled after Matson *et al.* (1980), showed that the trainees were able to move into the range of normal age peers on the target behaviours.

A second study by the same investigators (Gajar *et al.*, 1984) replicated the first investigation; training two men with similar problems and ages, using identical techniques. Thus, head trauma victims with some major neurological impairments were able to use a sophisticated self-monitoring strategy as a means of enhancing their social skills.

Generalisation

Although the ability to affect treatment change is very important in any programme, generalisation of these treatment effects is critical. In a number of treatment studies presented in this chapter, the researchers made overt attempts at assessing generalisation. However, several studies have been conducted to specifically address generalisation issues.

Matson and Earnhart (1981) looked at some generalisation issues in training social skills to mentally handicapped persons. They treated four women ranging in age from 24 to 47 years who had been hospitalised from

7 to 37 years in a facility for the mentally handicapped. Three of the women were severely mentally handicapped and a fourth was moderately handicapped. They were treated for pestering staff, talking too loudly and fussing, making derogatory comments, cursing, and belittling others. In addition to the basic social skills package described earlier, they were trained to monitor their own behaviour on the ward. An additional prompting component was also given on the ward: if a member of staff observed a target behaviour not recorded by the trainee, they were to contact the trainer immediately. This was possible since training only occurred during the day shift and all those involved in the study worked on the same ward. The trainer would then come to the ward, take the trainee to the spot where the misbehaviour had occurred, and provide performance feedback, modelling, social reinforcement, and role-playing. Very little generalisation resulted from the therapy sessions to the ward until prompting was provided on the ward. The immediacy and amount of feedback needed to sustain the self-monitoring was much greater than what had been reported for mildly handicapped persons (Bauman and Iwata, 1977). Despite considerable training, subjects were unable reliably to record behaviour without continued monitoring and prompting on the ward. It is suggested that these findings illustrate to some degree the cognitive limitations of these subjects. It should be noted that when all of these procedures were implemented consistently, training and generalisation proved to be highly successful.

Other efforts to enhance generalisation also have been made. Matson and Andrasik (1982) trained eight individuals, five males and three females, who ranged from mild to moderate in mental handicap. The subjects were between 25 and 43 years of age and lived on a large unit of a hospital for the mentally handicapped. These persons were being prepared for placement in a community setting. This study served as a follow-up to Matson and Earnhart (1981), although target behaviours were more general than those in the aforementioned study, being labelled appropriate and inappropriate social interactions. The standard SST package and a self-monitoring programme were initiated. In the first of three studies, self-reinforcement was evaluated. In two later experiments, self-monitoring and self-reinforcement were employed. Self-reinforcement consisted of trainees giving themselves tokens that could be exchanged for candy and soda pop. The tokens were kept in a leisure-time room where the trainees had been encouraged to interact socially with others. To increase appropriate use of self-reinforcement in the leisure area, similar situations were re-enacted in the therapy room for both appropriate and inappropriate applications. Instructions and modelling of self-reinforcement were used to enhance the instructional qualities of these analogue re-enactments. The findings from these three experiments were that social skills with self-monitoring and self-reinforcement were more effective than social skills alone or merely giving the subject attention as a means of promoting positive social behaviours. The gains were not extremely large relative to effects observed in the analogue situation, but these data suggest that training of this sort can be promoted in naturalistic situations with mentally handicapped persons.

Two other efforts at enhancing proficiency in social skills will also be noted. In one study, Matson (1980b) treated a 27-year-old male and a 23-year-old female for two broad categories of appropriate and inappropriate social behaviours. In this instance, other patients served as assistants in providing social skills training. This procedure helped save staff time, substantially improved the social behaviours of the mentally retarded assistants, and provided them with an opportunity to engage in constructive social activity.

In a related study, Matson and Zeiss (1979) employed a buddy system for monitoring inappropriate social statements, arguing, tantrums, and interruptions. Therapy sessions were fifteen to thirty minutes in length. The two trainees were mildly mentally retarded women of 33 and 38 years of age who also displayed serious mental problems. The buddies were to note target behaviours when they occurred. Marked improvements in the target behaviours were noted during the study and patients attributed these gains in large part to the assistance of their partner. Similar training procedures have been shown to be effective in a number of related studies (Matson, 1978; Matson and Adkins, 1980).

Future Directions

The present chapter has reviewed the application of social skills assessment and training with the mentally handicapped and organically impaired. Whilst SST with the mentally handicapped is relatively new, work with the organically impaired has virtually only just begun. On the basis of this review it is concluded that SST packages and contingency programmes are highly effective procedures, and that when generalisation is programmed into the training regimen, the effects can be successfully generalised and maintained. Social skills games and curricula are a further recent redevelopment, but little empirical support is available to recommend these procedures at present.

Looking to the future, we recommend programmatic research to assess the comparative effectiveness of different procedures with one goal being eventual community placement. With research of this kind, perhaps trainees may be matched to potentially effective treatments based on subject demographics, type of problem behaviours, and assessment and treatment constraints based on environmental circumstances. Several studies have been reported which exemplify this type of research.

The studies and programmes reviewed here were aimed primarily at teaching a number of specific social behaviours. In these instances, the purpose of training was to enhance specific responses without a training goal aimed at enhancing specific forms of community adjustment. However, several studies of this latter type have been conducted: for example, in one study the goal was to facilitate mentally handicapped adults to converse on the telephone. Matson (1982a) conducted a large group controlled study with 45 adults living in community arrangements. These trainees ranged in age from 21 to 55 years and were in the mild range of mental handicap. Telephone conversation skills were defined as the ability to interact verbally in a socially appropriate fashion on the telephone. Responses made by trainees on the telephone ranged from appropriate to inappropriate on nine questions predesigned to represent typical phone conversational topics. Training consisted of variations of the typical social skills package.

The three experimental conditions were no-treatment, a modelling group, and independence training. The modelling condition followed procedures described by Smith and Meyers (1979). The trainers then practised the questions and answers twice while the trainees watched. The trainees were not required to practise the responses nor was feedback provided.

Independence training was first described by Matson (1980a). In effect, it is a package programme with more procedures than the typical SST approach. The treatment involved instructions, performance feedback, modelling, social reinforcement, shaping by successive approximations, self-evaluation, and monitoring. Independence training proved to be more effective than the modelling or no-treatment groups. These findings were considered important since they were the first in which a comparison of modelling and independence training was performed, and also in which independence training was used to train verbal skills.

Another comparative study was described by Matson and Senatore (1981). They treated 32 mentally handicapped adults in the mild to moderate range who were outpatients at a mental health clinic. Twenty-three of these individuals had experienced previous psychiatric hospitalisations. Subjects were yoked into triplets based on pre-assessment levels of social skill, then one person from each triplet was randomly assigned to each of the experimental conditions: a psychotherapy group, a SST group using the standard social skills package described previously, and a no-treatment control group. The psychotherapy group followed procedures described by Yalom (1975), Carkhuff (1969), and Rogers (1961). These included an emphasis on process oriented therapy with increased genuineness, group cohesion, promotion of trust, security, universality, and interpersonal awareness and learning. Both psychotherapy and SST were conducted in small groups of three to five with sessions held twice weekly for one hour. Subjects were assessed on role-play scenes and ratings of discrete target behaviours, including appropriate and inappropriate statements. Other measures that were used were the revised version of the Social Skills Performance Survey and the NOSIE-30. Greater improvements on all the dependent variables were noted for SST. However, gains were not well maintained at follow-up. Thus, long-term gains for the traditional psychotherapy and social skills groups were similar but still much better than was evident with the no-treatment controls.

Another comparative study was conducted with two particular forms of SST with adults (Senatore *et al.*, 1982). Their sample of 44 adults ranged from borderline to severely mentally handicapped. Experimental conditions were a no-treatment group and two social skills conditions. One condition was the standard SST package, while the other condition contained an active rehearsal component in which rather than simply role-play and discuss the scenes while seated, trainees were engaged in actually acting out accurately recreated social situations. This latter approach was considered potentially beneficial particularly for those functioning at lower levels. Many such individuals were very concrete in their thinking and might benefit more from training if it closely approximated live situations. Trainees were rated on the social appropriateness of their responses both during analogue situations and while at a party. They were assessed on verbal responses that they made to predetermined questions from corresponding role-play scenes. Gains were greater for the active training programme, although both SST programmes were effective.

Studies of this type could prove to be beneficial in extending the already impressive results in SST with this population. Further research might focus on large group outcome studies assessing the differential effectiveness of various procedures with the goal of improved community adjustment.

References

Andrasik, F. and Matson, J. L. (1984) Social skills with the mentally retarded. In: L. L'Abate and M. A. Milan (Eds.), *Handbook of social skills training and research*. New York: Wiley.

Asher, S. R., Singleton, L. C., Tinsley, R. R. and Hymel, S. (1979) The reliability of a rating scale sociometric method with preschool children. *Developmental Psychology*, **15**, 443–444.

Ballard, M., Corman, L., Gottlieb, J. and Kaufman, M. J. (1977) Improving the social status of mainstreamed retarded children. *Journal of Educational Psychology*, **69**, 605–611.

Balthazar, E. E. (1971) *Balthazar scales of adaptive behavior. I: Scales for functional independence.* Champaign, Illinois: Research Press.

Balthazar, E. E. (1973) *Balthazar scales of adaptive behavior. II: Scales of social adaptation.* Palo Alto, California: Consulting Psychologists Press.

Bauman, K. E. and Iwata, B. A. (1977) Maintenance of independent housekeeping skills using scheduling plus self-recording procedures. *Behavior Therapy*, **8**, 554–560.

Bellack, A. S., Hersen, M. and Turner, S. M. (1976) Generalization effects of social skills training in chronic schizophrenics: An experimental analysis. *Behaviour Research and Therapy*, **14**, 391–398.

Bornstein, P. H., Bach, P. J., McFall, M. E., Friman, P. C. and Lyons, P. D. (1980) Application of a social skills training program in the modification of interpersonal deficits among retarded adults: A clinical replication. *Journal of Applied Behavior Analysis*, **13**, 171–176.

Braam, S. A. and Poling, A. (1983) Development of intraverbal behavior in mentally retarded individuals through transfer of stimulus control procedures: Classification of verbal responses. *Applied Research in Mental Retardation*, **4**, 279–302.

Brodksy, G. (1967) The relationship between verbal and non-verbal behaviour change. *Behaviour Research and Therapy*, **5**, 183–191.

Cain, L. F., Levine, S. and Elzey, F. F. (1963) *Manual for the Cain–Levine social competency scale*. Palo Alto, California: Consulting Psychologists Press.

Carey, G. C. and Posavac, E. J. (1978) Program evaluation of physical medicine and rehabilitation unit. *Archives of Physical Medicine and Rehabilitation*, **59**, 330–337.

Carkhuff, R. (1969) *Helping and human relations*. New York: Holt, Rinehart & Winston.

Connolly, J. A. (1983) A review of sociometric procedures in the assessment of social competencies in children. *Applied Research in Mental Retardation*, **4**, 315–328.

Deutsch, M. and Parks, L. A. (1978) The use of contingent music to increase appropriate conversational speech. *Mental Retardation*, **16**, 33–36.

Doll, E. A. (1953) *Measurement of social competence: A manual for the Vineland Social Maturity Scale*. Minneapolis: Educational Publishers.

Doll, E. A. (1965) *Social Maturity Scale*. Circle Pines, Minnesota: American Guidance Service.

Eisler, R. M., Hersen, M., Miller, P. M. and Blanchard, E. B. (1975) Situational determinants of assertive behaviors. *Journal of Consulting and Clinical Psychology*, **43**, 330–340.

Foxx, R. M., McMorrow, M. H and Schloss, C. N. (1983) Stacking the deck: Teaching social skills to retarded adults with a modified table game. *Journal of Applied Behavior Analysis*, **16**, 157–170.

Gajar, A., Schloss, P. J., Schloss, C. N. and Thompson, C. K. (1984) *Effects of feedback and self-monitoring on head trauma youth's conversation skills*. Manuscript submitted for publication.

Giampiccolo, J. S., Jr. (1974) *Manual for the Fairview Social Skills Scale*. Costa Mesa, California: Fairview State Hospital.

Halpern, A., Raffeld, P., Irvin, L. K. and Link, R. (1975) *Testbook for the social and prevocational battery*. Monterey, California: CTB/McGraw-Hill.

Hersen, M., Eisler, R. and Miller, P. M. (1973) Development of assertion responses: Clinical, measurement and research considerations. *Behaviour Research and Therapy*, **11**, 505–521.

Hersen, M., Eisler, R. and Miller, P. M. (1974) An experimental analysis of generalization in assertion training. *Behaviour Research and Therapy*, **12**, 295–310.

Honigfeld, G., Gillis, R. D. and Klett, C. J. (1966) NOISE-30: A treatment-sensitive ward behavior scale. *Psychological Reports*, **19**, 180–182.

Hops, H. and Greenwood, C. R. (1981) Social skills deficits. In: E. J. Mash and L. G. Terdal (Eds.), *Behavioral assessment of childhood disorders*. New York: The Guilford Press.

Jackson, D. A. and Wallace, R. F. (1974) The modification and generalization of voice loudness in a fifteen-year-old retarded girl. *Journal of Applied Behavior Analysis*, **7**, 461–471.

Kallman, W. M. and Gilmore, J. D. (1981) Vascular disorders. In: S. M. Turner, K. S. Calhoun and H. E. Adams (Eds.), *Handbook of clinical behavior therapy*. New York: Wiley.

Katz, S., Ford, A. B., Moskowitz, R. W., Jackson, B. A. and Jaffe, M. W. (1963) Studies of illness in the aged: Index of ADL: Standardized measure of biological and psychosocial function. *Journal of the American Medical Association*, **185**, 914–919.

Kazdin, A. E. (1977) Assessing the clinical or applied significance of behavior change through social validation. *Behavior Modification*, **1**, 427–452.

Kazdin, A. E., Esveldt-Dawson, K. and Matson, J. L. (1982) Changes in children's social skills performance as a function of preassessment experiences. *Journal of Clinical Child Psychology*, **11**, 243–248.

Kazdin, A. E. and Matson, J. L. (1981) Social validation in mental retardation. *Applied Research in Mental Retardation*, **2**, 39–54.

Kazdin, A. E., Matson, J. L. and Esveldt-Dawson, K. (1981) Social skill performance among normal and psychiatric inpatient children as a function of assessment conditions. *Behaviour Research and Therapy*, **19**, 145–152.

Kelly, J. A. (1982) *Social-skills training: A practical guide for interventions.* New York: Springer.

Kelly, J. A. and Christoff, K. A. (1983) Job interview training for the mentally retarded: Issues and applications. *Applied Research in Mental Retardation*, **4**, 355–368.

Kelly, J. A., Furman, W., Phillips, J., Hawthorn, S. and Wilson, T. (1979) Teaching conversational skills to retarded adolescents. *Child Behavior Therapy*, **1**, 85–97.

Kelly, J. A., Wildman, B. G. and Berler, E. S. (1980) Small group behavioral training to improve the job interview skills repertoire of mildly retarded adolescents. *Journal of Applied Behavior Analysis*, **13**, 461–472.

Lambert, N., Windmiller, M., Cole, L. J. and Figueroa, R. (1975) *AAMD adaptive behavior scale manual* (rev. ed.). Washington, DC: American Association on Mental Deficiency.

Levine, S., Elzey, F. F. and Lewis, M. (1969) *California preschool social competency scale.* Palo Alto, California: Consulting Psychologists Press.

Lowe, B. R. and Cautela, J. R. (1978) A self-report measure of social skills. *Behavior Therapy*, **9**, 535–544.

Lubar, J. F. and Deering, W. M. (1981) *Behavioral approaches to neurology.* New York: Academic Press.

Lutzker, J. R. and Martin, J. A. (1981) *Behavior change.* Monterey, California: Brooks/Cole.

Mahoney, F. I. and Barthel, D. W. (1965) Functional evaluation: The Barthel Index. *Maryland State Medical Journal*, **14**, 61–65.

Matson, J. L. (1978) Training socially appropriate behaviours to moderately retarded adults: A social learning approach. *Scandinavian Journal of Behavior Therapy*, **7**, 167–175.

Matson, J. L. (1980a) A controlled group study of pedestrian skill training for the mentally retarded. *Behaviour Research and Therapy*, **18**, 99–106.

Matson, J. L. (1980b) Acquisition of social skills by mentally retarded adult training assistants. *Journal of Mental Deficiency Research*, **24**, 129–135.

Matson, J. L. (1982a) Independence training vs. modelling procedures for teaching phone conversation skills to the mentally retarded. *Behaviour Research and Therapy*, **20**, 505–511.

Matson, J. L. (1982b) The treatment of behavioral characteristics of depression in the mentally retarded. *Behavior Therapy*, **13**, 209–218.

Matson, J. L. (1982c) Treating obsessive-compulsive behavior in mentally retarded adults. *Behavior Modification*, **6**, 551–567.

Matson, J. L. (1984) Social skills training. *Psychiatric Aspects of Mental Retardation Reviews*, **3**, 1–4.

Matson, J. L. and Adkins, J. (1980) A self-instructional social skills training program for mentally retarded adults. *Mental Retardation*, **18**, 245–248.

Matson, J. L. and Andrasik, F. (1982) Training leisure-time social-interaction skills to mentally retarded adults. *American Journal of Mental Deficiency*, **86**, 533–542.

Matson, J. L., DiLorenzo, T. M. and Andrasik, F. (1982) A review of behavior modification procedures for treating social skill deficits and psychiatric disorders of the mentally retarded. In: J. L. Matson and F. Andrasik (Eds.), *Treatment issues and innovations in mental retardation.* New York: Plenum Press.

Matson, J. L., DiLorenzo, J. M. and Esveldt-Dawson, K. (1981) Independence training as a method of enhancing skill acquisition in the mentally retarded. *Behaviour Research and Therapy*, **19**, 399–405.

Matson, J. L. and Earnhart, T. (1981) Programming treatment effects to the natural environment: A procedure for training institutionalized retarded adults. *Behavior Modification*, **5**, 27–37.

Matson, J. L., Helsel, W. J., Bellack, A. S. and Senatore, V. (1983) Development of a rating scale to assess social skill deficits in mentally retarded adults. *Applied Research in Mental Retardation*, **4**, 399–407.

Matson, J. L., Kazdin, A. E. and Esveldt-Dawson, K. (1980) Training interpersonal skills among mentally retarded and socially dysfunctional children. *Behaviour Research and Therapy*, **18**, 419–427.

Matson, J. L. and LaGrow, S. (1983) Developmental and physical disabilities. In: M. Hersen, V. B. Van Hasselt and J. L. Matson (Eds.), *Behavior therapy for developmentally and physically disabled*. New York: Academic Press.

Matson, J. L. and Mulick, J. A. (1983) *Handbook of mental retardation*. New York: Pergamon Press.

Matson, J. L., Ollendick, T. H. and Adkins, J. (1980) A comprehensive dining program for mentally retarded adults. *Behaviour Research and Therapy*, **18**, 107–112.

Matson, J. L. and Senatore, V. (1981) A comparison of traditional psychotherapy and social skills training for improving interpersonal functioning of mentally retarded adults. *Behavior Therapy*, **12**, 369–382.

Matson, J. L. and Stephens, R. M. (1978) Increasing appropriate behavior of explosive chronic psychiatric patients with a social-skills training package. *Behavior Modification*, **2**, 61–76.

Matson, J. L. and Zeiss, R. A. (1978) Group training of social skills in chronically explosive, severely disturbed psychiataric patients. *Behavioral Engineering*, **2**, 41–50.

Matson, J. L. and Zeiss, R. A. (1979) The buddy system: A method for generalized reduction of inappropriate interpersonal behaviour of retarded-psychiatric patients. *British Journal of Social and Clinical Psychology*, **18**, 401–405.

McClennen, S. E., Hoekstra, R. R. and Bryan, J. E. (1980) *Social skills for severely retarded adults: An inventory and training program*. Champaign, Illinois: Research Press.

McClure, R. F. (1968) Reinforcement of verbal social behavior in moderately retarded children. *Psychological Reports*, **23**, 371–376.

McFall, R. and Lillesand, D. (1971) Behavioral rehearsal with modeling and coaching in assertion training. *Journal of Abnormal Psychology*, **77**, 313–323.

McFall, R. and Marston, A. (1970) An experimental investigation of behavior rehearsal in assertion training. *Journal of Abnormal Psychology*, **76**, 295–303.

Melin, L., Sjoden, P. O. and James, J. E. (1983) Neurological impairments In: M. Hersen, V. Van Hasselt and J. L. Matson (Eds.), *Behavior therapy for the developmentally and physically disabled*. New York: Academic Press.

Mercer, J. R. and Lewis, J. F. (1978) *System of multicultural pluralistic assessment* New York: Psychological Corporation

Meyers, E. C., Nihira, K. and Zetlin, A. (1979) The measurement of adaptive behavior. In: N. R. Ellis (Ed.), *Handbook of mental deficiency: Psychological theory and research*. Hilsdale, New Jersey: Lawrence Erlbaum Associates.

Moskowitz, E. and McCann, C. B. (1957) Classification of disability in the chronically ill and aging. *Journal of Chronic Diseases*, **5**, 342–346.

Mueller, E. (1972) The maintenance of verbal exchanges between young children. *Child Development*, **43**, 930–938.

Mueller, E. and Brenner, J. (1977) The origins of social skills and interaction among play group toddlers. *Child Development*, **48**, 854–861.

Nelson, R., Gibson, F., Jr. and Cutting, D. S. (1973) Video tape modeling: The development of three appropriate social responses in a mildly retarded child. *Mental Retardation*, **11**, 24–27.

Nihira, K., Foster, R., Shellhaas, M. and Leland, H. (1974) *AAMD adaptive behavior scale*. Washington, DC: American Association on Mental Deficiency.

Nihira, K., Foster, R., Shellhaas, M. and Leland, H. (1975) *Manual for AAMD adaptive behavior scale*. Washington, DC: American Association on Mental Deficiency.

Paloutzian, R. F., Hasazi, J., Streifel, J. and Edgar, C. L. (1971) Promotion of positive social interaction in severely retarded young children. *American Journal of Mental Deficiency*, **75**, 519–524.

Paul, G. L. and Lentz, R. J. (1978) *Psychosocial treatment of chronic mental patients*. Cambridge, Massachusetts: Harvard University Press.

Peterson, S. L., Robinson, E. A. and Littman, I. (1983) Parent–child interaction training for parents with a history of mental retardation. *Applied Research in Mental Retardation*, **4**, 329–342.

Rogers, C. (1961) *On becoming a person*. Boston: Houghton Mifflin.

Ross, R. T. (1969) *Fairview Self-Help Scale*. Costa Mesa, California: Fairview State Hospital.

Ross, R. T. (1970) *Manual for the Fairview Self-Help Scale*. Costa Mesa, California: Fairview State Hospital.

Ross, R. T. and Giampiccolo, J. S., Jr. (1972) *Fairview social skills scale*. Costa Mesa, California: Fairview State Hospital.

Sanders, S. H. (1979) Behavioral assessment and treatment of clinical pain: Appraisal of current status. In: M. Hersen, R. M. Eisler and P. M. Miller (Eds.), *Progress in behavior modification* (Vol. 8). New York: Academic Press.

Schloss, P. J., Thompson, C., Gajar, A. and Schloss, C. N. (1984) *Influence of self-recording on heterosexual conversational behaviors of head trauma youth*. Manuscript submitted for publication.

Schoening, H. A., Anderegg, L., Bergstrom, D., Fonda, M., Steinke, N. and Ulrich, P. (1965) Numerical scoring of self-care status of patients. *Archives of Physical Medicine and Rehabilitation*, **46**, 689–697.

Schroeder, S. R., Schroeder, C. S., Rojahn, J. and Mulick, J. A. (1981) Self-injurious behavior: An analysis of behavior management techniques. In: J. L. Matson and J. R. McCartney (Eds.), *Handbook of behavior modification with the mentally retarded*. New York: Plenum Press.

Senatore, V., Matson, J. L. and Kazdin, A. E. (1982) A comparison of behavioral methods to train social skills to mentally retarded adults. *Behavior Therapy*, **13**, 313–324.

Singh, N. N. and Winton, A. S. (1983) Social skills training with institutionalized severely and profoundly mentally retarded persons. *Applied Research in Mental Retardation*, **4**, 383–398.

Smith, M. and Meyers, A. (1979) Telephone skills training for retarded adults: Group and individual demonstrations with and without verbal instructions. *American Journal of Mental Deficiency*, **83**, 581–587.

Stacy, D., Doleys, D. M. and Malcolm, R. (1979) Effects of social-skills training in a community-based program. *American Journal of Mental Deficiency*, **84**, 152–158.

Stephens, R. M., Matson, J. L., Westmoreland, T. and Kulpa, J. (1981) Modification of psychotic speech with mentally retarded patients. *Journal of Mental Deficiency Research*, **25**, 187–191.

Stokes, T. F., Baer, D. M. and Jackson, R. L. (1974) Programming the generalization of a greeting response of four retarded children. *Journal of Applied Behavior Analysis*, **7**, 599–610.

Strain, P. S. (1983) Identification of social skill curriculum targets for severely handicapped children in mainstream preschools. *Applied Research in Mental Retardation*, **4**, 369–382.

Twardosz, S. and Baer, D. M. (1973) Training two severely retarded adolescents to ask questions. *Journal of Applied Behavior Analysis*, **6**, 655–661.

Walker, H. M. and Hops, H. (1976) Use of normative peer data as a standard for evaluating classroom treatment effects. *Journal of Applied Behavior Analysis*, **9**, 159–168.

Wehman, P., Karan, O. and Retif, C. (1976) Developing independent play in three severely retarded women. *Psychological Reports*, **39**, 995–998.

Wetherby, B. and Baumeister, A. A. (1981) Mental retardation. In: S. M. Turner, K. S. Calhoun and H. E. Adams (Eds.), *Handbook of clinical behavior therapy*. New York: Wiley.

Whitman, T. L., Burish, T. and Collins, C. (1972) Development of interpersonal language responses in two moderately retarded children. *Mental Retardation*, **10**, 40–45.

Wolf, M. M. (1978) Social validity: The case for subjective measurement or how applied behavior analysis is finding its heart. *Journal of Applied Behavior Analysis*, **11**, 203–214.

Yalom, I. (1975) *The theory and practice of group psychotherapy*. New York: Basic Books.

4

Social Skills Training and Depression

J. M. G. WILLIAMS

Many behavioural psychological descriptions of depression begin with either or both of the following statements: that experimental psychologists have studied depressive phenomena only fairly recently, and that depression is the common-cold of psychopathology. The first is certainly true. Lazarus (1968) was one of the first to attempt a serious behavioural analysis of depression, this coming after most of the major advances in analysis and treatment of anxiety-based neuroses. The second statement is, as Gilbert (1984) has pointed out, somewhat misleading. Depression is indeed the most common psychiatric disorder, but it is not the psychological equivalent of a common-cold. These patients are at greatest risk of committing suicide, and some 10% make an attempt on their lives within one year of entering treatment (Paykel and Dienelt, 1971). Furthermore, depressed patients are at greatest risk of developing various physical disorders, including cancer (Whitlock and Siskind, 1979).

Since Lazarus' early paper there have been many attempts to explain depression by various models from experimental psychology. Since these have recently been reviewed (Williams, 1984) they will not be detailed here, but it is worth bearing in mind a number of points. Firstly, depression, like many psychiatric conditions, is a multi-faceted disorder. Many distinctions and subcategorisations have been made (e.g. endogenous-reactive, psychotic-neurotic, unipolar-bipolar). Despite this, most psychological analyses have not taken these subcategorisations into account. It may be that social skills deficits are only present in certain subtypes, restricting the range of relevance of SST, but as yet we do not know.

Secondly, a diagnosis of depression is made on the basis of occurrence or non-occurrence of many symptoms. For example, in the Research Diagnostic Criteria (Spitzer, Endicott and Robins 1978) five of the following symptoms (together with low mood which persists at least two weeks, and in the absence of other prior diagnoses) are required for a diagnosis of Major Depressive Disorder: poor appetite or weight loss or increased appetite or weight gain; sleep difficulty or sleeping too much; loss of energy, fatigability or tiredness; psychomotor agitation or retardation; loss of interest or pleasure in usual activities, including social contact or sex; feelings of self-reproach or excessive inappropriate guilt; complaints of evidence of diminished ability to think or concentrate; recurrent thoughts of death or suicide, or any suicidal behaviour. Yet many of these symptoms do not feature in experimental psychological models of depression in general, or social skills models in particular. Thus, for example, suicidal ideation, loss of concentration, and changed sleeping patterns tend to be ignored. By contrast, "reduced behavioural output" and "loss of reinforcers" which are central to most behavioural formulations including a social skills approach are readily subsumed under just one symptom — "loss of interest in usual activities", which may or may not be present for a psychiatric diagnosis of depression to be made.

On the other hand, psychological models do not claim to exhaust the possible routes to the development of clinical depression. They claim to describe sufficient, not necessary causes. Furthermore, they provide possible descriptions of the way in which other (e.g. biological) causes are mediated. This is particularly true of the social skills model which suggests that deficient or a lack of skills (however caused) render a person vulnerable to breakdown under the stress of a loss event. During a depressive episode (however caused) the subsequent reduction of social skills can maintain the depression by cutting people off from possible sources of positive reinforcement even when the initial causes are no longer operating. Involvement of social skills deficits at either of these points in the causal sequence would suggest SST as a useful therapeutic endeavour. But are depressed patients deficient in social skills?

The Evidence for Social Skills Deficits in Depression

Early descriptions in the literature certainly seemed to support the view that such deficits exist. The observations of Lewinsohn and co-workers (Lewinsohn, Weinstein and Alper 1970; Libet and Lewinsohn 1973) seemed to indicate that depressed individuals differed from nondepressed individuals in at least five areas: the total amount of verbal behaviour; the number of times the individual initiated behaviour (i.e. not a reaction to another); the degree to which the individual distributed their behaviour equally towards a group of others; the latency to respond to behaviour of another; and the rate of positive/reinforcing behaviour.

The problem with these conclusions was that they were largely derived from uncontrolled observations of depressed individuals in their homes (where the entire interpersonal structure may be biased as much by the "nondepressed" family members as by the behaviour of the "depressed" individual). Other data were derived from observations of groups of depressed individuals without extensive comparisons with nondepressed subjects.

There are now sufficient research findings to demonstrate that these initial descriptions are both right and wrong, depending on how closely one defines "social skills". For example, Coyne (1976) found that depressed individuals had a marked alienating effect on people to whom they were talking in a twenty-minute telephone conversation, but apart from the length of time the depressed person spent talking about themselves, the precise measures of social behaviour (total amount of speech, number of approval responses such as "Yeah", "hm-hmm" and "yes", number of hope statements, and degree of "genuineness") did not distinguish depressed from nondepressed patients or control subjects. That is, a discrepancy was found between general interpersonal cues and particular behaviour. A similar conclusion emerges from a very careful analysis of social interaction in depression by Youngren and Lewinsohn (1980). They examined the behaviour of 75 neurotically depressed out-patients in comparison with 69 nondepressed psychiatric controls and with 80 normal controls. On five subscales of the Interpersonal Events Schedule (social activity, assertion, cognition, give positive and receive positive) the depressives rated themselves as less skilled than did normals and nondepressed psychiatric controls, consistent with ratings made by peers in a group and by independent coders. However, the independent observers found no difference between depressed and nondepressed patients in activity level, initiation level, actions elicited, positive reactions elicited, negative reactions elicited, speech rate, speech volume, eye contact, smiling, facial expression and gestures (illustrators vs adaptors). These conclusions agree with an earlier study by Lewinsohn and Amenson (1978) which assessed a number of specific categories of overt behaviour but found that only the more global ratings tended to differentiate depressed patients, and to be associated with therapy improvement. A more recent study by Kornblith, et al. (1983) has also found that improvements in general ratings of depression over twelve weeks of self-control therapy were not paralleled by any changes in specific social behaviour.

Only one study appears to have shown differences between depressed patients and nondepressed controls in social skills at the "molecular" level (Bellack, Hersen and Himmelhoch, 1983). From a careful analysis of videotaped role plays of eight positive and eight negative scenarios, they found differences on speech duration, voice tone, gaze, posture focus, request/compliance content and overall assertiveness. Note however that of these, only speech duration was objectively measured, the remainder were subjective ratings on 5 point bidirectional Likert-type scales. There were in fact two other measures made objectively (response latency and number of smiles) and neither of these differed between the depressed and nondepressed group. Added to the fact that these behaviours were assessed in role-play situations, whereas Coyne (1976), Youngren and Lewinsohn (1980) and Kornblith *et al.* (1983), who found no molecular differences, took observations from genuine interactions, it can at least be said that the level of specific skills elements have not so far yielded as sensitive a measure of interpersonal difficulty as do more global ratings of behaviour. But if the patients and observers agree that there is something wrong with the interpersonal behaviour of depressives, and if these errors cannot be detected at the molecular level, where do they originate?

This question is partly answered in a series of studies of the effect of depressive behaviour on others. Coyne (1976) studied twenty-minute telephone conversations in 45 subject pairs. One member of each pair was an undergraduate subject, the other member of the pair (the target) was either a depressed patient (N = 15) or a nondepressed patient (N = 15) or a nondepressed control subject matched for age and social class with the patients (N = 15). All subjects in the experiment were women. Results showed that the nondepressed subjects felt more depressed, anxious and hostile following interaction with depressed patients than after interaction with nondepressed patients or controls. They also wished to have significantly less future contact with these individuals. Furthermore, there were significant associations between mood disturbance following the conversation and extent of rejection of opportunities for further contact. It was found that the depressed subjects spent more time talking about themselves (talking freely of deaths, marital infidelities, hysterectomies, family strife and "a variety of other intensely personal matters"). In the absence of measurable differences in the elements of the interaction Coyne concludes that it is this content — the inappropriate self-disclosure — which determined the other's reaction, and accounts for the global ratings of interpersonal inadequacy.

Two further studies complicate the picture. Hammen and Peters (1978) pointed out that Coyne had only used female subjects and targets. They used both male and females in the role either of interviewer or interviewee, with the interviewee taking the role of a depressed or nondepressed person in five-minute telephone conversations. They replicated Coyne's finding of mood disturbance by interviewers after talking to a "depressed" person, and of more resultant rejection of these individuals. But the predominant finding was that opposite-sex "depressed" individuals were rejected far more than were same-sex "depressed" people. Furthermore, by having interviewees play roles, the *content* of the interview could be controlled in this experiment. Specifically, there was no more personal information divulged by "depressed" than by "nondepressed" role players, so that Coyne's speculation that over-exposure of one's own life problems might be responsible for alienating the other person seemed not to explain these results. The "depressed" interviewees mentioned the same range of problems, but, unlike "nondepressed" interviewees, blamed themselves and expressed hopelessness about the eventual resolution of the problems. Wortman *et al.* (1976) have in fact found that such disclosure of a personal problem with blame attributed to the self elicits more negative reactions than if external circumstances are blamed.

Howes and Hokanson (1979) provide further supportive evidence. Thirty male and 30 female undergraduates interacted with a "depressed", "nondepressed" or "physically ill" confederate for seven minutes while waiting for an experiment to begin. Although subsequently the subjects rated the "ill" confederate as "functionally impaired" to the same extent as the "depressed" confederate, they significantly more often rejected the "depressed" individual. This rejection was not, however, correlated with mood disturbance, levels of which did not vary with the type of confederate with whom subjects were interacting.

These three experiments taken together provide strong evidence that depressed individuals alienate those with whom they interact; that this alienation is stronger for opposite sex interactions; that part of the effect may be mediated by the affect induced in the nondepressed partner, and that it seems to be the mentioning of personal problems with self-blameful and hopeless statements attached which causes both the mood disturbance and the alienation, which may sometimes, but need not correlate with each other. Interestingly, the fact that two out of the three studies used telephone interactions may be taken to demonstrate that deficiencies in observable nonverbal communication, such as eye contact and posture, are not necessary for such alienation to occur.

Assessment Issues

As in the application of social skills analysis to other areas, the assessment of deficits has been attempted at various levels. The following section does not attempt an exhaustive list of assessments used in all the outcome studies. (The reader is referred to the studies themselves to find these.) Rather, it attempts to give an illustrative sample of each level of assessment, and some comments on their validity.

Level One: Self-rating of difficulty with interpersonal situations. In this form of assessment the patients themselves rate their own interpersonal behaviour. For example, Youngren and Lewinsohn (1980) used the 160-item Interpersonal Events Schedule, the eight subscales of which — social activity, assertion, cognition, conflict, give and receive positive, give and receive negative — provide a comprehensive self-rating schedule.

Another commonly used scale is the Wolpe–Lazarus Assertiveness Scale (Bellack *et al.*, 1983; Wolpe and Lazarus, 1966).

These assessment methods invariably produce results which suggest significant decrements in depressed individuals' social skills relative to nondepressed patients and controls. They have been found to correlate with self-rated depressed mood (Sanchez and Lewinsohn, 1980) though the possibility of a negative self-rating bias rather than genuine interpersonal bias cannot be excluded by these methods alone.

McLean and Hakstian (1979) reduced the chances of such bias in a large outcome study of the efficacy of behaviour therapy in depression. They asked patients to rate their own behaviour on seven specific social areas: frequency of arranging an activity with others (over the last week); number of hours spent with friends (over the last week); frequency of having friends over (over the last week); frequency of going out to friends (over the last week); frequency of verbally praising someone (over the last two days); number of people spoken to outside work (over the last two days). Note here the attempt to limit the time period over which the self-rating is made, and to specify which behaviours at which frequency have occurred rather than rely on more global ratings of outcome satisfaction.

Level Two: Structured interviews of interpersonal adjustment. One of the most comprehensive investigations into social adjustment of depressed patients using a structured interview is that by Paykel *et al.* (1971) the result of which was their "Social Adjustment Scale". They rated 40 female depressed patients and 40 matched controls on 48 items (mostly five-point scales) covering a wide range of discrete behaviours in the area of interpersonal relationships and satisfactions. Importantly, they attempted to go beyond global self-ratings to actual behaviour. Initially they attempted to categorise the items into roles (work, spouse, extended family, social and leisure, parental, family unit) but this yielded some item-to-subscale correlations which were fairly low. In other words, there was only weak evidence that individuals could be interpersonally inefficient in some roles yet efficient in others. Rather, a factor analysis yielded areas of deficit which cut across role. Only in the case of "work performance" did a factor correspond closely to a specific role. The five other factors (interpersonal friction, inhibited communication, submissive dependency, family attachment and anxious rumination) represented clusters of behavioural deficits which could be seen to occur in a number of role situations. The authors conclude that although role theory may provide a useful framework, when roles are broken down into their many components, common elements of function across roles also become prominent. The scale has been found useful by many investigations of social behaviour in depressives (e.g. Bellack *et al.*, 1983).

Level Three: Self-monitoring of positive and negative actions and reactions. The assessments referred to above have all involved looking back over a time interval which, though specified to varying degrees, cannot escape the problem of current mood biasing the memory for past behaviour. An alternative is to instruct patients to monitor their own behaviour as it happens. Two strategies have been used. The first is to use behavioural diaries in which instances of nonassertiveness or interpersonal difficulties are recorded at the time or soon afterwards (e,g, Sanchez and Lewinsohn 1980). An example of such a diary is given in Williams (1984). The second strategy is to set up an interpersonal situation where each participant continuously monitors their own and the others' actions and reactions. McLean, Ogston and Grauer (1973) used cue boxes to achieve this aim in an outcome study of therapy for interpersonal communication problems where one member of a couple was depressed and where there were concurrent communication problems in the relationship. The "cue box" was a box on which pressing one of two buttons operated a red or green light. Each box had also an electric counter to record the use of each button. Couples were instructed to conduct twenty-minute conversations at home on a topic which normally caused some friction (e.g. finance, child rearing). They were to push the button to operate the red light if they perceived the other's comments to be negative, sarcastic, or indifferent. They were to operate the green light if they perceived the other's comments to be in any way positive, complimentary or constructive. The aim was not merely an assessment, of course, but a therapeutic manipulation. But note that individuals, though monitoring specific behaviours, are making judgements about the hedonic valence of the behaviour. As such, it is still difficult to separate the subjective affective component from the social skill component.

Level Four: Observer ratings of positive and negative actions and reactions. This set of methods avoids the disadvantage of a self-rating; though still has the difficulty of making a judgement about the valence of behaviour. McLean *et al.* (1973) instructed the couples in their study to conduct a thirty-minute conversation, at home, about some of their problem areas, and to tape-record it. Later the recording was split into 60 thirty-second intervals and the interaction during that period coded according to whether either individual was *initiating* or *reacting* to conversation in a *positive* or *negative* way. The scores were then averaged across patient and spouse and a negative interaction score computed as the proportion of total interaction for the tape session. McLean *et al.* (1973) report an inter-rater agreement average of 88% for this assessment procedure.

Level Five: Observer ratings of the elements of social behaviour. In this level of assessment, observers record amount of eye contact, head nods, noises of agreement ("yeah", "hm-hmm", etc.) and rate voice volume, voice tone, posture, and so on. Example of such specific rating is given by Youngren and Lewinsohn (1980) and Zeiss *et al.* (1979). Both of their studies required observers to rate the actual behaviour of depressed individuals. A variant of this procedure is to use role-plays which are then videotaped for each analysis. Bellack *et al.* (1983) report extensive results with the role-play behavioural assessment. Sixteen scenarios were chosen, in half of which the patient was required to stand up for their rights and in the other half they had to express praise and appreciation.

To enhance the validity of the procedure, the scenes were selected to be relevant to the individual patient, and before enacting the scene, patients read the situation on a card and details were amended to make it more realistic for them. The videotapes were then blind rated for response latency (to the first confederate prompt), speech duration (seconds) and number of smiles during positive asserting. In addition, six behaviours were scored on 5-point bidirectional behaviourally anchored scales (Trower, Bryant and Argyle, 1978). These were the frequency of autistic gestures, voice tone, gaze, posture tonus, request/compliance content (for negative scenes) and praise/appreciation content (for positive scenes). Bellack *et al.* (1983) report inter-rater agreement in excess of 80% for these assessment measures.

The problem with these specific measures is shown by several studies (to be reviewed in greater detail below) which report independent effects of treatment strategies for general depression level on the one hand and specific social skills behaviour on the other. Furthermore as has already been seen, some investigations (Coyne, 1976; Lewinsohn and Amenson, 1978; Youngren and Lewinsohn, 1980) have found that specific elements of social behaviour do not differentiate depressed from nondepressed patients or controls and do not change within an individual as depression remits (Kornblith *et al.*, 1983). Thus, whereas the reliability of these measures may be satisfactory, their validity as measures sensitive to social skill deficiency is still open to question.

Measuring the Association Between Social Skills Deficits and Depression

The correlations between ratings of social skills deficits and depression are rarely reported in the research literature, despite the fact that all the outcome studies do assess general depression level, using mostly the Beck Depression Inventory (BDI; Beck *et al.*, 1961), the Depression Adjective Check List (DACL; Lubin, 1967) and the Hamilton Scale (HRS(D); Hamilton, 1967), alongside the social skill measures. Sanchez and Lewinsohn (1980) reported a mean correlation of −0.5, for 12 patients over a five-week period, between daily ratings of depressed mood (DACL) and daily ratings of assertive behaviour. They also attempted to address the issue of causal primacy. Since they had daily ratings of mood as well as daily self-report of emitted assertive behaviour, in addition to computing the same day correlation between the two variables they could also compute the cross-lagged correlations for each subject. That is, they computed the correlations between any day's assertion rating and the day before's and day after's mood rating. They found that the correlation (−0.17), averaged for their 12 subjects, between any day's depressed mood and next day's amount of assertive behaviour was not significant. The correlation (−0.5) between any day's assertive behaviour and the next day's mood was significant, however. They conclude that their results "suggest that rate of emitted assertive behaviour may indeed be better able to predict subsequent level of depression than level of depression can predict subsequent rate of emitted assertive behaviour" (p. 120). This conclusion is somewhat premature. Firstly the choice of computing correlations with a lag of one day is quite arbitrary. It is very likely that interactions between mood and behaviour are quite complex — certainly complex enough to justify experimenting with lag 2 or lag 3 to assess this complexity. Secondly, they make no mention of how the autocorrelations were derived for each subject. It seems that they did not make allowances for the statistical dependence of scores for one day on scores of the same variable for previous days. Thirdly, none of the statistical assumptions underlying the use of cross-lagged correlation analysis appear to have been met. These include the assumptions of stationarity (Kenny, 1975) and equal stability (Cook and Campbell, 1979). Finally, and most damaging to their conclusions, they draw a conclusion about the difference between two correlations on the basis that one is statistically significant and the other is not. That is invalid. They should have tested the specific hypothesis that there was no difference between the correlations. In fact, when the difference between these correlations is computed, the t-test value is 0.81 which is not significant. These data do not therefore allow the conclusion that one variable predicts the other in one direction better than the reverse.

The Outcome Studies

The studies of the effect of SST in depression fall into three categories: uncontrolled case studies; controlled studies but where SST is only one of many components in treatment; and controlled studies which examine SST specifically.

Uncontrolled Case Studies

When Rehm and Kornblith (1979) reviewed studies of behaviour

therapy for depression, they found that uncontrolled case studies dominated the literature on the effectiveness of SST. Six such studies had been
reported but adding them all together only eight female and two male
out-patients and four female and five male college students had been
treated using SST (Lazarus, 1968; Lewinsohn and Atwood, 1969;
Lewinsohn et al., 1970; Lewinsohn and Shaffer, 1971; Lewinsohn and
Shaw, 1969; Wells et al., 1979). The results were relatively encouraging,
however.

Controlled Studies of Treatment "Packages"

There have now been several outcome studies of behavioural or
cognitive-behavioural treatments for depression, many of which include
SST as part of the treatment package. Four large scale studies to evaluate
the efficacy of cognitive-behaviour therapy by Rush et al. (1977), McLean
and Hakstian (1979), Blackburn et al. (1981) and Rotzer et al. (1982) have
been described elsewhere (Williams, 1984a; Williams, 1984b) so will not
be detailed here. A large number of techniques are used in these studies,
and it is difficult to tell in how many of the patients social skills was actually
a focus of treatment. The importance of these studies lies in their use of
male and female moderately to severely depressed out-patients. (The
uncontrolled case studies referred to above had mostly used younger,
predominantly female subjects.) In these mixed studies, cognitive-
behavioural treatment was found to be as effective as drug treatments on
general assessment of depression such as the BDI and HRS(D). More
specific assessment of interpersonal problems was made by McLean and
Hakstian (1979) (see Assessment Level One, above). In this study they
compared the efficacy of a behaviour therapy package with drugs,
psychotherapy and a relaxation control treatment. At the end of treatment
the behaviour therapy treatment group were superior to the other three
groups on a number of outcome variables. But at three-month follow-up,
an interesting pattern emerged. Although treatment gains were maintained
overall, virtually all outcome means for the four treatment groups were not
significantly different from each other. Only the category of social
interaction measures showed behaviour therapy to be still superior to all
three other treatments. On this variable the mean level now exactly
matched that of a nondepressed normative sample. That these specific
measures of social interaction still showed superiority when other
assessments of depression such as BDI, complaints, cognitive, coping,
satisfaction ratings, and goal attainment did not, suggests either that these
measures were the most sensitive, or that the behaviour therapy was most
effective in changing interpersonal behaviour. If the latter, it should be
noted that it was at follow-up that this extra improvement was most
noticeable.

Finally, Harpin *et al.* (1982) studied the effectiveness of combining cognitive techniques with SST in the treatment of six chronically depressed outpatients who had been unresponsive to other forms of somatic treatment and psychotherapy. Outcome was compared with a waiting list control of six comparable patients: seven of the 12 patients were men, mean age was 42 years, and mean duration of depression 17.8 years. Patients were suffering from a "unipolar depressive episode" which had been unresponsive for at least three months prior to the commencement of the study, and all patients had to have a score of 20 on the HRS(D) (administered blindly) for inclusion in the trial. Dependent measures included various self-report measures of social anxiety, assertiveness and social adjustment, daily diaries completed by the patient, and a role-play test from which ratings of a patient's "comfort" and "competency" were derived. Although such small numbers meant that statistically significant between-group differences were not achieved, the treated group did change significantly on within-group measures, whereas the waiting list control did not. The authors admit the statistical weaknesses of their study; yet following such a chronic history of nonresponse to therapy, even this limited result is quite surprising, and the fact that the improvements were maintained at six-month follow-up is quite encouraging for this combination of treatments.

Controlled Studies of Specific SST

Lomont, *et al.* (1969) compared group assertion training with group insight training in twelve in-patients with "social anxiety" but whose MMPI-D score were higher than any other factor with a mean in excess of 90. Six patients were allocated to each group which met for six weeks, daily for ninety minutes. Although the MMPI-D score was reduced more for assertion training than the insight group, the differences were not significant.

Maish (1972) allocated 15 male in-patients, aged 23–36 years, whose diagnosis was primarily depression, to 20 individual sessions over eight weeks of either assertion training, relaxation, or therapist contact control. Assertion training consisted of rehearsal of individualized problem situations, demonstration of assertive responses, coupled with some relaxation training. Levels of assertiveness were assessed both by self-report and staff ratings at the end of treatment and six-month follow-up. The small numbers meant that statistical significance was very difficult to achieve, but the MMPI-D scores fell from an overall median of 94 at the outset to 59 post-training, and 58 at follow-up in the assertion training group. There was no such improvement in the relaxation group, and although the therapist contact group improved initially (MMPI-D of 63 at end of treatment) this score rose again to 92 at six-month follow-up.

The five assertion training patients needed no further treatment at the end of the trial, whereas four out of the five patients in both of the other groups did so.

McLean *et al.* (1973) compared a treatment which aimed to modify the verbal interaction style in marital partners with a "treatment as usual" control. Sixteen female and four male outpatients (in whom "incapaci tating depressive behaviours" were present) and their spouses were randomly allocated to behaviour therapy or to be referred back to their own medical practitioner. The behaviour therapy took the form of eight one-hour conjoint sessions with male and female co-therapists. Following explanations of depression in social learning theory terms, a "ban" was placed on blameful statements, and patients were instructed to avoid incursions into the past to justify their present difficulties. The differential effects of positive and negative reinforcement in behaviour and feelings were explained, and instructions given on how to change interpersonal behaviour by the use of selective positive reinforcement. Throughout treatment, couples were encouraged to be specific rather than general in describing desirable behaviour changes. Homework tasks were given in which these principles were implemented. "Cue boxes" (see Assessment section, above) were used to facilitate treatment and as a method of assessment, and thirty minute tapes made pre- and post-treatment for which the proportion of positive and negative actions and reactions were derived. Other outcome measures included the DACL, and self-ratings of various depressive signs and symptoms in the areas such as work, sleep patterns, and concentration. Results showed that the behaviour therapy group were significantly more improved at the end of treatment, and that these improvements were maintained at three-month follow-up. There had been specific changes in verbal interaction style such that the proportion of negative actions within communication between the couple fell from 20% to 10%, and negative reactions fell from 62% to 35%. Improvements had also generalised to the other areas of social withdrawal, sleep, job satisfaction, concentration, decision-making, motivation, suicidal pre-occupation, communication, sexual satisfaction and hobbies.

The major drawback with this study is the fact that the control group did not have the same frequency of therapist contact, so the extent to which mere therapist contact was responsible for the improvements in the behavioural group remains untested. However, other studies which have controlled this variable (e.g. the earlier study by Maish, 1972 and the later study by McLean and Hakstian, 1979), found that mere therapist contact provided no lasting improvement in interpersonal skills, thus giving some reassurance that McLean *et al.* were in fact using an active treatment strategy to produce their effects.

Rehm *et al.* (1979) used 25 solicited volunteer depressed individuals, aged from 21 to 60 years, all of whom had MMPI-D scores exceeding 70. Fourteen subjects received group self-control training which concentrated on subjects' ability to monitor, self-evaluate and self-reinforce appropriately. Eleven subjects received group assertion training in which they role-played problem situations; making requests for change in others behaviour, expressing criticism or disapproval, refusing unreasonable requests, expressing approval and affection. Principles of effective social skills were presented didactically, and situations modelled with rehearsal and group feedback. Both group treatments took place weekly for six weeks. Outcome was assessed using the MMPI, BDI, Pleasant Events Schedule (MacPhillamy and Lewinsohn, 1972); Wolpe–Lazarus Assertiveness Scale, observations of verbal and nonverbal behaviour in groups, and three self-control questionnaires. Results showed that the self-control treatment group improved more on self-control variables and that the SST group improved more on social skills variables. However, the general measures of depression were more improved by the self-control than the SST. Treatment gains were found to be maintained at six-week follow-up. This result is reminiscent of those of McLean and Hakstian (1979), who also found that general measures of depression did not reflect specific measures of social skill, a point to which we shall return in discussion.

Zeiss et al. (1979) advertised for subjects for a trial which compared interpersonal skills training, pleasant activity scheduling, and cognitive therapy with a waiting list control. Forty-four met the criterion of an MMP1-D score greater than 80, and a structured interview was also conducted. The study attempted not only to evaluate outcome, but by making comprehensive (seven hour) assessments each month (four occasions in all) attempted to study the process of change. The assessments were to measure the specific subcomponents purported to mediate the efficacy of the various therapies. There were two self-ratings and one observer rating of interpersonal behaviour; three self and one observer rating of cognitive style; and the Pleasant Events Schedule assessed frequency and pleasantness of activities. All treatments were equally effective and more so than the waiting list control. But all treatments were found to affect nonspecifically all the ratings of the supposed "specific" mediating variables. The authors suggest that "the label of therapy does not ensure that the behaviours labelled will be these most directly affected" (p. 436). A major problem with this conclusion is that it was based on assessment made only once a month. It is likely that the interactions which exist between social behaviour, cognitive styles and engagement in pleasant activities are highly complex and not amenable to study by such infrequent assessment. However this study serves as a caution to those investigators who would claim specificity for their SST without explicitly checking the claim.

Sanchez, Lewinsohn and Larson (1980) allocated 11 males and 21 female patients who were depressed (MMPI-D score greater than 70) and subassertive either to group SST or group psychotherapy. Treatment sessions lasted for ninety minutes twice a week for five weeks and a one-month follow-up assessment was conducted. The SST consisted of didactic presentation, modelling, rehearsal, coaching and social reinforcement with token feedback for increased level of assertiveness. Homework assignments were also given and patients were trained in deep muscle relaxation. Assessments included BDI, MMPI-D scale, satisfaction indices, and an Assertion Inventory reflecting degree of discomfort and probability of making assertive responses. Results showed that whereas the SST group did better than the psychotherapy group at the end of treatment, the differences were not significant. However, at the one-month follow-up, all the measures strongly favoured the SST group. At this point, for example, the BDI mean score for the SST group had fallen from 29.2 to 14.0, whereas the scores for the psychotherapy group had only fallen from 30.5 to 28.5. The capacity of the SST to produce changes which continued after formal therapy had ended is a striking feature of this study, and reminiscent of the similar findings by McLean and Hakstian (1979) reviewed above.

Hersen *et al.* (1984) have made the most extensive outcome study of SST to date. The subjects were 120 depressed women, either referred from outpatient clinics or recruited by advertisement but with careful assessment to check for any differences between the referred and the recruited groups. (There were none.) All subjects obtained a diagnosis of primary depression (Feighner *et al.*, 1972) and needed to score over 7 on Raskin's Eligibility Depression Scale (Raskin *et al.*, 1967). In fact, these were a very depressed group: their mean chronicity was 50.2 months, their mean pre-treatment BDI score was 28.8 (severely depressed); and their mean HRS(D) score was 23.4. Patients were allocated to one of four treatment groups: amitriptyline (up to 200–300 mg/day); amitriptyline plus SST; placebo plus SST; and placebo plus psychotherapy. All treatments lasted for twelve weeks (weekly one-hour sessions for SST, and psychotherapy), and the drugs and placebo were administered double blind. SST included role-play, instructions, modelling, feedback and reinforcement. Hierarchies of difficult situations were constructed in four areas: family interactions, work interactions, interaction with friends and interactions with strangers. Specific training procedures concentrated on eye contact, smiles, gestures, voice interaction and voice loudness. Homework assignments based on situations practised in therapy were given, and patients trained to self-reinforce. Details of the role-play assessment used are given in the Assessment section, above. Other outcome variables included the BDI, HRS(D), and the Wolpe–Lazarus Assertiveness Scale, these measures being taken alongside the role-play behavioural measures at the end of treatment and again at six-month follow-up (during which time all patients had made six to eight maintenance therapy visits to their clinic). Results showed no differences between the groups on general measures of depression but between-group differences did emerge on the role-play behavioural test of social skills the details of which had been reported by Bellack *et al.* (1983). SST brought about significantly more improvements than amitriptyline on speech duration (in negative situations), voice tone in positive situations, gaze in both positive and negative situations, request/ compliance content in positive situations and overall assertiveness in negative situations. Nonsignificant differences between SST and psychotherapy favoured the social skills group on every measure. All these differences were maintained at six-month follow-up. One striking finding was the difference in attrition rate between the groups: 46% of the amitriptyline group dropped out of therapy (usually within the first seven weeks) whereas only 24% dropped out of the social skills and placebo groups. This reflects a much greater degree of dissatisfaction with the drugs alone treatment than the SST and is consistent with similar, though lower, differences in attrition rates for drugs vs behavioural treatments (32% and 5% respectively in Rush *et al.* 1977; and 36% and 5% respectively in McLean and Hakstian 1979).

Discussion

Surveying the literature on social skills deficits associated with depression, one finds a highly consistent picture of global deficits, rated both by observers, peers, and the depressed patients themselves. The evidence for deficits in specific elements of interpersonal behaviour (eye contact, speech duration, etc.) is less consistent, with several workers finding little evidence (e.g. Coyne 1976; Lewinsohn and Amenson 1978; Youngren and Lewinsohn 1980) and Bellack's research group (e.g. Bellack *et al.* 1983) finding some evidence of deficits on some skills but not on others in a structured role-play situation. Furthermore the evidence of Coyne (1976) and Hammen and Peters (1978) suggest that depressives can alienate people with whom they are interacting after brief telephone conversations suggesting that those elements of interpersonal behaviour which depend on face-to-face interaction may be sufficient but are not necessary for socially deficient behaviour to make itself apparent. This discrepancy between specific analysis of behaviour and more global ratings of skills ought not to surprise: specific elements are more complex than any measure of "total amount" may be able to reveal. There is also evidence from Coyne (1976), Hammen and Peters (1978) and Howes and Hokanson (1979) that it is the content of what is said rather than the way it is said that determines the listener's reaction: specifically, revelation of functional impairment which is attributed internally accompanied by self-blameful and hopeless statements seems to elicit changes in the listener's behaviour (more silences, less positive and neutral conversation maintainers, more directly negative comments, and less total output of verbal responses — Howes and Hokanson, 1979). Since the locus of the problem seems to be in the *content* of what the depressed person says and then in the rather stilted reactions thus elicited from the listener, it is unsurprising that it should be the more global ratings of the entire interpersonal encounter which should most readily pick up the deficiencies in social skills. The point is that the behaviour of the depressive seems to elicit social skills deficits in the people with whom he or she interacts. The resulting alienation implies that even if the depressive were to perceive accurately the other's behaviour, he or she would perceive them to be rejecting him or her. The consequences in terms of a further twist to the downward spiral of depression and self-preoccupation are not hard to imagine.

The results of SST in depression are encouraging, though there are several reasons for drawing only limited conclusions from the current research. Firstly, controlled studies have been remarkably consistent in showing that SST, though it alleviates depression, does not do so more than other treatments: pharmacotherapy and psychotherapy (Bellack *et al.*, 1983), pleasant events scheduling and cognitive therapy (Zeiss *et al.*, 1979), and seems less effective than self-control training (Rehm *et al.*, 1979). The only exception is the study of McLean *et al.* (1973) using interpersonal marital therapy, but the control patients did not receive adequate therapist contact to allow reliable conclusions to be drawn from this study.

The second reason for drawing only limited conclusions is the ambiguous evidence concerning the specific behaviour which is affected by SST. Bellack *et al.* (1983) did indeed find that although general depression levels were equally improved by SST, psychotherapy and amitriptyline, the SST specifically affected interpersonal skills, assessed in a behavioural role-play task. Rehm *et al.* (1979) also found that SST affected social skills specifically. But these findings must be set against other studies which have found that social skills can be equally improved by other procedures which do not claim to effect social skills specifically; cognitive therapy, pleasant events scheduling (Zeiss *et al.* 1979) and self-control training (Fuchs and Rehm 1977). Furthermore, some studies which have only used assertion training as part of a much larger "package" of treatment procedures have found specific effects on interpersonal behaviour over and above effects on general depression. Thus McLean and Hakstian (1979) found that three months after termination of treatment which had used a large behaviour therapy package there were no differences between treatment groups (behaviour therapy, psychotherapy, drugs, and relaxation) on general measures of depression, but behaviour therapy patients were significantly different from all three other groups only on measures of amount of social interaction. This result is consistent with other findings which have not used SST as part of treatment but have assessed social functioning as part of the outcome. For example, Weissman *et al.* (1981) who compared Interpersonal Psychotherapy (IPT) with drug treatment found no difference on clinical assessment of depression, but found that IPT significantly affected social adjustment on social and leisure activities, parental functioning, and functioning as member of family unit. In summary, SST may affect interpersonal functioning specifically, but so may more general psychological treatment packages.

This raises the question of whether social skill variables may be no more than a correlate of increased general motivation and increased motor activity which comes about as *any* effective treatment begins to work. There is some indication that this may be the case. For example in some very specific observations Williams, Barlow and Agras (1972) and Hersen *et al.* (1973) found that the four behaviours of talking, smiling, time out of room, and motor activity (assessed every thirty minutes for eight hours a day by observers using strict behavioural criteria) were highly inter-correlated. The fact that the social aspects of behaviour correlated with sheer amount of motor activity suggest that parsimonious explanation of the former behaviour in terms of the latter is possible.

Finally, any conclusions about SST are limited because not enough research has been done to indicate what subtypes of depression do best on which treatment. For example, the data for other psychological treatments suggest that cognitive therapy is equally effective for endogenomorphic and situational depressives (e.g. Blackburn *et al.*, 1981), whereas Interpersonal Psychotherapy seems to be better than drugs for situational depressives but better used in combination with drugs for endogenomorphic depressives (Prusoff *et al.*, 1980). As yet it is not clear whether SST will similarly be found to be more suitable for some depressive subtypes than others. Until psychological analysis in general, and social skills analysis in particular takes into account a greater range of the actual symptomatology evident in depression, these questions will remain unanswered.

Despite these limitations however, there is sufficient evidence to suggest that SST can be seen alongside other psychological treatments as a highly promising means of treating some depressed patients. The limitations are on what conclusions can be drawn from the effectiveness of SST and does not challenge the conclusion that they can be effective. Indeed, because it so readily lends itself to being used in a group format, it to some extent avoids the accusation made of the other psychotherapies (e.g. Goldberg, (1982) of cognitive therapy) that it is too expensive to be generally useful. Also, because the principles and methods of SST as used in depression do not differ a great deal from those developed for other psychiatric conditions, the need for extensive extra "special" training of would-be therapists is avoided. For all these reasons, it is likely that SST will continue to provide a useful range of techniques to be used in the treatment of clinical depression.

References

Beck, A. T., Ward, C. H., Mendelson, M. J. and Erbaugh, J. (1961) An inventory for measuring depression. *Archives of General Psychiatry*, **4**, 561–571.

Bellack, A. S., Hersen, M. and Himmelhoch, J. M. (1983) A comparison of social skills training, pharmacotherapy and psychotherapy for depression. *Behaviour Research and Therapy*, **21**, 101–107.

Blackburn, I. M., Bishop, S., Glen, I. M., Whalley, L. J. and Christie, J. E. (1981) The efficacy of cognitive therapy in depression: A treatment trial using cognitive therapy and pharmacotherapy, each alone and in combination. *British Journal of Psychiatry*, **139**, 181–189.

Cook, T. D. and Campbell, D. T. (1979) *The design and analysis of quasi-experiments in field settings*. Chicago: Rand McNally.

Coyne, J. C. (1976) Depression and the response of others. *Journal of Abnormal Psychology*, **85**, 186–193.

Feighner, J. P., Robins, E., Gaze, S. B., Woodruff, R. A., Winokur, G. and Munoz, T. (1972) Diagnostic criteria for use in psychiatric research. *Archives of General Psychiatry*, **26**, 57–63.

Fuchs, C. Z. and Rehm, L. P. (1977) A self-control behavior therapy program for depression. *Journal of Consulting and Clinical Psychology*, **45**, 206–215.

Gilbert, P. (1984) *Depression: From psychology to brain state*. Hillsdale, New Jersey: Lawrence Erlbaum Associates.

Goldberg, D. (1982) Cognitive therapy for depression. *British Medical Journal*, **284**, 143–144.

Hamilton, M. (1967) Development of a rating scale for primary depressive illness. *British Journal of Social and Clinical Psychology*, **6**, 278–296.

Hammen, C. L. and Peters, S. D. (1978) Interpersonal consequences of depression: Responses to men and women enacting a depressed role. *Journal of Abnormal Psychology*, **87**, 322–332.

Harpin, R. E., Liberman, R. P., Marks, I., Stein, R. and Bohannon, W. E. (1982) Cognitive-behaviour therapy for clinically depressed patients: A controlled pilot study. *Journal of Nervous and Mental Disease*, **170**, 295–301.

Hersen, M., Bellack, A. S., Himmelhoch, J. M. and Thase, M. E. (1984) Effects of social skills training, amitriptyline, and psychotherapy in unipolar depressed women. *Behavior Therapy*, **15**, 21–40.

Hersen, M., Eisler, R. M., Alford, G. S. and Agras, W. S. (1973) Effects of token economy on neurotic depression: An experimental analysis. *Behavior Therapy*, **4**, 392–397.

Howes, M. J. and Hokanson, J. E. (1979) Conversational and social responses to depressive interpersonal behavior. *Journal of Abnormal Psychology*, **88**, 625–634.

Kenny, D. A. (1975) Crossed-lagged panel correlation: A test for spuriousness. *Psychological Bulletin*, **82**, 887–903.

Kornblith, S. J., Rehm, L. P., O'Hara, M. W. and Lamparski, D. M. (1983) The contribution of self-reinforcement training and behavioral assignments to the efficacy of self control therapy for depression. *Cognitive Therapy and Research*, **7**, 499–528.

Lazarus, A. A. (1968) Learning theory and the treatment of depression. *Behaviour Research and Therapy*, **6**, 83–89.

Lewinsohn, P. M. and Amenson, C. (1978) *Some relationships between pleasant and unpleasant mood related events and depression*. Unpublished manuscript, University of Oregon.

Lewinsohn, P. M. and Atwood, G. E. (1969) Depression: A clinical research approach. *Psychotherapy, Research and Practice*, **6**, 166–171.

Lewinsohn, P. M. and Shaffer, M. (1971) The use of home observations as an integral part of the treatment of depression: Preliminary report and case studies. *Journal of Consulting and Clinical Psychology*, **37**, 87–94.

Lewinsohn, P. M. and Shaw, D. A. (1969) Feedback about interpersonal behavior as an agent of behavior change: A case study in the treatment of depression. *Psychotherapy and Psychosomatics*, **17**, 82–88.

Lewinsohn, P. M., Weinstein, M. S. and Alper, T. (1970) A behavioral approach to the group treatment of depressed persons: Methodological contribution. *Journal of Clinical Psychology*, **26**, 525–532.

Libet, J. and Lewinsohn, P. M. (1973) The concept of social skill with special reference to the behavior of depressed persons. *Journal of Consulting and Clinical Psychology*, **40**, 304–312.

Lomont, J. F., Gilner, F. H., Spector, N. J. and Skinner, K. K. (1969) Group assertion training and group insight therapies. *Psychological Reports*, **25**, 463–470.

Lubin, B. (1967) *Manual for the Depressive Adjective Check Lists*. San Diego: Educational and Industrial Testing Service.

McLean, P. D. and Hakstian, A. R. (1979) Clinical depression: Comparative efficacy of out-patient treatments. *Journal of Consulting and Clinical Psychology*, **47**, 818–836.

McLean, P. D., Ogston, K. and Grauer, L. (1973) A behavioral approach to the treatment of depression. *Journal of Behaviour Therapy and Experimental Psychiatry*, **4**, 323–330.

MacPhillamy, D. J. and Lewinsohn, P. M. (1972) *The structure of reported reinforcement.* Unpublished manuscript, University of Oregon.

Maish, J. I. (1972) The use of an individualised assertive training program in the treatment of depressed in-patients (Unpublished doctoral dissertation, Florida State University), *Dissertation Abstracts International*, **33**, 281.

Paykel, E. S. and Dienelt, M. N. (1971) Suicide attempts following acute depression. *Journal of Nervous and Mental Disease*, **153**, 234–243.

Paykel, E. S., Weissman, M., Prusoff, B. A. and Tonks, C. M. (1971) Dimensions of social adjustment in depressed women. *Journal of Nervous and Mental Diseases*, **152**, 158–172.

Prusoff, B. A., Weissman, M. M., Klerman, G. L. and Rounsaville, B. J. (1980) Research diagnostic criteria subtypes of depression: Their role as predictors of differential response to psychotherapy and drug treatment. *Archives of General Psychiatry*, **37**, 796–801.

Raskin, A., Schulterbrandt, J., Reatin, N. and Rice C. (1967) Factors of psychopathology in interview, ward behavior and self report ratings of hospital depressives. *Journal of Consulting and Clinical Psychology*, **31**, 270–278.

Rehm, L. P., Fuchs, C. Z., Roth, D. M. Kornblith, S. J. and Romano, J. M. (1979) A comparison of self-control and assertion skills treatments of depression. *Behavior Therapy*, **10**, 429–442.

Rehm, L. P. and Kornblith, S. J. (1979) Behavior therapy for depression: A review of recent developments. In: M. Hersen and P. M. Eisler (Eds.), *Progress in behavior modification Vol. 7*. New York: Academic Press.

Rotzer, F. T., Nabitz, U., Koch, H. and Pflug, B. (1982) Zur Bedentung von Attribuierungs — Prozessen bei der Depressionsbehandling. In: Luer G., *Bericht des 33, Kongresses der Deutschen Gesellschaft für Psychologie*. Mainz, FRG.

Rush, A. J., Beck, A. T., Kovacs, M. and Hollon, S. (1977) Comparative efficacy of cognitive therapy and pharmacotherapy in the treatment of depressed out-patients. *Cognitive Therapy and Research*, **1**, 17–37.

Sanchez, V. and Lewinsohn, P. M. (1980) Assertive behavior and depression. *Journal of Consulting and Clinical Psychology*, **48**, 119–120.

Sanchez, V. C., Lewinsohn, P. M. and Larson, D. W. (1980) Assertion training: Effectiveness in the treatment of depression. *Journal of Clinical Psychology*, **36**, 526–529.

Spitzer, R. L., Endicott, J. and Robins, E. (1978) *Research Diagnostic Criteria (RDC) for a selected group of functional disorders*, 3rd Edition. New York State Psychiatric Institute, Biometrics Research.

Trower, P., Bryant, B. and Argyle, M. (1978) *Social skills and mental health*. London: Methuen.

Weissman, M. M., Klerman, G. L., Prusoff, B. A., Sholomskas, D. R. and Padian, N. (1981) Depressed out-patients: Results one year after treatment with drugs and/or interpersonal psychotherapy. *Archives of General Psychiatry*, **38**, 51–55.

Wells, K. C., Hersen, M., Bellack, A. S. and Himmelhoch, J. M. (1979) Social skills training in unipolar nonpsychotic depression. *American Journal of Psychiatry*, **136**, 1331–1332.

Whitlock, F. A. and Siskind, M. (1979) Depression and cancer: A follow-up study. *Psychological Medicine*, **9**, 747–752.

Williams, J. G., Barlow, D. H. and Agras, W. S. (1972) Behavioural measurement of severe depression. *Archives of General Psychiatry*, **27**, 330–333.

Williams, J. M. G. (1984a) *The psychological treatment of depression: A guide to the theory and practice of cognitive-behaviour therapy*. London: Croom Helm.

Williams, J. M. G. (1984b) Cognitive-behaviour therapy for depression: Problems and perspectives. *British Journal of Psychiatry*, **145**, 254–262.

Wolpe, J. and Lazarus, A. A. (1966) *Behavior therapy techniques: A guide to the treatment of neuroses*. New York: Pergamon.

Wortman, C. B., Adesman, P., Herman, E. and Greenberg, R. (1976) Self-disclosure: An attributional perspective. *Journal of Personality and Social Psychology*, **33**, 184–191.

Youngren, M. A. and Lewinsohn, P. M. (1980) The functional relation between depression and problematic interpersonal behavior. *Journal of Abnormal Psychology*, **89**, 333–341.

Zeiss, A. M., Lewinsohn, P. M. and Munoz, R. F. (1979) Nonspecific improvement effects in depression using interpersonal skills training, pleasant activity schedules, or cognitive training. *Journal of Consulting and Clinical Psychology*, **45**, 543–551.

Acknowledgement. I should like to thank Dr. Paul Gilbert for helpful discussions at an early stage of drafting this chapter.

5

Social Skills Training and Substance Abuse

PETER M. MONTI, DAVID B. ABRAMS, JODY A. BINKOFF and
WILLIAM R. ZWICK

Introduction

Social learning theory treatment conceptualisations for substance abuse
have recently included social skills training (SST) components. While
alcoholism assessment and treatment programmes (e.g., Chaney, O'Leary
and Marlatt, 1978; Foy, Nunn and Rychtarik, 1984; Monti, Corriveau and
Zwick, 1981; Monti et al., 1984) appear to be more developed in this
direction than other hard drug abuse programmes such as those for opiate
addiction, a number of researchers (e.g., Chaney, Roszell and Cummings,
1982; Kolko et al., 1983) have suggested that SST should also be relevant
for all types of addicts experiencing difficulty in interpersonal situations

Behavioural approaches are only beginning to be used in hard drug
abuse programmes. Chaney et al. (1982) speculated that one reason why
behavioural techniques have been under-utilised with opiate addicts is that
such approaches may be more difficult to integrate with the philosophies of
the two major treatment approaches to opiate abuse, namely, therapeutic
communities and methadone maintenance. Nevertheless, several distinct
lines of research point to commonalities among various types of substance
abuse from both a conceptual (e.g., Shiffman, in press) and a developmental (e.g., Mills and Noyes, 1984) perspective. While there are no doubt
important differences among the addictions, the present chapter will focus
on commonalities with respect to social skills (SS). That is, for many
individuals, across addictive disorders, there may be an underlying SS
dysfunction that warrants the use of SST as a major component of
treatment.

Unfortunately, since there is a paucity of studies of SST with hard drug
abusers, the primary data base for the present chapter is, of necessity, SS
and alcohol abuse. Relevant literature pertaining to other forms of drug
abuse (e.g., opiate addiction) will be included where available. Furthermore, few data exist with respect to SS and other forms of substance abuse,

such as smoking and overeating. These disorders will not be directly addressed. One reason for this paucity of data is that overeating and smoking do not typically occur as part of participating in a subculture while heavy drinking and hard drug abuse often do (Shiffman, in press).

In this chapter the literature will be reviewed with respect to the rationale for examining SS and substance abuse. First, attention will be focused on conceptual and developmental issues. The rationale for a SST framework will be developed by reviewing selected assessment and analogue studies and research on situations surrounding relapse. This will be followed by an examination of assessment issues and instruments in the social skills/substance abuse literature. Next, the treatment literature will be reviewed with particular attention to issues of generalisation and maintenance of behaviour change. Finally, an attempt at integration and some recommendations for future directions will be presented.

Rationale

Developmental Considerations

The rationale for examining social competence of problem drinkers dates back at least 20 years to the work of Sugarman, Reilly and Albahar (1965) who, arguing from Zigler and Phillips' (1960, 1961, 1962) perspectives on a developmental approach to psychopathology, suggested that the essential-reactive distinction in alcoholism resembles the process-reactive distinction in schizophrenia. Sugarman *et al.* (1965) administered both a questionnaire purporting to tap the essential-reactive distinction of Rudie and McGaughran (1961), and Zigler and Phillips' social competence questionnaire to 118 inpatient problem drinkers and found a significant correlation between the measures. These results were interpreted as supporting the notion that the "essential alcoholic", who is socially immature and characterised by an inadequate personality, demonstrates less social competence than the "reactive alcoholic," who drinks more in response to the environment. Sugarman *et al.*'s (1965) basic findings were extended by Levine and Zigler (1973) who reported a negative relationship between social competence and incidence of alcoholism. While Sugarman *et al.*'s data are cited here for illustrative purposes, it should be noted that many authors share Miller's (1978) contention that "there are virtually no established commonalities, either of alcoholics in general or of alcoholic subtypes" (p. 659).

In an extensive review of the psychosocial development of people later defined as alcoholics, O'Leary, O'Leary and Donovan (1975) found that parents of problem drinkers fail to present a model for moderate social drinking. Indeed, such individuals are frequently heavy drinkers or problem drinkers themselves (Robins, Bates and O'Neal, 1962; Rosenberg, 1969) and tend to show approval of their children's drinking. Bandura (1969) points out that familial situations, where alcohol is consumed across a variety of circumstances and is often used as a means of coping, are likely to transmit a similar pattern of drinking. It may well be that some children of problem drinkers learn that heavy drinking is a requisite for adequate coping in social situations. They may never learn appropriate SS that could be effectively utilised in the absence of alcohol.

Several studies focusing on adolescent and college-age problem drinkers are pertinent to O'Leary's formulations. Jones (1968) found that prealcoholic boys, who functioned adequately during latency using outgoing behaviors, were judged less favourable as they grew up. Later in high school they were judged less productive, less socially perceptive, less calm, and more sensitive to criticism. Braucht et al. (1973) found that adolescent problem drinkers were overly aggressive, impulsive, and generally lacking in personal controls. These findings have recently been extended by Asher and Renshaw (1984) who found that children and adolescents at risk for alcohol abuse are likely to have poor SS. Kalin (1972) studying a college age group of male problem drinkers, found them to be "anti-socially assertive", disorderly, and less often involved in long term relationships. O'Leary et al. (1975) concluded that problem drinkers find it increasingly difficult to establish and maintain social relationships expected of individuals, and their social responses are inadequately or partially learned rather than learned and then forgotten. These authors speculate that "with prealcoholics there is a two-fold process involved which prevents the acquisition of more appropriate social responses and which serves to maintain an inadequate and maladaptive response repertoire" (p. 115). In support of this obervation, Braucht et al. (1973) showed that adolescent problem drinkers select heavy drinkers for friends thus making it less likely for them to learn more appropriate social behaviour from peers. The second stage of the process suggests deficiencies in learning that are created and maintained by the alcohol's pharmacological influence.

These developmental findings, suggesting the likely SS deficits of prealcoholic teenagers and college age males, may also be pertinent to a consideration of the relationship between SS and other drug abuse. Our understanding of the developmental relationship among various types of substance abuse has recently been enhanced by a study (Mills and Noyes, 1984) examining the utilisation rates of selected drug substances among adolescents. The findings suggest that drug use shows a cumulative pattern and can be taken as support for a progressive model of adolescent drug use (Kandel, 1975). For a subset of the populations a fairly invariant sequence was found from no drug use, to alcohol and cigarette use, to marijuana use, and then lastly to hard drug use. It is therefore likely that a subset of those prealcoholic socially deficient adolescents who were discussed above go on to abuse hard drugs.

In addition, findings parallel to those with alcohol have been reported with hard drug abusers. Several investigators have suggested that drug addicts may be deficient in SS (Van Hasselt, Hersen and Milliones, 1978). Interestingly, Cheek *et al.* (1973) point out that many male addicts' ghetto backgrounds "undoubtedly instill in them the idea that they must define their manhood aggressively, so that they would probably respond overassertively to the inevitable hostility of others" (p. 971). Such observations have been supported in some early work suggesting that certain drug addicts exhibited SS deficits (Cameron, 1961; Seeyers, 1962).

Directly relevant to the role of social competencies and substance abuse, O'Learly *et al.* (1975) point out that individuals later identified as alcoholics have significant deficits in those SS that might increase the accessibility of desired outcomes. They note that complex interpersonal situations requiring the use of well developed SS may provoke social anxiety that is likely to precipitate drinking among heavy drinkers. This position is consistent with Kraft's (1971) social anxiety model of alcoholism which suggests that patients may fail to acquire adequate SS during their development because social responses have been inhibited by their environment including family, friends, school, and peer groups.

It is also possible that, for some individuals, social anxiety is primarily responsible for the hypothesised relationship between skills deficits and substance abuse. In this context, the SS deficit could be viewed as secondary (Trower *et al.*, 1978) as opposed to the primary skills deficit discussed thus far. A secondary skills deficit is one in which the performance of socially inappropriate behaviours are secondary to some other kind of psychopathology (e.g., related to biochemical, physiological, or cognitive disturbance). For example, for some problem drinkers, debilitating anxiety may interfere with the performance of skills that they may acutally have in their repertoire. It is important to consider the nature of the observed skills deficit when considering assessment and treatment (Bandura, 1969).

Regardless of the cause of the skills deficit, substance abuse may serve as a means of coping with everyday life and/or with strong external pressures. In the case of alcohol, initiation of drinking is enhanced by the individual's expectations that alcohol will improve social interactions, promote an "adult-like image" with associated self-image fantasies and power motivation (e.g., McClelland *et al.*, 1972), and reduce tension. This latter notion is supported by recent evidence on expectations regarding alcohol consumption (Brown *et al.*, 1980; Rohsenow, 1983), by cross cultural studies (e.g., MacAndrew and Edgerton, 1969), and by laboratory studies directly examining social anxiety and alcohol expectancy effects (Abrams and Wilson, 1979; Wilson and Abrams 1977; Wilson, Perold and Abrams, 1981). In these studies (cf. Abrams, 1983) research has shown the powerful effects that the mere belief that alcohol has been consumed has on social behaviour, self-report measures of anxiety, and physiological responding. Depending on the situational context, the sex of the subjects, social learning history and other person variables, alcohol can serve to increase or reduce social anxiety and physiological arousal in stressful social encounters.

In the following section we will briefly consider selected assessment studies linking assertiveness with substance abuse and then review several analogue experiments relevant to the substance abuse and SS rationale.

Selected Assessment and Analogue Studies

Several alcohol researchers (e.g., Caddy, 1982; Sobell, 1978; Watson and Maisto, 1983) have emphasised that assertiveness training is an important part of behavioural treatments for problem drinkers. This position is shared by other drug abuse researchers (e.g., Callner and Ross, 1976; Cheek et al., 1973). The rationale for conducting assertion training with substance abuse problems usually follows one of two arguments. The first is consistent with Wolpe's (1969) suggestion that assertion is incompatible with anxiety and, consequently, both inhibits anxiety and increases socially appropriate behaviour (Adinolfi, McCourt and Geoghegan, 1976). The second argument views drug abuse as correlated with assertion skill or with negative affect associated with such situations. It is argued that abusers often cope with interpersonal situations by drug consumption instead of exhibiting assertive behaviour (Watson and Maisto, 1983).

In one of the earliest studies of assertiveness and hard-drug abuse, Callner and Ross (1976) described a self-report assessment instrument measuring five aspects of assertiveness. Differences between matched groups of addicts and nonaddicts were obtained in the areas of drugs, authority, and positive feedback. Results pointed to the existence of assertiveness deficits and to the situational specificity of addicts' assertion difficulties.

Following Callner and Ross (1976), several studies were conducted on assertiveness among problem drinkers. Sturgis, Best and Calhoun (1977) first demonstrated that problem drinkers were less assertive than a college student control group. In a follow-up study, Sturgis, Calhoun and Best (1979) administered male problem drinkers a battery of self-report instruments. Two groups were identified on the basis of assertiveness scores and then examined on the other measures. Results supported two hypotheses as to why people drink excessively and indicated that people with different interpersonal styles drink for different reasons. The findings suggested that passive individuals drink to facilitate social interactions and thus drinking becomes a reinforcing social agent. Furthermore, highly assertive individuals may drink to change their sensations and to reduce boredom. This formulation is consistent with Zuckerman's (1972) and Kilpatrick, Sutker and Smith's (1976) speculations that alcohol facilitates risk-taking, sensation-seeking, and associated behaviours that are incompatible with depression or hypo-arousal.

Hamilton and Maisto (1979) assessed problem drinkers and matched non-problem drinkers on self-report and behavioural tests of assertiveness and discomfort. While results showed no differences between groups on assertiveness, the problem drinkers reported more discomfort in situations requiring assertive behaviour. Miller and his colleagues have reported two studies examining the relationship between assertive behaviour and problem drinkers' consumption. Miller *et al.* (1974) exposed problem drinkers and matched social drinkers to stressful and non-stressful social encounters. Immediately following these encounters, subjects were given access to alcohol for which they had to press a lever. Findings showed that while the stressful encounter increased physiological responding for both groups, only problem drinkers increased their operant responding under the stress condition.

In a more extensive study, Miller and Eisler (1977) examined problem drinking and non-problem drinking psychiatric patients on self-report and role-play measures of assertiveness as well as on operant drinking. The results indicated that while the problem drinkers perceived themselves as being more assertive than did the psychiatric patients, the role-play measure showed the two groups to be equally deficient on negative assertion. Of particular interest is the finding for problem drinkers of a significant negative correlation between role-play measures of negative assertion and alcohol consumption. The extent to which this relationship may be generalisable has not as yet been investigated.

Marlatt and his colleagues (cf. Marlatt, 1978a) have studied the influence of a number of potential determinants of alcohol consumption utilising drinking on a taste-rating task as a dependent measure. Higgins and Marlatt (1975) asked heavy social drinking males to participate in the taste-rating task. Prior to the task, subjects were assigned to either a high social evaluation stress condition or a control condition. Experimental subjects drank almost twice the amount of alcohol as controls, suggesting that the fear of interpersonal evaluation had a significant impact on alcohol consumption.

In another study, Marlatt, Kosturn and Lang (1975) examined the effects of induced anger on alcohol consumption. Heavy social drinking college students were assigned to three conditions: insult, insult with opportunity to retaliate, no-insult and no-retaliation. The taste-rating task followed. Results showed that students who were angered with no opportunity to retaliate demonstrated the greatest consumption. Those who were allowed to retaliate drank significantly less than those in either of the other groups. Taken together, Marlatt's studies suggest that a combination of a negative emotional state plus an inability to express oneself effectively can lead to an increase in alcohol consumption.

Several suggestions relevant to the focus of the present chapter emerge from the above studies. First, it seems likely that a subset of abusers may have assertiveness problems which are situationally specific. Problem drinkers in particular may require focus on increasing comfort in being assertive. Second, evidence on the relationship between assertiveness and problem drinking may be inferred from the several analogue studies that have manipulated social stress or opportunity to retaliate to an insult and measured subsequent consumption. Researchers have suggested that problem drinkers' responses in these situations may be analogous to their lack of assertiveness in the real world which may lead to excessive drinking as an alternative coping behaviour.

Interpersonal Skills and the Process of Relapse

Within the substance abuse literature a major emphasis has recently been placed upon the processes of maintaining treatment produced change and prevention of relapse. This interest has been sparked by the retrospective findings that among people who change their drinking, cigarette smoking, or opiate abuse behaviour, 70–80% relapse within six months (Marlatt and Gordon, 1980). Such statistics have led researchers to focus on the processes of relapse and on broader-based conceptual models of addiction. Cronkite and Moos (1980) have formulated a model that considers the domains of extra-treatment factors (e.g., family, work settings, and stressful events) in conjunction with patient and treatment factors. Indeed, these researchers have shown that the inclusion of extra-treatment factors more than doubles the explained variance in treatment outcome, leading them to suggest that, for problem drinking treatment in particular, treatment may be more effective when oriented toward patients' present life circumstances. Abrams (1983) has proposed a triple-response mode model of the factors that initiate and maintain problem drinking. Special emphasis is placed on psychosocial stressors, social anxiety, cognitive factors, and physiological arousal mechanisms.

The implication of both of these models is that environmental factors, especially stress and social networks in the family, the workplace and friendships, should be seriously considered as a means of improving treatment. SST can be used to enhance the social support for sobriety and to substitute more healthy alternatives for coping with interpersonal stressors at work and with family and friends.

In a seminal study, Marlatt and Gordon (1980) retrospectively examined the process of relapse among three addictive behaviours (alcohol, smoking and heroin abuse). Based on extensive relapse interviews these authors found that two social situations preceded relapse in 39% of the cases where relapse occurred. In half of the cases, interpersonal conflict preceded the relapse, in the other half, social pressure to drink was the precipitant. In addition, non-social negative emotional states such as anxiety, boredom, depression and loneliness accounted for 46% of the precipitants of relapse. It is unclear to what extent factors such as social phobias, SS deficits, or lack of assertiveness (retaliation) are implicated in these contexts as well. In an earlier sample studied, Marlatt (1978b) reported that interpersonal conflicts or social pressure to drink precipitated over 50% of alcohol relapses.

More recently, Rosenberg (1983) studied differences between relapsed and nonrelapsed chronic alcohol abusers. Results of this retrospective study showed that nonrelapsers responded to problem situations in a more assertive and drink refusing manner compared to the relapsers. Also, nonrelapsers perceived their life events as significantly more positive and significantly less negative than relapsers.

In one of the few available studies on relapse with problem drinking women, Rist and Watzl (1983a) found that those who relapsed three months after treatment evaluated various situations involving social pressure to drink alcohol as more difficult to deal with and as creating more discomfort than did abstainers. Interestingly, the groups did not differ in their self-rated assertiveness in non-alcohol related situations. The authors interpret these results as suggesting the need for more specific SST programmes for problem drinking women.

Several researchers (Chaney et al., 1982; Kolko et al., 1983; Stephens, 1971) have pointed to the role of interpersonal problems in the relapse process of hard drug abusers as well. Indeed, Stephens (1971) suggests that half of hard drug abusers who relapse after treatment do so because of interpersonal difficulties. Chaney et al. (1982) conducted a behavioural interview with 38 opiate addicts who were receiving methadone maintenance treatment, in order to study the antecedents and concomitants of relapse. Twenty-nine per cent of situations leading to relapse involved inter-personal determinants, leading the authors to suggest that SST should be relevant for addicts having difficulty in interpersonal situations.

It seems clear from both recent conceptual models of drug addiction (Abrams, 1983; Cronkite and Moos, 1980; Shiffman, in press) as well as from several empirical analyses of relapse situations, that difficulties in interpersonal situations play a major role in the relapse process of many substance abusers. Such findings have led several researchers to point to SST as a potentially valuable adjunctive treatment for substance abuse problems. In the following section, we will consider the assessment of SST among substance abusers.

Assessment of Social Skills in Substance Abuse Populations

The assessment of SS in substance abuse populations has developed in response to clinical needs. This section presents an overview of the methods of skills assessment with an emphasis on their continued refinement and directions for further development.

General and Specific Social Skills Assessment

There are four broad categories of social skill assessment: (a) questionnaire self-report, (b) *in vivo* observation, (c) naturalistic interaction, and (d) role-play tests (Bellack, 1979). The techniques for the specific assessment of social skills in substance abuse populations can be further divided into two broad approaches. The first approach selects measures of general SS and applies them to substance abuse populations and will be referred to as *general skills* assessment. The second approach utilises measures of SS which are tailored specifically to those social interactions expected to be of major importance for a particular substance abuse population: this will be referred to as *specific skills* assessment.

Both the general skill assessment and the specific skill assessment approaches have been used in SS assessment and treatment studies of problem drinkers. Few such studies exist for other substance abuse populations. The remainder of this section will focus on skills assessment of problem drinkers. Studies with other substance abusers will be included wherever possible.

Specific skills assessment instruments have mainly grown out of studies identifying social situations in which there is said to be a high risk for relapse (Greenwald *et al.*, 1980; Litman *et al.*, 1977; Marlatt and Gordon, 1980; Rist and Watzl, 1983a, 1983b); or from behavioural analysis studies of situations in which problem drinkers frequently drink (Eisler *et al.*, 1975; Monti *et al.*, 1984). High risk situations have typically been identified by gathering retrospective descriptions of the circumstances surrounding patients' relapses. Behaviour analytic approaches have focused on the circumstances surrounding ongoing substance use rather than just relapse situations. Both approaches have identified drinking situations which involve SS deficits. These situations and deficits have then been incorporated into the various specific skills assessment instruments.

General and Specific Skills Assessment Studies

The earliest studies focused on small samples and utilised assessment devices aimed at specific skills associated with each individual's substance abuse (e.g. Eisler, Hersen and Miller, 1974a; Foy *et al.*, 1976; Polakow and Dactor, 1973). These treatment studies reported assessments which were sensitive to pre-post changes in specific skills. However, they rarely presented reliability or validity data in support of the assessment techniques used. The focus was on a functional analysis of each patient's substance use and on documenting treatment produced change in SS behaviours associated with that substance use.

The initial treatment demonstration studies were followed by a group treatment outcome and assessment development studies which incorporated general skills assessment techniques (e.g., Hamilton and Maisto, 1979) and/or specific skill assessment techniques (e.g., Callner and Ross, 1976; Hirsch *et al.*, 1978; Miller and Eisler, 1977; Parker, Gilbert and Spiltz, 1981). Some studies began to provide a link between the more developed general skills assessment literature and emerging specific skill assessment techniques for substance abusing populations.

Callner and Ross (1976) examined both a self-report questionnaire and a role-play assessment procedure in a study which addressed both general and specific skill areas associated with hard drug abuse. They reported a high level of convergence between the role-play and self-report approaches ($r = .75–.95$), and a moderate level of discriminant validity ($r = .50–.80$) across five areas of assertion (authority, drugs, positive feedback, negative feedback and heterosexual interaction). As mentioned in the previous section, addict and non-addict groups differed significantly in assertiveness in the drugs, authority and positive feedback areas.

Hirsch *et al.* (1978) presented one of the first treatment outcome studies to show both a general skills assessment approach (Rathus Assertiveness Scale and a naturalistic observation) and a specific skills approach (role-play test) to assess changes in the assumed general and specific skills deficits of poblem drinkers. They reported that the assertion training groups differed on all three measures following treatment. Interrater reliabilities of .93 and .94 were reported for the alcohol specific role-play test. No reliability information was provided for either the Rathus scale or the naturalistic observation session.

Matuszewski (1982) reported on a detailed behaviour analytic approach to identify the drinking situations to be included in a specific skills assessment questionnaire. He reported that the resulting multiple choice format inventory for college students documented different patterns of responding in social situations for heavy and non-heavy drinking samples.

Given the implications of skill deficits of substance abusers a theme in the skills assessment research has been to identify more precisely the exact nature of such deficits. Using questionnaires and a general skills approach, Hamilton and Maisto (1979) report that problem drinkers showed deficits in the area of negative assertion. Although problem drinkers have been reported to be more assertive in general than other psychiatric patients (Miller and Eisler, 1977; Monti et al., 1981) they were equally non-assertive in negative assertion situations and as reported earlier, the problem drinker's alcohol consumption was inversely related to their level of negative assertion (Miller and Eisler, 1977).

In a further attempt to identify both general and specific skill deficits in problem drinkers, Twentyman et al. (1982) used a 50-item audiotaped role-play test to compare problem drinkers and a control sample. The 50 items represented two categories of specific skills (drink refusal and frustrating interpersonal situations requiring assertion) and three categories of general skills (other types of refusals, expression of positive sentiment and response to positive sentiment). The items were drawn from 100 such items suggested by the authors and treatment staff members. Subjects' responses were scored for the number of words used and speech dysfluencies as well as given a 1–5 rating of social skill. Overall, compared to control subjects, problem drinker subjects gave shorter responses and their responses contained fewer speech dysfluencies even after correction for response length. Problem drinkers' responses were considered less skilful only on two of ten items representing drink refusal. No correlations between the subjects' performance on the general skill categories and other, standardised measures of general skill were reported nor were any validity data presented in support of the specific skills categories.

This study raises an important issue concerning the selection of an appropriate control group for comparison to problem drinkers or other substance abusers. Based on the test scores the control group apparently contained at least some individuals with significant alcohol related problems. The inclusion of such subjects can only serve to lessen the ability of measures to differentiate the groups. In general, substance abusers should be screened out of control groups in studies of this kind. Nevertheless, the researcher is left with a difficult choice. Arguments can be made that the appropriate control groups for comparison to problem drinkers should consist of non-problem social drinkers or non-drinkers with no history of problem drinking or non-drinkers with a history of problem drinking or some combination of the three. Depending upon the focus of a study, some form of drinking history may be necessary for control subjects to be able to respond to all the assessments techniques.

Suggested Directions for General and Specific Skills Assessment

The thrust of the assessment work in this field has been on documenting the nature of skills deficits of groups of problem drinkers rather than upon the accurate assessment of skills deficits in individual patients. As researchers have focused more and more on the identification of specific areas of skill deficits in substance abusing populations, a number of psychometric details have been underemphasised. Most of the assessment studies, even in programmatic research, have utilised new or markedly changed assessment instruments or techniques from one study to the next. Although there has been a consistent attempt to present some form of reliability estimate for most instruments used in these studies, aside from occasional demonstrations of the ability to differentiate known groups, little or no evidence of validity has been reported.

Treatment outcome studies have tended either to use questionnaire measures of general SS and/or more alcohol specific assessment techniques which are tailored to a particular aspect of the treatment. These assessment instruments have been primarily employed to document change in the treated groups. In addition, however, the association between these measures and drinking patterns have sometimes been examined (e.g., Chaney *et al.*, 1978). There has not been an opportunity to date to evaluate systematically the specific skills instruments used in these studies. Behaviour analytic approaches have led to the development of one general and specific skills questionnaire for college students (Matuszewski, 1982) and a general and specific role-play test appropriate for adult clinical populations (Monti *et al.*, 1984). Both tests have reported high reliabilities and, given their foundation on an applied behaviour analytic approach, both hold promise for eventually demonstrating validity.

The triple response mode approach which simultaneously assesses behavioural, cognitive, and physiological modes of response, was utilised by Abrams *et al.* (1984) with a sample of cigarette smokers to demonstrate the value of expanding skills assessment across multiple modes. This approach can be integrated into either single case or group assessment research. Identifying individuals with concordant or disconcordant responses across modes may aid in the differentiation of so-called "relaxed incompetents" (Bandura, 1977) and individuals whose skills deficits are based on the interference of performance by anxiety (i.e., a secondary skills dysfunction). This approach appears particularly promising in light of the hypothesised role of anxiety in problem drinkers.

The final common pathway to relapse requires the presence of alcohol and its cues. The avoidance of drinking in social situations in the presence of alcohol cues may prove to be an important specific social skill. In this context, a promising line of research is being developed in our laboratory

(Binkoff *et al.*, 1984) to examine the role of alcohol cues in the disruption of social performance.

Social Skills Training Programmes in Substance Abuse Populations

SST for substance abusers has been reported in the context of broad spectrum treatment programmes, single case designs, and treatment outcome studies. Representative literature from each of these contexts will be discussed, followed by a consideration of issues in the generalisation and maintenance of SS.

Broad-Spectrum Programmes

There have been numerous reports of "broad-spectrum" behavioural treatment programmes for problem drinkers that include some element of SST, assertion, or communication skills training. In fact, this type of report far outnumbers those studies that focus explicity on the particular contribution of SST. Their prevalence documents the widespread inclusion of SST in behavioural treatments of alcoholism and demonstrates that such training can be incorporated into a variety of treatment programmes and settings. Yet, the design of these studies precludes evaluation of individual programme components. Thus, the relative contribution of SST, when included in a broad-spectrum programme, cannot be estimated. Keeping this caveat in mind, representative examples of such programmes will be outlined to illustrate the broader context in which SST with problem drinkers is often applied. The reports reviewed range from case histories, to descriptions of treatment programmes, to group design studies. There is a fair amount of variability in the amount and specificity of SST, the population involved, and the drinking goals sought (moderation or abstinence).

One of the earliest reports is a case history by Lazarus (1965) in which he treated a 42-year-old male who had a 15-year history of chronic, solitary drinking. Using behavioural rehearsal, the patient was taught to express assertively his negative feelings with the goal of reducing anxiety that built up when he "bottled up his feelings". Treatment included several additional components as well. A fourteen-month follow-up showed that the patient remained a successful social drinker and maintained improvement in other areas of adjustment.

Since Lazarus's report, broad-spectrum treatment programmes that include a SST component have been applied to outpatient, early stage problem drinkers (Miller, Pechacek and Hamburg, 1981), hospitalised male problem drinkers (Cautela, 1967; Miller, Stanford and Hemphill,

1974), and hospitalised female problem drinkers (Burtle, Whitlock and Franks, 1974). Each of these programmes also used anxiety reduction methods such as relaxation training and/or systematic desenitisation. This is noteworthy since these programmes' components could address both primary and secondary skill deficits.

Participants in the Miller *et al.* (1981) study attended ten group meetings aimed at teaching moderation through methods such as self-control of drinking rate and stimulus control. Seventy per cent of the subjects were rated as having "successful" drinking outcomes at post-treatment and at a three- to six-month follow-up. Miller *et al.* (1974) utilised discussion, role-playing, modelling, feedback, and verbal reinforcement in their SST groups, which focused mainly on dealing with stressful situations involving confrontation and anger. The authors emphasised the importance of having a female therapist in the all male SST group in order to provide examples of handling male–female relationships. The importance of sex of therapist has not been examined systematically in any study to date.

Lack of attention to sex differences is also reflected by the paucity of data on SS of female alcoholics. It is not known whether their skill deficits are the same or different from male alcoholics. In one of the few studies on women, Burtle *et al.* (1974) focused on assertion training and on improving self-esteem, which the authors observe to be a critical problem area for female problem drinkers. Self-reported improvements in assertion and self-esteem were evident following treatment, but dissipated following return to the community. At a sixteen-week follow-up, 10 of the 16 women treated were abstinent or had recovered from a brief slip.

Several treatment outcome studies comparing interventions other than SST *per se* have included SST (or communication or assertion training) in one or more of their treatment conditions. The focus of many of these studies has been on the utility of training controlled drinking skills (i.e., non-problem drinking) and/or the utility of broad-spectrum behaviour therapy (e.g., Alden, 1980; Foy *et al.*, 1984; Miller, Taylor and West, 1980; Sobell and Sobell, 1973, 1978; Vogler, Compton and Weissbach, 1975). As was the case in the treatment programmes described earlier, there is a range of individuals treated across the various studies and a range of additional treatment components offered.

Other dimensions that varied across the above five studies were whether the SST was conducted individually or in groups, and whether or not the amount and content of training was standardised or tailored to match the individual's needs. Training in one alcohol-specific subset of social skills — drink refusal skills — was clearly included in some (e.g., Alden, 1980; Foy *et al.*, 1984), but not all of the studies. Although the design of these studies precludes evaluating the specific role of SST in treatment outcome, Foy *et al.* (1984) do provide preliminary data about the effects of SST with problem drinkers: of the studies noted here, only this one included assessment of patient's SS. Results with hospitalised problem drinkers showed highly significant improvements in SS following training. An understanding of the specific factors contributing to these improvements and the relationship between such improvements and sobriety requires further research.

In contrast to the several reports of SST within broad-spectrum programmes for problem drinkers, far fewer such reports are available about drug addiction programmes. One of the most extensive descriptions of such a treatment programme is provided by Check *et al.* (1973) who worked with 43 inpatient heroin addicts involved in methadone maintenance or opiate detoxification. In addition to the standard drug treatment programme, patients attended a behavioural self-control programme that included assertiveness training, relaxation, desensitisation, and self-image training. Post-treatment findings suggest the programme was well received by the patients and that it reduced anxiety and improved self-image and assertiveness. Encouraged by these findings, the authors call for future research involving experimental designs that would more adequately evaluate this type of programme.

It is likely that, ultimately, the most effective SST for substance abuse populations will not occur in isolation but rather in the context of broad-spectrum programmes that address the multiple problems faced by the abuser. However, because the overall success of such programmes has been moderate, the efficacy of the various components needs to be further investigated. Research designs which systematically dismantle the treatment components of these broad-spectrum programmes will provide crucial information for treatment refinement. Another source of such information is single subject research designs.

Single Case Experimental Designs

The single case design has been used to demonstrate the contribution of specific training techniques to SS acquisition among problem drinkers. It examines the process of more focused training and acquisition within individuals, and thus may be seen as complimentary to the broad-spectrum approaches that seek to maximise treatment gains across large numbers of patients by offering SST in conjunction with other interventions.

The sequential training of several components of general assertion (Eisler *et al.*, 1974a), drink refusal skills (Foy *et al.*, 1976) and Vocational Social Skills (Foy *et al.*, 1979) has been investigated using multiple-baseline designs. Skill components have included eye contact, compliance with unreasonable demands, requesting behaviour change, speech duration, and non-verbal affective or expressive responses. In each of these studies, problem drinkers typically displayed skill deficits on several target behaviours during baseline assessment, received training in each target behaviour sequentially, and showed remarkable improvement in each behaviour only upon training in it. Data regarding post discharge drinking status, reported in two of the three studies, indicated that one patient remained abstinent during a three-month follow-up period (Foy *et al.*, 1976), one relapsed and sought additional treatment during the same period (Foy *et al.*, 1976), and a third patient relapsed and was readmitted within three weeks (Eisler *et al.*, 1974a).

In addition to demonstrating that some individuals with histories of abusive drinking can improve specific SS through SST these studies address two other important issues. First, Eisler *et al.* (1974a) found that when a patient received training using standardised, general assertive situations unrelated to his real-life problems, the newly acquired skill components (e.g., eye contact) transferred to untrained, role-played simulations of his real-life assertive difficulties at work. Similarly, patients receiving training in drink refusal skills (Foy *et al.*, 1976) reported some success in using those skills after leaving the hospital.

A second important issue addressed is maintenance of treatment gains. Foy *et al.* (1976) videotaped three-month follow-up sessions and found that, between two patients, nine out of ten target behaviours remained at the same improved levels as observed in the last treatment session. In their subsequent study, Foy *et al.* (1979) conducted similar follow-up sessions at six months post-treatment for two of the three subjects and again found maintenance of treatment gains in nine out of ten target behaviours.

Treatment Outcome Studies

Treatment outcome studies form the core data base for evaluating the present state of the art regarding SST with substance abusers. SST was one component of a behavioural treatment programme for problem drinkers evaluated by Chaney *et al.* (1978) that also used training in general problem solving skills (D'Zurilla and Goldfried, 1971). Patients were randomly assigned to one of three groups in addition to participating in the regular hospital treatment programme: skills training (ST); discussion control (DC); or no additional treatment control (NTC). The ST group was based on the assumption that ability to analyse novel problematic situations and the skills required to generate and evaluate adaptive responses are critical for maintenance and generalisation of coping skills. Standardised training situations were based on Marlatt's (1978b, p. 291–292); and Marlatt and Gordon's (1980) previous categorisation of relapse situations and included both interpersonal situations (e.g., conflict, drink refusal) and intrapersonal situations (negative emotional states).

Results indicated that the ST had a significant effect on drinking behaviour, with patients in the ST group having shorter and less severe relapse episodes during a one-year follow-up than did patients in the other two groups. Based on patient's responses to a verbal role-play test, two dimensions of competency (latency to response and noncompliance) were unaffected by condition, and two other dimensions (duration and specification of new behaviour) were superior in the ST group at post-treatment but not at a three-month follow-up. An additional interesting finding was that the subjects with shorter latencies drank less, were employed more, and had more regular aftercare attendance following treatment. Overall, this study provides encouraging results about the utility of SST as one component in the remediation of problem drinking. As noted by the authors, the relative contributions of problem solving training and behaviour rehearsal of specific adaptive behaviours (including social behaviours) remains to be determined, as does any causative role of response latency in enhancing outcome. Furthermore, it is not clear from the report whether social responses were occasionally presented as a means of coping with the intrapersonal situations or whether they were used solely with the interpersonal situations. This ambiguity illustrates an important issue that is typically not addressed: to what extent can ostensibly intrapersonal precipitants to substance abuse (e.g., boredom, anxiety, loneliness, depression) be effectively coped with by using interpersonal strategies (e.g., broadening friendships, seeking moral support)?

In a study with inpatient problem drinkers, Greenwald et al. (1980) compared the effects of two quite specific SST interventions and a no-treatment control on five categories of social skilfulness. Subjects were randomly assigned to the three experimental conditions and also continued to attend all other therapeutic ward activities. The five categories assessed were general refusal, express sentiment, response to sentiment, alcohol refusal, and positive assertive reponses in frustrating interpersonal situations. One SST intervention focused on alcohol refusal and the other on assertion in frustrating interpersonal situations. Thus, 3 of the 5 assessment categories were untrained and presented an opportunity to assess generalisation. SST was conducted individually during two sessions of behaviour rehearsal, modelling and coaching. Curiously, audiotaped role-plays at pre- and post-treatment showed that training produced significantly greater gains than no-treatment on two untrained categories but nonsignificant differences between groups were found for the trained categories. Several factors make it difficult to interpret these findings. Most notably, only two SST sessions were provided in the context of an inpatient programme that may have addressed similar social interactional goals. The present experimental conditions may not provide a suitably powerful test of SST. Further, since a primary aim of the SST is to ultimately influence sobriety, lack of follow-up drinking data is a serious problem. Despite these shortcomings, this study usefully refocuses our attention on two increasingly important issues; developing specific SST interventions that address topics of relevance to problem drinkers, and developing assessments that discriminate between such alcohol-specific SS and more general SS.

In another examination of skills training, Oei and Jackson (1982) compared the effectiveness of SST, combined cognitive restructuring — social skills training (CR + SST), cognitive restructuring alone (CR), and traditional supportive therapy (TST). Thirty-two inpatient problem drinkers who had mild to severe assertion deficits were randomly assigned to one of the four groups. In the SST group, didactics, modelling, role-play, videotaping, feedback, and homework assignments were used to teach a variety of SS. In the CR group, each session dealt with the same skill taught in SST sessions, although no direct SST methods were used. Instead, therapists led discussions about effective and noneffective behaviours and attitudes, using rational persuasion to modify irrational beliefs and to encourage "healthy self-talk". For all groups, SS level at follow-up was assessed during a behavioural interview and through general paper and pencil questionnaires. The pattern of results on SS and alcohol intake measures indicated that the SST, CR, and CR + SST groups led to significantly better outcome than did the TST group. Further, although SST provided greater immediate improvements, patients in the CR groups showed better maintenance of treatment gains at later follow-ups. The authors conclude that treatment of SS deficits, either by SST, cognitive restructuring, or both, is an effective therapy for alcohol dependency when patients present with social anxiety or SS deficits. They speculate that the superiority of the CR groups may be due to their treatment of maladaptive cognitions which inhibit assertive responding. This raises a crucial issue with respect to primary versus secondary skill deficits (see introduction and concluding sections of this chapter). Some other factors to be considered in interpreting this study are: (a) whether the design of the treatment groups led to more discussion of SS in the CR group than of cognitive restructuring in the SST group, and whether this potential confound could be avoided in future research; and (b) whether enhanced group process in the CR groups (suggested by more questions and self-disclosure by therapists in those groups) markedly affected outcome and whether group process is necessarily better managed in CR versus SST groups.

As previously noted, evaluations of SST with drug addicts are in an earlier stage of development than are studies with problem drinkers. However, several empirical studies do support the notion that SST may enhance the interpersonal effectiveness of other substance abusers besides problem drinkers. For example, Hall *et al*. (1977) randomly assigned 49 unemployed methadone maintenance patients to either a two-week workshop on job placement skills or to a minimal treatment control group that only received vocational information. Workshop participants role played and received feedback on effective interviewing skills, practiced relaxation to reduce anticipatory and social anxiety related to interviews and were instructed in completion of sample job application forms. At post-treatment, interview assessments were conducted and results showed that experimental subjects performed better than controls.

Other investigators have focused even more directly on evaluating SST with drug users. Callner and Ross (1978) randomly assigned eight inpatients to a control group receiving standard inpatient treatment only or to a social assertiveness group that received the inpatient treatment plus three weeks (nine hours) of SST. The training involved rehearsal of drug refusal skills as well as other more general assertive skills. Analysis of pre-post verbal role-play performances yielded significant treatment effects on all three dimensions rated — duration, fluency, and affect. No significant group differences were obtained across subscales of an assertion questionnaire.

Taken together the above treatment outcome studies indicate that SST when added to an existing treatment programme, can contribute to improvements in patients' social effectiveness and help problem drinkers reduce drinking. Whether reductions in other drug abuse also occur is not yet known. The inclusion of cognitive restructuring of problem-solving training in some studies further suggests that some patients may benefit from attention to cognitive factors as well as to acquisition of performance capabilities.

Despite the encouraging results to date, optimal treatment parameters for SST with substance abusers have yet to be identified. Two such parameters that require more systematic exploration are treatment length and topics covered. In the studies reviewed, length of treatment ranged from two sessions of unspecified duration to twenty-four hours over three weeks. Topics ranged from vaguely described global assertion to general SS such as starting conversations and giving compliments, to SS specific to substance abuse such as resisting social pressure to drink. However, there has been scant discussion of how to tailor the more general topics to fit the needs of this specific population.

Generalisation and Maintenance of Social Skills

Findings that relapse is often precipitated by interpersonal stress make it particularly valuable to determine which SST methods best promote generalisation and maintenance. Those that do should increase the likelihood that the individual will be able to handle social stressors without turning to alcohol or other drugs. Although the extent to which individuals receiving SST use those skills beyond the treatment setting is a critical issue, it has been relatively unexplored in substance abuse research. However, some empirical data are available. As noted above, Eisler *et al.* (1974a) found that a problem drinker whose training involved standardised assertive scenes unrelated to his actual problems transferred his new skills to untrained role-play scenes of his real-life assertive difficulties. In another study, Eisler *et al.* (1974b) provided a 52-year-old male problem drinker with assertion training sessions in which a surrogate wife (research assistant) role-played marital encounters typical of the patient's interactions with his real wife. Behavioural ratings of pre- and post-training encounters between the patient and his real wife indicated that changes in the patient's assertive behaviour generalised to interactions with his wife. Yet another example of generalisation was demonstrated by Intagliata (1978) who trained 32 hospitalised problem drinkers in interpersonal problem solving skills. Patients receiving training generalised those skills to a structured interview setting in which they were asked to discuss their plans for coping with post-discharge problems.

The above studies provide examples of three of the four dimensions of generalisation identified by Scott, Himadi and Keane (1983) in their review of generalisation in SST. Those dimensions are scene (problem content), persons, setting, and time (maintenance), with generalisation across scenes showing the most success among the many studies reviewed.

Attention to the first strategy, scene selection, is implicated by Eisler *et al.* (1974b) as a factor in the successful generalisation reported above. In that study, a problem drinker transferred his newly acquired assertiveness skills to interactions with his wife. The patient was trained on simulated transactions highly relevant to his marital problems, whereas a different patient who was trained on non-relevant scenes showed less generalisation to interactions with his spouse. Although the conceptual argument for increasing scene relevance is strong and case reports of its efficacy are available, it is not yet clear how best to identify relevant scenes for individual substance abusers in treatment. Development of measures that tap specific SS deficits of substance abusers may provide clearer information for scene development than do general measures of SS. Asking patients to generate their own relevant role-play scenes is another useful tactic, although our experience indicates that many patients initially find this difficult.

Besides providing useful scene information, participation of significant others may also enhance generalisation by directly addressing the dimension of role-play partners (Scott *et al.*, 1983). That is, for the many substance abusers for whom relationships with family members are particularly problematic, the most realistic role-play partners would be those family members themselves. Their participation may contribute to skill generalisation and maintenance in other ways as well. For example, it is not infrequent that the spouses or other relatives also have difficulties with substance abuse or psychological adjustment (e.g., Bailey, 1967; Rimmer, 1974). Improvements in their own SS and their acceptance of new communication goals might very well serve to reinforce changes in the behaviour of the identified patient. Rather than meeting with resistance or scepticism, behaviour change would be more likely met with co-operation and other positive social consequences. This, in turn, would increase the likelihood that the behaviour change would endure, or generalise over time (Scott *et al.*, 1983). In other cases, patients who unrealistically expect to incur negative consequences for assertive reponses and thus inhibit such behaviour may be able to revise these expectancies following more satisfying interchanges with their significant others during training.

Examples of participation by significant others in communication skills training with problem drinkers have been reported by several writers. In their comparison of four behavioural treatments of problem drinking, Hedberg and Campbell (1974) randomly assigned 49 outpatient alcoholics to one of the following: behavioural family counselling, systematic desensitisation, covert sensitisation, or a shock presentation programme. Behavioural family counselling emphasised behaviour rehearsal of communication and assertiveness skills and was found to be the most effective of the four treatments in reducing alcohol intake at six-month follow-up.

Case histories provide thoughtful descriptions that aid therapists in conducting SST with problem drinkers and their spouses. Paolino and McCrady (1976) describe the joint hospital admission of a 28-year-old problem drinker and her 29-year-old husband. Goals of the admission were feedback to them about those patterns of interaction. When the couple argued the staff immediately intervened and taught them to discuss the problem more effectively. As the patient and her husband practiced more direct, assertive behaviour, learned to correct misconceptions and to negotiate compromises, the patient improved significantly and was discharged to outpatient care after three weeks. In his case report of SST with a 49-year-old problem drinker and his wife of 29 years, Miller (1978) clearly describes the use of SST to teach the couple more positive interactional skills. A nine-month follow-up showed that the patient had remained abstinent and that the couple maintained improvements in several communication areas.

Based on preliminary experimental data and case reports, involvement of significant others in SST with problem drinkers seems both feasible and useful. What is now needed are controlled outcome studies that compare

SST with and without family member involvement. One such study is currently under way in our research programme at the Providence VA Medical Center. Although no outcome data are available yet, subjective reports about family involvement from unit staff and group members have been quite encouraging.

In addition to scene selection and realistic role-play partners, conducting SST in settings that resemble the actual problem setting was a third suggestion offered by Scott *et al.* (1983) to facilitate generalisation. Barring practical limitations this would optimally involve training in the natural environment (e.g., home, shops). Otherwise, approximations to the natural environment can be constructed in the treatment setting (e.g., patients who are anxious speaking in groups might be trained in the recreation hall or canteen). Clinical observation and innovation by Cooney, Baker and Pomerleau (in press) led those authors to propose a very straightforward way of bringing an important aspect of the problem drinker's natural environment into the treatment setting: use real alcoholic beverages as props in drink refusal training. Cooney *et al.* (in press) observed that addition of these setting cues seemed to increase patients' desire to drink, to decrease initially their confidence about their ability to resist drinking, and generally enhance the impact of drink refusal practice. By increasing the difficulty and realism of the task to a level more representative of patients' real-life experiences, these role-plays may better prepare the patients for actual post-discharge experiences. In a recently conducted study (Binkoff *et al.*, 1984) we examined the extent to which presence of alcohol cues impairs the ability of problem drinkers to refuse a drink skilfully and calmly. By exploring which subgroups of problem drinkers are most affected we hope to begin to identify those patients for whom inclusion of alcohol setting cues in SST groups would be most beneficial. An important next step for clinical researchers will be to conduct treatment studies to examine the effects on skill generalisation and maintenance using such cue exposure procedures in SST groups.

Conclusion and Future Directions

Interpersonal skills training for substance abusers has been reported in clinical case studies as early as 25 years ago and probably was used informally before then. However, clinical research in the areas of assessment and treatment outcome are of relatively recent origin. The studies reviewed suggest that SST can make a significant contribution to improving treatment strategies with these populations. However, because so few studies have been done, there are several conceptual, method-ological, and practical issues that remain.

A fundamental conceptual issue relates to our understanding of the nature of substance abuse. From both social learning theory and developmental perspectives, substance abuse can be viewed as a maladaptive coping response to the demands of everyday life. Aside from their pharmacological and psychophysiological actions, drugs can also be used to modify social situations, cultural norms, moods, individual behaviour, and cognitions. Individuals can take social risks and misattribute responsibility for their errors to the drug rather than to themselves. Furthermore, resorting to drugs as a maladaptive coping response can result from the need to attentuate behavioural excesses (for example, to reduce tension or social anxiety) or for purposes of disinhibition (to express repressed anger or enhance social or sexual contacts).

Not all the effects of drugs are deleterious to society. In the majority of individuals, the controlled use of certain substances, particulary alcohol, can have beneficial effects and enhance the culture and quality of life. Drugs cease to have positive value when psychological and/or chemical dependency develops. Unfortunately, maladaptive and habitual use of drugs for mood manipulation, to change physiological arousal, behaviour or cognitions, results in short-lived success and long-term failure. A comprehensive analysis of biopsychosocial factors over time is needed to isolate the specific reasons why an individual uses drugs and what the nature of their response deficits or excesses are (cf. Abrams, 1983).

Several clinical researchers have attempted a conceptual integration to explain drug abuse from a social learning perspective. Emphasising clinical issues, Wills and Shiffman (in press) and Abrams (1983) have presented models that focus on both interpersonal and intrapersonal factors. A behavioural chain is examined that includes environmental factors (work, family, drug cues and availability), cognitive (expectations of drug effects on self and others), and physiological processes (change in arousal and anxiety). In attempting to understand the chain of continual interaction between the individual and the environment, it is important to identify the antecedents, both environmental and individual, the nature of the current coping repertoire, the capacity for alternative (non-drug) coping responses, and the reinforcing and punishing long and short-term consequences following drug use. A comprehensive approach to assessment and treatment should therefore incorporate environmental, cognitive and physiological factors into the functional analysis of the drug abuser (Abrams, 1983). Even when SST is considered the major focus of treatment, other biopsychosocial factors should not be ignored.

Several studies reviewed suggest that SS deficits may be situation specific. Individuals with mild to moderate problems with drug abuse may be very skilful in most situations. They may simply be unable to resist peer pressure for drug use and thus their skill deficit may be limited to lack of assertiveness in the face of such coercion. Perhaps the deficit is only apparent when strong cues related to the abused substance are actually present (Binkoff *et al.*, 1984). More severely addicted individuals, by contrast, could have basic skills problems across a variety of situations. These deficits eventually would lead to alienation, social isolation, or extreme dependency on the drinking or drug using subculture. For these individuals, simple SST around peer pressure to refuse their drug would not be an adequate treatment. A more general SS programme would have to be implemented to help the individual establish new and health-supporting social contacts as is done informally in groups like Alcoholics Anonymous.

A related issue of considerable importance is identifying whether the skills deficits are primary or secondary (Trower *et al.*, 1978). Individuals who have primary skills deficits would not have learned certain appropriate SS because of inadequate role-models in childhood and association with individuals with similar deficits during adolescence. These individuals would first require a comprehensive SST programme focused on skill acquisition. Individuals with secondary skill deficits are more likely to have cognitive-emotional or psychophysiological factors inhibiting their ability to express skills that do in fact currently exist in their behavioural repertoire. Such individuals may benefit from cognitive-behavioural treatment. Ultimately, the challenge of the future is to develop reliable and valid assessment devices that can produce biopsychosocial profiles to distinguish primary from secondary skill deficits. These profiles can then be used to better match client characteristics to treatment techniques.

Behavioural assessment in the area of alcohol and drug abuse is beginning to contribute to our understanding of individual differences and the need to tailor treatment accordingly. Some self-report inventories and behavioural role-play tests have been developed. More work needs to be done on instrument development and psychometrics. However, there is also a gap between assessment, laboratory analogue research, treatment outcome studies, and clinical practice. For the most part, assessment studies have been conducted in isolation from treatment studies with very small sample sizes. Assessment protocols have not been developed with a comprehensive biopsychosocial conceptual model in mind. The implications of laboratory analogue studies on cognitive processes and alcohol's effects (e.g., Abrams and Wilson, 1979; Higgins and Marlatt, 1975) have not yet been integrated into assessment or clinical treatment protocols. Bridging these gaps will help research and clinical work to develop new hypothesis and better treatment. The studies reported by Monti *et al.* (1984) and Binkoff *et al.* (1984) illustrate recent attempts to integrate theory and practice to improve assessment.

Another strategy with potential benefits is to concentrate more resources on process evaluation and existing programme tracking within the context of treatment outcome studies. Many studies to date have simply conducted assessments at pre- and post-treatment and then related these to drinking outcomes. While this is a necessary component of a treatment study, it is not sufficient to answer some fundamental questions and to understand the process of change and the components of treatment. Studies of SST have been conducted within the context of an existing treatment milieu or where skill training was only one part of a more comprehensive treatment package. In the absence of appropriate controls, the power to predict the independent contribution of SST to outcome is consequently diminished. There is no guarantee that an adequate amount of SST actually took place within treatment or that it was remembered by the participants who may be overwhelmed with a smorgasbord of treatment techniques. As Moos and Finney (1983) point out, SST programmes provide an appropriate model for conducting such process evaluations.

In group designs, more process evaluation and programme tracking would add to our knowledge of how treatment interacts with clients and relates to outcome. The use of single case designs, especially during the early phases of a new programme of research, can greatly contribute to our understanding of the process of treatment and help identify key variables for further research. Furthermore, eventually randomised trials will have to be conducted using additive treatment designs to isolate active ingredients and thereby conduct components analyses.

Given the well-established finding that 70–80% of drug users relapse within three to six months of treatment (Marlatt and Gordon, 1980), it is never too early to concentrate on generalisation and maintenance. In a typical programme, even three weeks of daily intensive SST around drug refusal, establishing new social networks, dealing with work pressures and marital/family communications is probably not enough to prevent relapse following discharge from the inpatient or day hospital facility. Factors should be considered such as outpatient treatment, use of "booster sessions", a telephone hotline for emergency social support and active involvement of family, close friends and employers in the follow-up process. Maintenance skills training may require different sets of skills compared with the skills to prevent drug use. SST could focus on modifying the behaviour of significant others in the social network (e.g., rather than drink refusal training, the issue may be how to teach a spouse to be supportive when the ex-drug abuser is feeling too stressed to cope). Generalisation and maintenance of treatment produced changes should not be assumed, rather they should be programmed into treatment (Monti, Corriveau and Curran, 1982b). Studies evaluating the effectiveness and cost-effectiveness of various maintenance components need to be conducted.

The Broader Context: Environmental and Systems Variables

At the present time, most research and clinical work has focused primarily on intrapsychic and individual treatment factors, and occasionally family members are involved in treatment. Recently, several researchers have suggested that life-context factors such as family adjustment, work related issues, recreational and friendship circles are important in the process of recovery or relapse (cf. Longabaugh and Beattie, 1982; Moos and Finney, 1982). Thus, in a comprehensive process-oriented framework for evaluation of alcohol treatment, Moos and Finney included life context factors (family and work settings, life stress events), intervention factors, and client characteristics. As noted in the first section of this chapter, Moos and Finney (1982) have shown that inclusion of such parameters enable evaluators to account for substantially more of the variance in treatment outcome.

Social network and social support variables have long been known to mediate health and illness (McKinlay, 1980). Individuals who have a rich social network, who can turn to others for support when under stress; and those who are members of supportive work environments, religious groups, and social organisations, are likely to have a better prognosis. Indirect evidence of the importance of this strategy comes from findings that suggest married alcoholics with jobs do better in treatment than divorced or isolated alcoholics (Polich, Armor and Braiker, 1981; Ruggels, Armor and Polich, 1975). At present we know of no treatment protocol that has attempted to use SST to maximise social support, and thereby facilitate "systems interventions" to ensure the drug abusers entry into the mainstream of society.

Primary Prevention of Substance Abuse

The systems variables also point in the direction of early intervention or even prevention of chronic substance abuse. From a developmental perspective, children and adolescents who are at risk for alcohol or drug abuse are likely to have skill deficits (Asher and Renshaw, 1984). They would have difficulty with assertiveness within their peer group and thus when asked to experiment with alcohol or a new drug they would be unable to resist for fear of expulsion from their support system. Experimentation would eventually lead to regular use and finally to abuse.

SST programmes for the prevention of tobacco smoking and alcohol abuse have recently been successfully implemented in junior high schools (Flay, 1985; Perry *et al.*, 1980). A large portion of these prevention programmes involve SST to resist peer pressure to experiment with drugs, alcohol or cigarettes. "Rap sessions" are held and role-plays and feedback are provided to teach young adolescents how to resist requests to experiment with alcohol or hard drugs and at the same time how to remain accepted in their peer group. SST can play a powerful role not only in secondary and tertiary interventions with adult substance abusers, but also in primary prevention and early intervention in highrisk populations of children, adolescents, and families. This is perhaps one of the most rewarding possibilities for future research and clinical treatment.

To conclude, there is reason to be cautiously optimistic about the expanding contribution of SST to substance abuse problems. Although more research is needed, existing evidence suggests that there is a significant role to be played in improving treatment outcome and facilitating recovery. A comprehensive conceptual model has not yet been developed, but progress has been made toward this end in both assessment and treatment studies to date. The possibility for primary prevention of substance abuse in children at risk is an area worthy of further research exploration.

Notes

The authors wish to thank Damaris Rohsenow and Ray Niaura for their helpful comments on an earlier draft of this manuscript.

References

Abrams, D. B. (1983) Psycho-social assessment of alcohol and stress interactions: Bridging the gap between laboratory and treatment outcome research. In: L. Pohorecky and J. Brick (Eds.), *Stress and alcohol use*. New York: Elsevier North Holland.

Abrams, D. B., Pinto, R. P., Monti, P. M. and Jacobus, S. (1984) *Reactivity of smokers, quitters, and controls to smoking cues*. Paper presented at a symposium, "Cue Exposure and Self-Control", chaired by Peter M. Monti at the 18th Annual Convention of the Association for the Advancement of Behavioural Therapy, Philadelphia. Pennsylvania.

Abrams, D. B. and Wilson, G. T. (1979) Effects of alcohol on social anxiety in women: Cognitive versus physiological processes. *Journal of Abnormal Psychology*, **88**, 161–173.

Adinolfi, A. A., McCourt, W. F. and Geoghegan, S. (1976) Group assertiveness training for alcoholics. *Journal of Studies on Alcohol*, **37**, 311–320.

Alden, L. (1980) Preventive strategies in the treatment of alcohol abuse: A review and proposal. In: P. O. Davidson and S. M. Davidson (Eds.), *Behavioral medicine: Changing health lifestyles*. New York: Brunner/Mazel.

Asher, S. and Renshaw, P. D. (1984) Children without friends: Social knowledge and social skills training. In: S. Asher and J. Gottman (Eds.), *The development of children's friendships*. New York: Cambridge University Press.

Bailey, M. B. (1967) Psychophysiological impairment in wives of alcoholics as related to their husbands' drinking and sobriety. In: R. Fox (Ed.), *Alcoholism: Behavioral research, therapeutic approaches*. New York: Springer.

Bandura, A. (1969) *Principles of behavior modification*. New York: Holt, Rinehart & Winston.

Bandura, A. (1977) Self-efficacy: Toward a unifying theory of behavioral change. *Psychological Bulletin*, **84**, 191–215.

Bellack, A. S. (1979) A critical appraisal of strategies for assessing social skills. *Behavioral Assessment*, **1**, 157–176.

Binkoff, J. A., Abrams, D. B., Collins, R. L., Liepman, M., Monti, P. M., Nirenberg, T. and Zwick, W. R. (1984) *Exposure to alcohol cues: Impact on reactivity and drink refusal skills in problem and non-problem drinkers*. Paper presented at a symposium, "Cue Exposure and Self-Control", chaired by Peter M. Monti at the 18th Annual Convention of the Association for Advancement of Behaviour Therapy. Philadelphia. Pennsylvania.

Braucht, G. N., Brakarsh, D., Follingstad, D. and Berry, K. L. (1973) Deviant drug use in adolescence. *Psychological Bulletin*, **79**, 92–106.

Brown, S. A., Goldman, M. S., Inn, A. and Anderson, L. R. (1980) Expectations of reinforcement from alcohol: Their domain and relation to drinking patterns. *Journal of Consulting and Clinical Psychology*, **48**, 419–426.

Burtle, V., Whitlock, D. and Franks, V. (1974) Modification of low self-esteem in women alcoholics: A behavior treatment approach. *Psychotherapy: Theory, Research and Practice*, **11**, 36–40.

Caddy, G. R. (1982) Evaluation of behavioral methods in the study of alcoholism. In: E. M. Pattison and E. Kaufman (Eds.), *Encyclopedia handbook of alcoholism*. New York: Gardner Press, Inc.

Callner, D. A. and Ross, S. (1978) The assessment and training of assertive skills with drug addicts: A preliminary study. *The International Journal of the Addictions*, **13**, 227–239.

Callner, D. A. and Ross, S. (1976) The reliability and validity of three measures of assertion in a drug addict population. *Behavior Therapy*, **7**, 659–667.

Cameron, D. C. (1961) Addiction — current issues. *American Journal of Psychiatry*, **35**, 523–531.

Cautela, J. R. (1967) Covert sensitization. *Psychological Reports*, **20**, 459–468.

Chaney, E. F., O'Leary, M. R. and Marlatt, G. A. (1978) Skill training with alcoholics. *Journal of Consulting and Clinical Psychology* **46**, 1092–1104.

Chaney, E. F., Roszell, D. K. and Cummings, C. (1982) Relapse in opiate addicts: A behavioral analysis. *Addictive Behaviours*, **7**, 291–297.

Cheek, F. E., Tomarchio, T., Standen, J. and Albahary, R. S. (1973) Methadone plus a behavior modification training program in self-control for addicts on methadone maintenance. *The International Journal of the Addictions*, **8**, 969–996.

Cooney, N. L., Baker, L. and Pomerleau, O. F. (in press) Cue exposure for relapse prevention in alcohol treatment. In: R. J. McMahon and K. D. Craig (Eds.), *Advances in clinical behavior therapy*. New York: Brunner/Mazel.

Cronkite, R. C. and Moos, R. H. (1980) Determinants of the post treatment functioning of alcoholics patients: A conceptual framework. *Journal of Consulting and Clinical Psychology*, **48**, 305–316.

D'Zurilla, T. J. and Goldfried, M. R. (1971) Problem solving and behavior modification. *Journal of Abnormal Psychology*, **78**, 107–126.

Eisler, R. M., Hersen, M., Miller, P. M. and Blanchard, E. B. (1975) Situational determinants of assertive behaviour. *Journal of Consulting and Clinical Psychology*, **43**, 330–340.

Eisler, R. M., Hersen, M. and Miller, P. M. (1974a) Shaping components of assertive behavior with instruction and feedback. *American Journal of Psychiatry*, **131**, 1344–1347.

Eisler, R. M., Miller, P. M., Hersen, M. and Alford, H. (1974b) Effects of assertive training on marital interaction. *Archives of General Psychiatry*, **30**, 643–649.

Flay, B. (1985) What do we know about the social influences approach to smoking prevention? Review and recommendations. In: C. Bell and R. Battjes. (Eds.), *Prevention research: Deterring drug abuse among children and adolescents*. Washington, D.C.: NIDA Research Monograph.

Foy, D. W., Massey, F. H., Duer, J. D., Ross, J. M. and Wooten, L. S. (1979) Social skills training to improve alcoholics vocational interpersonal competency. *Journal of Counseling Psychology*, **26**, 128–132.

Foy, D. W., Miller, P. M., Eisler, R. M. and O'Toole, D. M. (1976) Social skills training to teach alcoholics to refuse drinks effectively. *Journal of Studies on Alcohol*, **37**, 1340–1345.

Foy, D. W., Nunn, L. B. and Rychtarik, R. G. (1984) Broad-spectrum behavioural treatment for chronic alcoholics: Effects of training controlled drinking skills. *Journal of Consulting and Clinical Psychology*, **52**, 218–230.

Greenwald, M. A., Kloss, J. P., Kovaleski, M. E., Greenwald, D. P., Twentyman, G. T. and Zibung-Hoffman, P. (1980) Drink refusal and social skills training with hospitalized alcoholics. *Addictive Behaviours*, **5**, 227–228.

Hall, S. M., Loeb, P., Norton, J. and Yang, R. (1977) Improving vocational placement in drug treatment clients: A pilot study. *Addictive Behaviours*, **2**, 227–234.

Hamilton, F. and Maisto, S. (1979) Assertive behavior and perceived discomfort of alcoholics in assertion-required situations. *Journal of Consulting and Clinical Psychology*, **47**, 196–197.

Hedberg, A. G. and Campbell, L. (1974) A comparison of four behavioral treatments of alcoholism. *Journal of Behavior Therapy and Experimental Psychiatry*, **5**, 251–256.

Higgins, R. L. and Marlatt, G. A. (1975) Fear of interpersonal evaluation as a determinant of alcohol consumption in male social drinkers. *Journal of Abnormal Psychology*, **84**, 644–651.

Hirsch, S. M., Von Rosenberg, R., Phelan, C. and Dudley, H. Jr. (1978) Effectiveness of assertiveness training with alcoholics. *Journal of Studies on Alcohol*, **39**, 89–97.

Intagliata, J. C. (1978) Increasing the interpersonal problem-solving skills of an alcoholic population. *Journal of Consulting and Clinical Psychology*, **46**, 489–498.

Jones, M. C. (1968) Personality correlates and antecedents of drinking patterns in adult males. *Journal of Consulting and Clinical Psychology*, **32**, 2–12.

Kalin, R. (1972) Descriptions of college problem drinkers. In: D. C. McClelland, W. N. Davis, R. Kalin and E. Warner (Eds.), *The drinking man*. New York: Free Press.

Kandel, D. B. (1975) Stages in adolescent involvement in drug use. *Science*, **190**, 912–914.

Kilpatrick, D. G., Sutker, P. B. and Smith A. D. (1976) Deviant drug and alcohol use: The role of anxiety, sensation-seeking, and other personality variables. In: M. Zuckerman and C. D. Spielberger (Eds.), *Emotions and anxiety: New concepts, methods, and applications*. Hillsdale, New Jersey: Erlbaum.

Kolko, D. J., Sirota, A. D., Monti, P. M. and Paolino, R. (1983) *The behavior-analytic identification of problematic interpersonal situations of drug addicts*. Paper presented at the 3rd World Conference of Behaviour Therapy, Washington, D.C.

Kraft, T. (1971) Social anxiety model of alcoholism. *Perceptual and Motor Skills*, **33**, 797–798.

Lazarus, A. A. (1965) Towards the understanding and effective treatment of alcoholism. *South African Medical Journal*, **39**, 736–741.

Levine, J. and Zigler, E. (1973) The essential-reactive distinction in alcoholism: A developmental approach. *Journal of Abnormal Psychology*, **81**, 242–249.

Litman, G. K., Eisler, J. R., Rawson, N. S. B. and Oppenheim, A. N. (1977) Towards a typology of relapse: A preliminary report. *Drug and Alcohol Dependence*, **2**, 157–162.

Longabaugh, R. and Beattie, M. (1982) *Optimizing the cost-effectiveness of treatment for alcohol abusers*. Paper presented at the Conference on Directions in Alcohol Abuse Treatment Research. Newport, Rhode Island.

MacAndrew, C. and Edgerton, R. B. (1969) *Drunken compartment*. Chicago: Aldine Publishing Co.

Marlatt, G. A. (1978a) Behavioral assessment of social drinking and alcoholism. In: G. A. Marlatt and P. Nathan (Eds.), *Behavioral approaches to alcoholism*. New Brunswick, New Jersey: Publication Division, Rutgers Center of Alcohol Studies.

Marlatt, G. A. (1978b) Craving for alcohol, loss of control, and relapse: A cognitive-behavioral analysis. In: P. E. Nathan, G. A. Marlatt and T. Loberg (Eds.), *Alcoholism: New directions in behavioral research and treatment*. New York: Plenum Press.

Marlatt, G. A. and Gordon, J. R. (1980) Determinants of relapse: Implications for the maintenance of behavior change. In: P. O. Davidson and S. M. Davidson, (Eds.), *Behavioral medicine: Changing health life styles*. New York: Brunner/Mazel.

Marlatt, G. A., Kosturn, C. F. and Lang, A. R. (1975) Provocation to anger and opportunity for retaliation as determinants of alcohol consumption in social drinkers. *Journal of Abnormal Pscychology*, **84**, 652–659.

Matuszewski, J. E. (1982) *Development of the college drinking inventory: An analysis of situation-specific response competence and college problem drinking.* Unpublished master's thesis, Indiana University, Bloomington, Indiana.

McClelland, D. C., Davis, W. M., Kalin, R. and Wanner, E. (1972) *The drinking man.* New York: Free Press.

McKinlay, J. (1980) Social network influences on morbid episodes and the career of help seeking. In: L. Eisenberg and A. Kleinman (Eds.), *The relevance of Social Science for medicine.* Boston, Massachusetts: D. Reidel Publishing Company.

Miller, P. M. (1978) Alternative skills training in alcoholism treatment. In: P. E. Nathan, G. A. Marlatt and T. Loberg (Eds.), *Alcoholism: New directions in behavioral research and treatment.* New York: Plenum Press.

Miller, P. M. and Eisler, R. M., (1977) Assertive behavior of alcoholics: A descriptive analysis. *Behavior Therapy*, **8**, 146–149.

Miller, P. M., Hersen, M., Eisler, R. M. and Hilsman, G. (1974) Effects of social stress on operant drinking of alcoholics and social drinkers. *Behaviour Research & Therapy*, **12**, 67–72.

Miller, P. M., Stanford, A. G. and Hemphill, D. P. (1974) A social-learning approach to alcoholism treatment. *Social Casework*, **55**, 279–284.

Miller, W. R., Pechacek, T. F., and Hamburg, S. (1981) Group behavior therapy for problem drinkers. *The International Journal of the Addictions*, **16**, 829–839.

Miller, W. R., Taylor, C. A. and West, J. C. (1980) Focused versus broad-spectrum behavior therapy for problem drinkers. *Journal of Consulting and Clinical Psychology*, **48**, 590–601.

Mills, C. J. and Noyes, H. L. (1984) Patterns and correlates of initial and subsequent drug use among adolescents. *Journal of Consulting Psychology*, **52**, 231–243.

Monti, P. M., Boice, R., Fingeret, A. L., Zwick, W. R., Kolko, D., Munroe, S. and Grungerger, A. (1984) Midilevel measurement of social anxiety in psychiatric and non-psychiatric samples. *Behaviour Research and Therapy*, **22**, 651–660.

Monti, P. M., Corriveau, D. P. and Curran, J. P. (1982a) Assessment of social skill in the day hospital: Does the clinician see something other than the research sees? *International Journal of Partial Hospitalization*, **1**, 245–250.

Monti, P. M., Corriveau, D. P. and Curran, J. P. (1982b) Social skills training for psychiatric patients. In: J. P. Curran and P. M. Monti (Eds.) *Social skills training: A practical handbook for assessment and treatment.* New York: Guilford Press.

Monti, P. M., Corriveau, D. P. and Zwick, W. R. (1981) Assessment of social skills in alcoholics and other psychiatric patients. *Journal of Studies on Alcohol*, **42**, 526–529.

Monti, P. M., Zwick, W. R., Binkoff, J. A., Abrams, D. B. and Nirenberg, T. (1984) *The development of behavior-analytically derived categories and role-play situations for alcoholics.* Paper presented at the 5th annual meeting of the Society of Behavioral Medicine, Philadelphia, Pennsylvania.

Moos, R. H. and Finney, J. W. (1982) *New directions in program evaluation: Implications for expanding the role of alcohol researchers.* Presented at the Conference on New Directions in Alcohol Abuse Treatment Research, Newport, Rhode Island.

Moos, R. H. and Finney, J. W. (1983) The expanding scope of alcoholism treatment evaluation. *American Psychologist*, **38**, 1036–1044.

Oei, T. P. S. and Jackson, P. R. (1982) Social skills and cognitive behavioural approaches to the treatment of problem drinking. *Journal of Studies on Alcohol*, **43**, 532–546.

O'Leary, D. E., O'Leary, M. R. and Donovan, D. M. (1975). Social skills acquisition and psychosocial development of alcoholics: A review. *Addictive Behaviours*, **1**, 111–120.

Paolino, T. J. and McCrady, B. S. (1976) Joint admission as a treatment modality for problem drinkers: A case report. *American Journal of Psychiatry*, **133**, 222–224.

Parker, J. C., Gilbert, G. and Spiltz, M. L. (1981) Expectations regarding the effects of alcohol on assertiveness: A comparison of alcoholics and social drinkers. *Addictive Behavior*, **6**, 29–33.

Perry, C., Killen, J., Slinkard, L. and McAlister, A. (1980) Peer teaching and smoking prevention among junior high students. *Adolescence*, **58**, 277–281.

Polakow, R. L. and Dactor, R. M. (1973) Treatment of marijuana and barbiturate dependency by contingency contracting. *Journal of Behavioral Therapy and Experimental Psychiatry*, **4**, 375–377.

Polich, J. M., Armor, D. J. and Braiker, N. B. (1981) *The course of alcoholism: Four years after treatment*. New York: Wiley.

Rimmer, J. (1974) Psychiatric illness in husbands of alcoholics. *Quarterly Journal of Studies on Alcohol*, **35**, 281–283.

Rist, F. and Watzl, H. (1983a) Self-assessment of relapse risk and assertiveness in relation to treatment outcome of female alcoholics. *Addictive Behaviors*, **8**, 121–127.

Rist, F. and Watzl, H. (1983b) Self-assessment of social competence in situations with and without alcohol by female alcoholics in treatment. *Drug and Alcohol Dependence*, **11**, 367–371.

Robins, L. N., Bates, W. M. and O'Neal, P. (1962) Adult drinking patterns of former problem children. In: D. J. Pittman and C. R. Snyder (Eds.), *Society, culture, and drinking patterns*. New York: Wiley.

Rohsenow, D. J. (1983) Drinking habits and expectancies about alcohol's effects for self versus others. *Journal of Consulting and Clinical Psychology*, **51**, 752–756.

Rosenberg, C. M. (1969) Determinants of psychiatric illness in young people. *British Journal of Psychiatry*, **115**, 907–915.

Rosenberg, H. (1983) Relapsed versus non-relapsed alcohol abusers: Coping skills, life events, and social support. *Addictive Behaviors*, **8**, 183–186.

Rudie, R. E. and McGaughran, L. S. (1961) Differences in developmental experience, defensiveness and personality organization between two classes of problem drinkers. *Journal of Abnormal and Social Psychology*, **62**, 659–665.

Ruggels, W., Armor, D. and Polich, J. (1975) *A follow-up study of clients at selected alcoholism treatment centers*. Funded by NIAAA, Menlo Park, California: Stanford Research Institute.

Scott, R. R., Himadi, W. and Keane, T. M. (1983) A review of generalization in social skills training: Suggestions for future research. In: M. Hersen, R. Eisler and P. Miller (Eds.), *Progress in behavior modification Vol. 15*. New York: Academic Press.

Seeyers, M. H. (1962) Medical perspectors on habituation and addiction. *Journal of American Medical Association*, **181**, 92–98.

Shiffman, S. (in press) Maintenance and relapse: Coping with temptation. In: T. Nirenberg (Ed.), *Advances in the treatment of addicitve behaviors*. New Jersey: Ablex Press.

Sobell, L. C. (1978) A critique of alcoholism treatment evaluation. In: P. E. Nathan and G. A. Marlatt (Eds.), *Behavioral assessment and treatment of alcoholism*. New Brunswick: Rutgers Center of Alcohol Studies.

Sobell, M. B. and Sobell, L. C. (1973) Alcoholics treated by individualized behaviour therapy: One year treatment outcome. *Behaviour Research and Therapy*, **11**, 599–618.

Sobell, M. B. and Sobell, L. C. (1978) *Behavioral treatment of alcohol problems: Individualized therapy and controlled drinking*. New York: Plenum Press.

Stephens, R. (1971) *Relapse among narcotic addicts: An empirical test of labelling theory*. Unpublished doctoral dissertation, University of Wisconsin, Madison.

Sturgis, E. T., Best, C. L. and Calhoun, K. S. (1977) The relationship of self-reported assertive behaviour to alcoholism. *Scandinavian Journal of Behavior Therapy*, **6**, 126.

Sturgis, E. T., Calhoun, K. S. and Best, C. L. (1979) Correlates of assertive behavior in alcoholics. *Addictive Behaviors*, **4**, 193–197.

Sugarman, A. A., Reilly, D. and Albahar, R. S. (1965) Social competence and essential-reactive distinction in alcoholism. *Archives of General Psychiatry*, **12**, 552–556.

Trower, P., Yardley, K., Bryant, G. M. and Shaw, P. (1978) The treatment of social failure. *Behavior Modification*, **2**, 41–60.

Twentyman, G. T., Greenwald, D. P., Greenwald, M. A., Kloss, J. D., Kovaleski, M. E. and Zibung-Hoffman, P. (1982) An assessment of social skill deficits in alcoholics. *Behavioral Assessment*, **4**, 317–326.

Van Hasselt, V. B., Hersen, M. and Milliones, J. (1978) Social skills training for alcoholics and drug addicts: A review. *Addictive Behaviors*, **3**, 221–233.

Vogler, R. E., Compton, J. V. and Weissbach, T. A. (1975) Integrated behavior change techniques for alcoholics. *Journal of Consulting and Clinical Psychology*, **43**, 233–243.

Watson, D. W. and Maisto, S. (1983) A review of the effectiveness of assertiveness training in the treatment of alcohol abusers. *Behavioural Psychotherapy*, **11**, 36–49.

Wilson, G. T. and Abrams, D. B. (1977) Effects of alcohol on social anxiety and physiological arousal: Cognitive versus pharmacological processes. *Cognitive Therapy and Research*, **1**, 195–210.

Wilson, G. T., Perold, E. and Abrams, D. B. (1981) The influence of attribution of alcohol intoxication on interpersonal interaction patterns. *Cognitive Therapy and Research*, **5**, 251–254.

Wolpe, J. (1969) *The practice of behavior therapy*, New York: Pergamon.

Zigler, E. and Phillips, L. (1960) Social effectiveness and symptomatic behaviours. *Journal of Abnormal and Social Psychology*, **61**, 231–238.

Zigler, E. and Phillips, L. (1961) Social competence and outcome in psychiatric disorder. *Journal of Abnormal and Social Psychology*, **63**, 264–271.

Zigler, E. and Phillips, L. (1962) Social competence and process-reactive distinction in psychopathology. *Journal of Abnormal and Social Psychology*, **65**, 215–222.

Zuckerman, M. (1972) *A preliminary manual and research report of the sensation seeking scale*. University of Delaware.

6

Social Skills Training for Health Professionals

PETER MAGUIRE

Whilst relatively recently introduced, the skills training model has had a considerable impact on the training of health professionals. The aim here is first to illustrate, using case examples, the need for communication skills in health professional–patient interaction. The utility of skills training is shown with specific reference to training in interviewing skills for medical students. The details of both assessment and the design and evaluation of skills training programmes are discussed in detail. This discussion includes evaluation of various training procedures such as modelling, practice, and feedback; various styles of training; and the role of the trainer. Additionally, studies are included which have examined the training of various professional groups as skills trainers themselves. In evaluating the long term effects of training, the experimental evidence is examined along with the problems in measurement of the effects of training. Finally, the potential of the skills training approach is linked to the need for training in other areas of health professional–patient interaction.

The Need for Key Communication Skills

Eliciting Problems

If health professionals are to be effective they must be able to talk with their patients in a way which promotes trust, leads patients to believe they are interested in them as people and able disclose their problems. Otherwise, patients will withhold important information and the diagnosis and treatment plan will be wrongly based as in the following example.

A 61-year-old woman had been attending a psychiatric out-patient department for three months for treatment of a severe depressive illness and phobic anxiety. She had responded well to treatment with anti-depressive medication, behaviour therapy, and the opportunity to talk over various concerns. On her next visit she looked anxious again although there was no sign that the depression had returned. The doctor assumed that her anxiety was temporary and enquired no further. At the subsequent follow-up appointment the woman still appeared anxious and he asked her why she was like this. She said she had been very worried over the last few weeks because she had noticed that every time she went to the toilet she passed red blood. She had come to fear that she had cancer. The doctor was extremely concerned because he realised he had not explored her anxiety on the previous visit and was frightened that he might have missed diagnosing a treatable cancer. He therefore arranged to carry out the necessary investigations immediately. Fortunately, the bleeding was due to "piles" and not cancer, as he and the patient had feared.

Establishing Patients' Responses

As well as the ability to identify problems accurately whether they are physical, social or psychological in nature, the health professional has to provide a satisfactory explanation to patients and explore how they have responded to the diagnosis and information given. Failure to check how a patient has responded to such information can lead to the doctor or nurse providing inappropriate reassurance.

A 45-year-old woman was seen in an out-patient clinic because she had developed a breast lump. She indicated that she was concerned about this lump because she was worried that it could be cancer. The doctor explained to her that even if it was cancer, which he thought unlikely, it had probably been caught at "a very early stage". If it was cancer he should be able to get rid of it completely and the prognosis looked good. He offered this reassurance in the genuine belief that it would help. He was surprised that woman still seemed anxious when she left the clinic; had he enquired why she was so upset she would have told him that her older sister had been in an identical situation two years earlier. She had developed a breast lump, had been told that it had been caught at an early stage and informed she had a good prognosis. Yet, she died six months later. The patient, therefore, was convinced that she would suffer the same fate and did not believe what the doctor told her.

Correcting Misconceptions

Explanation about illness and treatment can be hard for patients to assimilate. It is therefore important that the doctor or nurse checks that the patient has understood what is being said. Failure to do this can have serious consequences.

A man of 63 began to experience bouts of severe abdominal pain. He worried that it could be cancer because he was losing weight and passing blood when he went to the toilet. He was quickly referred to the surgical clinic where he was seen promptly. He was told that it was not serious and most likely to be ulcerative colitis. The surgeons thought that they had explained this successfully and thought no more about it. He duly came into hospital, had a colostomy fashioned, and was fitted with a colostomy bag. He still seemed anxious, but it was thought that his anxiety was due to his colostomy since he indicated that he was worried that it might leak, smell, be visible to others, or make a noise.

On his return home he seemed to make a good physical recovery, but his wife noted he was getting more withdrawn and she could not understand this. One morning when she woke up she noticed that her husband had already got out of bed and left their bedroom. She got up and went downstairs expecting to find him there. Instead she found that the back door of the house was wide open. She walked down the path and found that the door of the garden shed was open. To her horror she found her husband hanging there, and a note nearby in which he wrote that he had killed himself because he was convinced that his disease was cancer and not ulcerative colitis. He had harboured this misconception from the time he had first presented to the doctor but no one had established this. So it is not possible to determine if his misconception could have been corrected by explanation or if it was the product of a depressive illness which would have responded to appropriate treatment.

This is a dramatic example of what can happen if health professionals fail to explore what perceptions patients have of their illness. Even if this is done well many illnesses and treatments may cause substantial morbidity in the longer term.

Monitoring the Impact

Some drugs, like combination chemotherapy for cancer, have very unpleasant effects which can include severe nausea, vomiting and hair loss. Some patients develop a conditioned response to treatment such that any mention, sight, smell or sound associated with the treatment causes them to feel nauseous or to vomit reflexly. They then come to dread each treatment and may refuse it even though they realise it might save their lives. So it is important that health professionals interview in a way that maximises the chances of patients disclosing such physical morbidity. Otherwise they will not realise that the toxicity needs to be reduced by lowering the dosage or combatted by adding appropriate medication.

Disease can also carry a high toll socially, for the capacity of an individual to work and function as they did before illness can be adversely affected and lead to marked social withdrawal and isolation. Social withdrawal may also occur when the patient feels self-conscious because of body changes due to treatment or surgery, or because of feelings of stigma about a particular illness. Patients who experience such problems are usually reluctant to disclose them because they feel ashamed that they are not coping more effectively and are concerned that others will reject them or make fun of them. At least 1 in 4 patients who develop a severe physical illness are at risk of developing an anxiety state or depressive illness (Maguire *et al.*, 1974). Some patients are also at high risk of developing sexual problems. If such social and psychiatric problems remain unrecognised they hinder recovery and intensify the suffering both of the patients and their families.

A 44-year-old man had a severe myocardial infarction (heart attack) while out at dinner. He thought it was merely indigestion from which he was prone to suffer anyway, but he collapsed and became unconscious. The next he knew was when he woke up in a coronary care unit. When he was informed that he had had a major heart attack he was extremely upset. He could not accept it since he had always been an active sportsman and had kept himself fit to avoid such an occurrence.

He had not smoked and had been careful about his weight. He felt extremely bitter, therefore, that this had happened to him. He became so fearful of having a further heart attack that he limited his exercise as much as possible when he went home. He became a recluse and his wife had great difficulty getting him to do anything. He became increasingly depressed and got to the point where he thought that life was not worth living. Unfortunately, no one involved in his aftercare realised that he had become so depressed. They attributed his behaviour to worry about his illness and fear that he might precipitate another heart attack. If his wife had not realised how depressed he was and that he needed help he would not have had the psychiatric treatment that enabled him to recover fully from the depression and myocardial infarction.

Given the importance of these communication tasks a key question is whether current methods of training ensure that health professionals are able to execute them effectively. Experimental work has been carried out to assess the performance of medical students on these key tasks.

Medical Students' Skills

Maguire and Rutter (1976) surveyed a group of 50 medical students completing a clerkship in psychiatry. The students were within fifteen months of their final examinations and had completed clerkships in medicine, surgery, paediatrics, obstetrics and gynaecology. This group was selected because it was hypothesised that at that stage in their training they would have acquired the relevant communication skills.

Each student was given the task of trying to elicit a patient's presenting problems and concerns. They were given fifteen minutes to do this since it was considered important to determine how well they handled the time available. They were informed that they should try to end the interview within the allotted time and write up a history afterwards. In order to make this a reasonable test of communication skills patients were selected if they were recovering from a depressive illness or anxiety state, were willing to co-operate and talk with the students, and were able to give a coherent history about their problems and concerns within the fifteen minute time limit. Each of these interviews was recorded on videotape and then analysed to find out the extent to which students displayed key communication skills. This was done by means of a rating scale specifically developed for this purpose (Maguire *et al.*, 1978).

When the technique was discreet, such as the student explaining who they were, it was rated as present (1) or absent (0). When the technique was more complex, for example "control" (helping the patient keep to the point without alienating him) a 5 point scale (0–4) was used. A score of "0" meant that the student was very poor, allowing the patient to spend the whole interview talking of matters that were unrelated to the presenting problems. A score of "4" meant that the student was able to keep the patient to the point throughout the interview but did so in a way that was acceptable to the patient. The written histories were also analysed to determine the number of items of accurate and relevant information which they contained. Judgements of what was relevant were based on information from the patients' case notes and discussion with the doctors involved in their care.

This analysis revealed major deficiencies in the students' skills. A quarter of the students failed to establish their patients' main problems, and overall they obtained only a third of the data which was judged to be readily available to them in the time allowed for interview. Of particular note was the students' repeated failure to enquire about the impact of the psychiatric or concurrent physical illness on the patient's life. They avoided important areas like effects of illness on the patient's work, ability to cope with day to day chores, close relationships, marriage, and sexual adjustment. Nor did they usually ask what support, both practically and emotionally, patients felt they had received since they became ill. Students rarely found out what patients thought was wrong with them or checked if they had any serious misconceptions about their illness and treatment. Few students checked if the patients had any other concerns which were unrelated to their illness and treatment but might hinder recovery or cause problems in the future.

When their ability to begin the interview was assessed it was found that few students bothered to check whether their patients understood the circumstance of the interview or its purpose. The time available and need to take notes were rarely mentioned. Most of the students rushed into their interviews without settling their patients down and making sure they were at ease. The majority (80%) of students were rated as "poor" or "very poor" on their ability to cover personal topics like whether or not the patient had ever felt so depressed that they had wanted to commit suicide, and the effect of their illness on marriage and sexual adjustment. It was common (78%) for students to accept at face value words like "anxiety", "depression", or "confusion" and assume that this was what the patient had been suffering from. Thus, in one interview, a woman began by saying that she had been brought into hospital because she had been worrying terribly. The student took this to mean that she was suffering from an anxiety state and began to ask questions which would elicit symptoms of anxiety. He spent the whole of the fifteen minutes doing this. Had he explored what she meant by "worrying terribly" he would have found that she had been suffering from a severe agitated depression and that she had been close to killing herself by hanging. Few students were prepared to educate the patient to be precise in relation to the information they provided, and consequently they often obtained a mistaken impression of the relationship between the onset of illness and key provoking or precipitating events. Most patients tried to help the students by giving clear verbal or non-verbal leads about their problems. For example, they might look obviously upset or depressed at some stage in the interview, or mention directly that they had been feeling very low or anxious. Three-quarters of the students were rated as "poor" or "very poor" on their ability to pick up and respond to such leads. Even when they acknowledged these leads they were reluctant to establish what the patient meant and obtain a real idea of the patient's suffering. Overall, students talked more than was necessary, used leading questions relatively often (34%) that biased the patients' answers, or multiple questions (24%) where it was difficult for the patients to know which element they should answer. This analysis of senior medical students confirmed that they were seriously deficient in the communication tasks which are important for effective clinical practice. This accorded with previous work where students had been observed directly (Anderson *et al.*, 1970; Tapia, 1972).

It could of course be argued that students would acquire skills once they had qualified and begun to practise medicine. However, Weiner and Nathanson (1976) found that more experienced doctors showed exactly the same pattern of deficiencies as medical students. They over-questioned their patients and did not allow them to tell their own stories in their own way. When confronted with poorly defined complaints they made little attempt to clarify what patients meant and they were imprecise about establishing data about the onset, time course, relieving or precipitating factors of the presenting illness. They took notes excessively, made inadequate eye contact with their patients, and often repeated questions they had already asked. Nor did they answer patients' questions adequately. Similar problems were found by Korsch, Guzzi and Francis (1968) when they studied interactions between experienced paediatricians and mothers who visited them with a sick child in an out-patient setting. In 65% of cases the doctor failed to establish what the mother's expectations were about the visits, and only a quarter of mothers revealed why they were worried about their child's health. Direct observations of surgeons interacting with women suffering from breast disease (Maguire, 1976) confirmed that surgeons rarely elicited psychological and social problems. They seldom determined how worried patients were, or why they were anxious. They often used strategies of reassurance which bore little relationship to what the women were really concerned about. In view of this evidence it seemed reasonable to conclude that the students' current training was failing to equip them with essential communication skills and that more effective methods should be developed.

The Development of More Effective Training

There appeared to be three main reasons why the medical students' skills were deficient. Discussion revealed that none of them had been given more than just a list of the questions they should ask to elicit key signs and symptoms in relation to the main physical systems of the body. Similarly, in psychiatry they had been given a list of questions to cover the patient's biography and presenting illness. On no occasion had they been given explicit guidelines about the importance of finding out about other matters like the patients' response to being ill, their perception of what was wrong, and their present concerns. Nor had they received any guidance about the need to clarify the impact of illness on the patients' daily lives, occupational adjustment and personal relationships. The students, therefore, had not realised the importance of these areas. None of the students had been given any explicit guidance about actual interview techniques that would help them elicit both the history of the presenting complaints and this information. They had relied on observing their teachers in action in the context of ward rounds or out-patient clinics. They presumed that what they were witnessing was good and desirable practice and had tried to model themselves on this. Few students had ever had a chance to watch themselves in action or had anyone standing by while they interviewed a patient. Consequently they had no idea of how well or badly they interviewed patients and could not discuss their strengths and weaknesses in any systematic way. Most students tended to believe that interviewing skills were something that they were either innately good at already or would acquire through training. They had also come to the conclusion that they could not be that important since little curriculum time or discussion had been devoted to training in these skills during their pre-clinical or clinical experience. It seemed obvious from these discussions that if any training were to be more effective than the traditional approach it would have to remedy each of these deficiencies.

Training Procedures

A training procedure was therefore evolved which included the components of modelling, practice, and feedback.

Modelling. Each student was provided with detailed handouts which specified both the information to be obtained and the areas to be covered as well as the techniques that should be used. It also made clear how the interview was to be begun and ended (Maguire, 1984).

Practice under controlled conditions. The students were given a precise task as in the original analysis. They were asked to concentrate on eliciting the patient's current problems and to do so within a fifteen minute time limit. They were instructed that it would be up to them to end the interview within that time and they should take notes as they normally would during any interview. It was explained that the patients they would be asked to interview would be co-operative and capable of giving a clear history providing they were approached in the right way.

Feedback. Each interview was recorded on videotape so that it could be played back and discussed with the student by a tutor who was knowledgeable about the skills being taught and the information to be elicited. To facilitate such assessment and feedback a rating form was developed for use by both student and tutor. This included an assessment of the extent to which key areas of information were covered as well as the extent to which desirable techniques were used (Maguire *et al.*, 1978). Rutter and Maguire (1976) evaluated this individual feedback teaching with 24 medical students randomly allocated to either routine clinical training, or routine clinical training plus the experimental training procedure. Prior to training each student was asked to conduct an interview with a patient they had not seen before in order to determine the patient's presenting problems, and write up a detailed history. Following this baseline interview students in this experimental group met individually with a tutor who began by giving them the printed handouts which described the areas to be covered, the questions to be asked, and the techniques to be used. The interview was then replayed and the student's performance discussed in the light of the guidelines contained in the handouts. The control group students were sent away after their baseline interview without comment, but asked to return the following week for a second interview. A week later students in both the experimental and control groups were asked to interview a different patient than the one they had seen on the previous occasion. Assessment was made of the amount of accurate and relevant data that both groups of students had obtained: it was considered that if this did not reveal any major difference between the two groups then it would be difficult to justify the interview training. The experimental students reported a median of 35.5 (range 20–40) relevant and accurate items of information in their written histories compared with 13.5 (range 6–23) in the control group which represented a three-fold and highly significant difference.

In a second experiment the aim was to determine if the videotape feedback element of the training procedure was a crucial component of training (Rutter and Maguire, 1976). Fourteen pairs of medical students were randomly selected: each pair was asked to interview the same patient, but independently, to provide a measure of their performance before training. The order in which they did so was balanced so that the first and second position was equally represented between the experimental and control groups. After this interview students in the control group were given the detailed handouts and discussed their performance, but no actual replay of their performance using videotape was given. Those in the experimental group each received both the handouts and a videotaped replay of their performance followed by discussion with a tutor. A week later each pair of students interviewed another patient and again the order was balanced so that the first and second positions were equally represented. This provided a measure of their performance after training.

The students who had the full training reported a median of 25.5 (range 15–49) relevant and accurate items in their histories which they wrote up after their second interviews. This was significantly more than the median of 21.5 items (range 7–28) reported by the partially trained group who had not seen or discussed a videotape replay. However, overall the results suggested that most improvement could be obtained simply by providing students with handouts which detailed the information to be obtained and the techniques to be used, and then discussing their performance (when interviewing a patient under controlled conditions) by reference to a rating scale.

However, these experiments were not a proper test of video feedback in that they only measured the information obtained and did not assess the actual techniques used. Moreover, feedback was given on only one occasion. It was, therefore, likely that the provision of more feedback sessions together with an analysis of change in interviewing skills might reveal a definite benefit due to the use of videotape feedback over and above that accounted for by feedback by a tutor using detailed handouts.

Despite the initial success of this feedback training it was considered that it suffered from three weaknesses. The students were not provided with an actual demonstration of the key skills in action. There was the problem of finding a sufficient number of real patients who were prepared to be interviewed and willing to co-operate. There was also the amount of time required by the teachers. It was therefore decided to carry out the teaching in small groups, to use television to provide a demonstration of these skills in action, and to recruit and train simulated patients to facilitate practice.

The Use of Simulation

Simulation appeared particularly attractive because it would allow the teacher to standardise the clinical problems presented to the students, eliminate any risk that real patients might be upset or harmed by their experiences and enable simulators to comment on the students' performance (Barrows, 1968). In considering how best to present a model of the key interviewing skills it was unclear whether it would be better to present it in a didactic way as the best way to interview, or whether students should be allowed to work out a procedure for themselves first. Maguire, Clarke and Jolley (1977) carried out a study to clarify this by comparing three distinct training modes — didactic, discovery and traditional.

Didactic mode. Training took place weekly on three occasions. In the first seminar the students were given the detailed handouts which described the questions they should ask and the areas they should cover. They were then shown a television replay of an interview which had been conducted by the teacher and showed these questions being asked and the areas being covered. This was followed by a videotape of a senior medical student's interview in which there were important and common omissions. The students were invited to point out what the omissions were and discuss why they had occurred. In the second week each student was asked to interview a simulated patient for twelve minutes in order to obtain a history of the main problems. They knew that these videotapes were being recorded for assessment purposes but they were not informed that the patients were simulated. The third seminar concentrated on teaching the key interviewing skills. Students were presented with a second handout which described how to begin an interview, obtain accurate and relevant data and end within the agreed time limit. This was followed by a videotape in which the teacher interview used in the first seminar was reshown with the addition of introductory and termination sequences. The medical student tape was then shown again with the focus on comparing the student's performance with the teacher's in terms of the history-taking techniques used. It was made clear that the procedures illustrated should be followed if their interviews were to be effective.

Discovery mode. The first seminar began with a request to the students to suggest the kinds of questions that should be asked when attempting to obtain a history of the patient's presenting problems. Once they had formulated a sequence of questions the first medical student tape "what questions to ask" was shown and the group invited to compare this with their own model. The teacher tape followed and further discussion was actively encouraged. Only after this was the first handout presented and students asked to comment on it in the light of their own model. In the second week the students each interviewed a simulated patient under the same conditions as in the didactic mode. In the third week the same sequence was followed as in the initial seminar but using the "how to conduct an interview" version of the medical student and teacher tapes. Each of these tapes was stopped at three points: after the introduction; during the main body of the interview; and after the final sequence, in order to provoke discussion. The second handout was then distributed to allow the students to compare this with the model they had derived themselves. The model was offered as just one way of proceeding rather than "the best buy".

Traditional mode. Each student first interviewed a simulated patient to measure their skills before training. There were three weekly seminars which were conducted by a teacher of comparable seniority and experience to the one who taught the didactic and discovery groups. On each occasion he took a history from the patient in front of the group and then invited one or more students to interview the same or another patient. The students were encouraged to discuss how the interview was conducted and both the questions and techniques that had been used. Though the teacher had been briefed to teach exactly the same history-taking content and skills, he did not provide any detailed handouts or television demonstrations.

Thirty students who were beginning the introductory clinical course were randomly selected and allocated to a traditional or experimental course. After completing these courses each student was asked to take a history from a simulated patient to afford a measure of their skills after training. Ratings of videotapes of these interviews showed that the two experimental groups had obtained much more relevant information and acquired many more of the desired skills than students assigned to the traditional course. Importantly, the experimental students were also rated more favourably by the simulators on items such as their ability to empathise and put patients at ease, and had recorded more accurate and relevant data in their case histories. It was concluded that these short courses were much superior to the traditional seminar method usually adopted. There were no differences between the didactic and discovery modes of presenting the content and skills. Thus, short courses involving demonstration of interviewing skill, discussion and practice with simulators were effective, but the value of also providing feedback required to be determined.

The Role of Feedback

In a study by Maguire *et al*. (1978) 48 medical students were drawn at random in groups of four from those completing a clerkship in psychiatry. All the students in each quartet received training in history-taking from their clinical firms by the traditional apprenticeship method. This typically consisted of asking students to interview several patients and then discussing the histories that they had obtained in seminars, ward rounds, or outpatient clinics. Three of the students within each group were also assigned to one of three methods of feedback training: feedback by a tutor using television replay; audio feedback; or ratings of the student's practice interviews. The fourth student received no additional teaching and so acted as a control for the feedback programme.

Prior to feedback training, each of the three "feedback students" within the quartet was asked to interview the same patient. As in the other experiments, they were asked to establish the patient's main problems within fifteen minutes and informed that they were to end the interview within the allotted time and write up a history afterwards. They were told that their interviews would be videotaped to provide a baseline measure of their skills. The order in which the students interviewed these patients was so balanced that the first, second and third positions were equally represented among the three feedback groups.

Students assigned to the control group saw the same patients under identical conditions but a day later. It was considered that this would minimise the possibility that control students would feel antagonistic because they were not receiving feedback until after the experiment was over. The patients who participated were in-patients or day patients in a psychiatric unit who were suffering from an affective disorder, psychoneurosis, or alcoholism. They were selected by medical staff who were independent of the study but mindful that only co-operative patients should be chosen. Once these pre-training interviews had been completed students in the feedback programme received appropriate individual feedback from their tutor. Each feedback session lasted forty-five minutes. In the group which received feedback from a tutor unaided by either television or audiotape the tutor first watched the television replay of the interview without the student. He then rated it before next meeting with the student to reflect on the interview, discuss the ratings, and analyse overall performance. Each student conducted three practice interviews and was given feedback on each occasion. A post-training interview was conducted by each student to determine if any changes had occurred.

Performance was assessed both in terms of accurate and relevant information obtained by reference to the case histories and by using a rating scale to assess how the student began and ended the interview and the extent to which he used the desired techniques. There was little improvement in the skills or ability to elicit key information with those students who had only received training from their clinical firms. In marked contrast all three feedback groups improved in their ability to elicit accurate and relevant information, but only the television and audiotape feedback groups showed similar gains in their use of essential interviewing skills. Maguire *et al.* concluded that feedback of performance by audiotape replay or television was worthwhile, but audiotape alone was almost as good as television at the basic level of the skills being taught.

Teaching in Small Groups

A major limitation of feedback training is the amount of time required to teach each student. Within a large medical school where several hundred students are to be taught each year this could be a serious obstacle. Thus two further issues were considered: first, was a supervisor necessary or could students give themselves feedback?; second, would the feedback be as effective if given in small groups rather than individually?

A study by Roe (1978) provided some information on these questions. Sixty-four students completing a clerkship in psychiatry were randomly allocated in groups of four to one of four training conditions: practice of interviewing under controlled conditions followed by self-feedback through the use of videotape replay; self-feedback and peer review within a group of 4 students; individual feedback by a tutor using video replay; and discussion and videotape feedback by a tutor within a group of 4 students. Each student conducted three practice interviews and was given external feedback or self-feedback during the experiment. In the small group conditions each student had been given feedback on one of their own interviews and had an opportunity to discuss the others in relation to the interview of another student when that was replayed. Contrary to prediction, students who had received the feedback in small groups did as well as those who were given feedback individually. However, the presence of a supervisor appeared critical: those who had been given feedback by a tutor, whether individually or within a small group, became much more skilled than those who had been self-taught or helped by their peers. Students without a tutor showed an initial improvement but then failed to realise why they were not making any more progress. In contrast, those who had received feedback from a tutor indicated that they had maintained their motivation better, had enjoyed the teaching more than those who were self-taught individually or in small groups, and were better able to spot their strengths and weaknesses. Roe's findings are encouraging as they indicate that feedback teaching, as well as the presentation of the model, can be done in groups, making the training more feasible than it would be on an individual basis within a large medical school.

So far all the feedback training had been done by experienced teachers with a particular interest in this form of teaching. Thus there remained the important question of whether this teaching could be done by less experienced teachers.

Training of Teachers

A study was conducted by Fairbairn *et al.* (1983) to determine if personnel with less experience could be effective as trainers in interviewing skills. The people selected as teachers had different levels of experience of interviewing and teaching and came from different disciplines. The first and most experienced teacher was a psychiatrist who had helped develop the training procedure and teaching methods. The second, intermediate, teacher was a clinical and research psychologist who had evaluated the teaching of empathy to medical students (Sanson-Fisher and Poole, 1980). He had some years experience of clinical interviewing and was therefore considered intermediate in experience. The third teacher was a State Registered Nurse who had little direct training in these skills. She was therefore given some training before the study started. She was asked to "interview" a psychiatric patient in order to obtain a history of the presenting problems and then met with the tutor to watch and discuss a videotape replay. She was given handouts which described the data to be obtained and the skills to be used, and a rating scale to help her monitor her own progress. She conducted three more practice interviews at weekly intervals and received feedback on each occasion. Each feedback session lasted one hour.

Prior to the training of the students all three teachers met for two hours to discuss the teaching methods, handouts, rating scales and watch the modelling tapes which showed the key skills in action. Thirty-six medical students were then randomly allocated to one of these three teachers. Each teacher taught two groups of six medical students using videotape feedback and discussion of practice interviews. A psychologist who did not know which students had been assigned to which teacher independently rated pre- and post-training interviews. All three teachers proved effective in teaching interviewing skills, and Fairbairn *et al.* concluded that teachers could be taught to carry out this training regardless of their level of experience or professional discipline.

Generalising to Other Teachers

In order to determine if teachers could be successfully trained to teach key interviewing skills, Naji *et al.* (1986) conducted a study to see if doctors normally involved in the clinical teaching of medical students, namely Senior Registrars and Registrars, could be taught to carry out feedback. Additionally, whether it was essential to put the trainers through feedback training themselves, or whether they could simply be instructed in the technique. It was also uncertain whether or not they would benefit from supervision of their initial teaching sessions. Consequently, teachers were randomly allocated to four conditions: training in interviewing skills followed by supervision of initial teaching; such training without supervision; didactic instruction in teaching interviewing skills followed by supervision; and didactic instruction alone. Naji *et al.* found that those teachers who underwent the feedback training themselves were more effective in helping students acquire key interviewing skills than those who were just instructed how to do it, but supervision of teaching made little difference. It was also found that most teachers were able to carry out this teaching effectively within a busy hospital and teaching unit. Therefore, there seemed no reason why this training could not be given to all students within a large medical school.

Long-Term Effects

While studies of feedback training have produced encouraging results, they only demonstrated that the training helped medical students acquire essential interviewing skills in the short-term when interviewing psychiatric patients. Maguire, Fairbairn and Fletcher (1986) attempted to determine if this learning was maintained over time, and generalised to work with non-psychiatric patients. Thirty-six doctors were included in the study: half had received the feedback training as students, while the other half had acted as controls in the experimental studies.

A follow-up was conducted at a median of four years after feedback training when most of the former students were working as Senior House Officers or Registrars. They were each asked to interview three patients who suffered from a chronic disabling condition, a life-threatening condition, or a psychiatric illness.

Comparison of their interviews showed that those who had been trained were still significantly better than those who had not been given feedback training as undergraduates. This latter group were especially deficient in the skills required for adequate coverage of psychosocial aspects. The group given feedback training were just as effective when interviewing physically ill patients as psychiatrically ill patients. Thus, the effects of training had generalised to non-psychiatric patients. It therefore seems reasonable to conclude that feedback training given to medical students as undergraduates is both effective and maintained over time. Even so, some critical issues remain and require discussion.

Critical Issues

Is Training Still Needed?

It could be argued that since this work began in the early 1970s medical training has improved in such a way that the introduction of such feedback training is no longer necessary. This view is hard to sustain given the growing evidence that serious deficiencies in interviewing skills still remain. Thus, Byrne and Long (1976) in an audiotape study of consultations between general practitioners and their patients found that the doctors were inflexible in their interviewing style. They tended to interview in the same way regardless of the type of patient they were interviewing. They commonly missed important verbal and non-verbal leads and much preferred to concentrate on physical aspects of the case. They tended to ask leading questions and did not give patients sufficient opportunity to tell their stories in their own way. The same pattern of difficulties was found by Platt and McMath (1979) when they observed 300 clinical interviews conducted by hospital doctors. They were forced to conclude that physicians at all levels who had previously been thought quite competent appeared defective in their interactions with patients. Platt and McMath commented that their initial reaction was to distrust observations but repeated observations showed great consistency. In particular, they found that the doctors in their study began the interview poorly, and paid inadequate attention to how the patient felt before they began asking questions. They did not appear very understanding or supportive. They tended to avoid discussion of the patients' feelings about illness and its impact, and were poor at providing reassurance.

A similar study by Duffy, Hamerman, and Cohen (1980) of house officers found that in only 27% of instances was the patient asked what they had understood about their illness; and the impact of the illness on the patient's psychological adjustment was established in only a third of cases. The ability of these doctors to interview these patients effectively bore no relationship to the length of time they had been qualified. This study also explored the reasons for these difficulties. The doctors indicated that they much preferred to deal with medical rather than psychological and social aspects of disease and there was too little time to deal with psychological aspects. If they did explore such matters this would distress patients, and there was little point since nothing could be done about psychological problems. So it is not surprising that psychological problems are more likely to be missed by doctors, especially when the patient is also suffering from a physical illness. For example, in a follow-up study of patients undergoing mastectomy the psychiatric morbidity which developed in a substantial proportion of women was recognised — by surgeons, nurses, social workers and general practitioners involved in their care — in only 20% of cases (Maguire *et al.*, 1980). Even when physicians were asked to say whether patients who were well known to them had psychological problems, the morbidity still remained undetected in a third of patients (Brody, 1980). While general practitioners often argue that they are least likely to miss problems because they know their patients well, Marks, Goldberg and Hillier (1979) found that their ability to recognise psychological problems varied from 20% to 80%, with an average of 50% of psychiatric problems remaining undisclosed and undetected. More recent studies on medical wards have shown a similar hidden morbidity (Bridges and Goldberg, 1984). Thus, deficiencies in interviewing skills remain and result in poor interviewing and a failure to recognise social and psychiatric morbidity. This suggests that their medical training did not equip doctors adequately with key interviewing skills and this has been confirmed by longitudinal studies.

Wright *et al.* (1980) examined the changes which occurred in medical students during their clinical training. They found that the students continued to rely too much on direct questions and while there was some improvement in their overall interview structure they still failed to clarify patients' complaints adequately. They rarely summarised or recapped the information they had obtained, and there was little change in their level of interest in the patient as a person. They still made little attempt to introduce themselves or enquire about the impact of illness. A third of their group had been less empathic, and bad habits evident in the first clinical year had persisted throughout. This accords with the claim made by Helfer (1970) that medical training may lead to a worsening of medical students' interpersonal skills and ability to interview effectively. Such a "dehumanisation process" has been observed directly by Alroy, Ber and Kramer (1984). It therefore seems reasonable to conclude that a strong case for feedback training in interviewing skills can still be made, indeed it could be argued that it is even stronger than when the original work began.

Validity

A key question is whether the interviewing skills being taught are valid. In all the studies where the experimental group was compared with the control group and the key variable was feedback training, those given feedback were more able to elicit accurate and relevant information. There were two key elements in their training: the handouts described the *areas* they should cover, and the *techniques* they should use. It has not yet been established what exact contribution each of these components makes to the improvement in eliciting key information. However, some progress has been made in determining which skills correlate with the accuracy of diagnosis. Goldberg *et al*. (1980) found that the ability of general practitioners to detect psychiatric morbidity was strongly correlated to their establishing good eye contact at the outset of the interview, detecting and clarifying verbal and non-verbal clues, using open questions, asking appropriate questions to elicit key symptoms and keeping patients to the point while allowing them to tell their stories as far as possible in their own words. It has also been found that both specialist (Maguire *et al*., 1980) and ward nurses (Faulkner and Maguire, 1984) detect at least 80% of the psychological and social problems which present in patients with breast cancer when they have been given feedback training and use a standard assessment form.

While doctors and nurses can acquire essential interviewing skills through feedback training, and maintain them over time this is no guarantee that they actually use these techniques in their daily work. The study of ward nurses (Faulkner and Maguire, 1984) is therefore important, as is the work with specialist nurses (Maguire *et al*., 1980), since both found that the nurses continued to use their skills in their daily work, and recognised the majority of their patients with problems even though they were no longer subject to formal assessment. It was encouraging that they integrated the key questions and skills within their daily practice and found that it was possible to do so within the context of a busy clinical load.

While the model being taught is valid in terms of the greater recognition of problems, it is also important to see if it is valid from the patients' viewpoint. Thompson and Anderson (1982) sought to determine this in the context of interviews by medical students with surgical patients. Patients were asked to rate the students on several dimensions and put them into a rank order. They preferred those students who avoided repetition, picked up verbal leads, helped them tell their story in their own way but kept them to the point, and were precise, self-assured and competent. Perceiving the students as "warm" was related to ability to ask open questions, enquire about the personal impact of the illness, and how their mood had been affected. Students were perceived as "sympathetic" if they asked open-ended rather than closed questions and covered the impact on the patients' lives. The students seen as "most easy to talk to" were those who bothered to greet the patient, introduce themselves, ask simple questions and focus on the patient's key complaints early in the interview. These are all major features of the model that has been taught to medical students.

Problems in Measurement

Although the interviewing scale presented by Maguire *et al.* (1978) has proved valid in its ability to discriminate between interviewers who can put patients at ease and elicit key information from those who are poor at these tasks, it has not been validated in its own right by comparing it with an interaction analysis of the same interview. However, it is much simpler to use than an interaction analysis like that developed by Scott *et al.* (1973) although such interaction analyses can be simplified by scoring only a limited number of behaviours (Morrison and Cameron-Jones, 1972). This latter approach can produce profiles which indicate to each doctor how much he or she is using desirable and undesirable behaviours and facilitate feedback (Bain, 1976). A detailed comparison of these differing approaches to measurement is needed in order to determine their proper validity and usefulness within the context of teaching health professionals on a regular basis.

General Effectiveness

The case for feedback training would be strong if it could be shown to be effective within different clinical settings. Robbins *et al.* (1979) found that a training course which included a considerable amount of feedback helped doctors training in internal medicine to improve their interviewing skills significantly. Verby, Holden and Davis (1979) found that trainees in general practice improved their skills with feedback training. Similarly, Janek, Burra and Leichner (1979) found that first year residents in psychiatry benefited from feedback training. In the short-term, while feedback training is effective in different medical settings and with nurses there has been little systematic study of the longer-term effects apart from the study already cited (Maguire *et al.*, 1986). Poole and Sanson-Fisher (1981) concentrated on one particular skill — that of being empathic with patients. They found that while there had been some decay since initial training, those who had been trained showed significantly greater levels of empathy than control students when followed up three years later. Kauss *et al.* (1980) checked retrospectively the training which interns and residents had received while they were medical students. They then assessed their performance when they elicited a history from a patient. They found no evidence to suggest that the skills had been maintained, and there was no relationship between the present level of interviewing skills and the amount of training in interpersonal skills they had been given as medical students. Further studies of the longer-term effects and generalisation of feedback training of interviewing skills are clearly required.

Teaching Methods

While feedback training appears effective in the shorter- and longer-term it might be more so if other components were added. Kagan has advocated the use of Interpersonal Process Recall (Kagan, *et al.*, 1969) where a third person reviews an interview with both the interviewer and patient to raise points that might otherwise have been missed in a straight teacher-student feedback session. Such "interrogators" require training and are encouraged to note abrupt changes in theme, changes in body posture, changes in voice level and cues to strong feelings. Another way of enhancing feedback is to use simulators who can both portray patients effectively and give students and doctors feedback (Barrows, 1968; Carroll, Schwartz and Ludwig, 1981; Hannay, 1980; Helfer, Black and Helfer, 1975; Meadow and Hewitt, 1972; Stillman, Sabers and Redfield, 1977). Training through practice with simulators is effective provided the simulators have been properly trained (Meier, Perkowski and Wynne, 1982). Sanson-Fisher and Poole (1980) found that students learned as well on simulated as real patients when they were focusing on empathy. However, more detailed comparisons of the benefits and disadvantages of practice with simulators versus real patients have still to be made.

Actors who are used to getting in and out of a role might be best able to give students feedback about their performance but they are not necessarily an economic resource (Whitehouse, Morris and Marks, 1984). While simulation is valuable in facilitating practice of interviewing skills, it is not clear whether those who help in this way can be affected adversely. Naftulin and Andrew (1975) have claimed that volunteers are suitable provided they are properly screened in terms of having had sufficient acting experience but have not suffered serious emotional problems. However, it is possible that harm could result if simulators take on roles which mimic serious physical and mental illness, and further work is needed to clarify this.

Feedback might also be facilitated by recording a running commentary during the interview which can be listened to later (Kirby, 1983). Alternatively, the commentary could be given at the time using the "bug in the ear" technique advocated by Hunt (1980). There is also the possibility that real patients may be able to give the most useful feedback about a student's performance (Kent, Clarke and Dalrymple-Smith, 1981).

Micro-Teaching

In most of the work carried out in this field, students have been presented with packages detailing the areas to be covered and the skills to be used. It is possible that teaching one skill at a time would be more effective as Moreland, Ivey and Phillips (1973) have advocated. However, comparative studies are necessary to see if such claims are justified.

Teachers

It has been established that doctors, social scientists and nurses who have a reasonable grasp of the skills to be taught can be effective as teachers. But they are likely to be more effective when given clear guidelines (Naji et al., 1986; Pendleton, 1981; Tanner and Silverman, 1981). There is also the possibility that more experienced medical students and nurses might be able to teach basic history-taking skills to junior students (Barnes et al., 1983).

Concluding Remarks

The work discussed in this chapter has mainly concerned training in basic interviewing skills which students and nurses require if they are to elicit accurate histories from patients and put them at ease. However, this is only one aspect of interactions between health professionals and patients. A similar social skills model ought to be as effective if students were taught how to give information, how to reassure patients, and how to deal with difficult situations like talking with the dying and the bereaved. Future research and practice will hopefully build on the results achieved so far to enhance further the communication between health professionals and their clients.

References

Alroy, G., Ber, R. and Kramer, D. A. (1984) An evaluation of the short-term effects of an interpersonal skills course. *Medical Education*, **18**, 85–89.

Anderson, J., Day, J. L., Dowling, M. A. C. and Pettingale, K. W. (1970) The definition and evaluation of the skills required to obtain a patient's history of illness. *Postgraduate Medical Journal*, **46**, 606–612.

Bain, D. J. G. (1976) Doctor patient communication in general practice consultation. *Medical Education*, **10**, 125–131.

Barnes, H. V., Albanese, M., Schroeder, J. and Reiter, S. (1983) Senior medical students teaching the basic skills of history and physical examination. *Journal of Medical Education*, **53**, 432–434.

Barrows, H. S. (1968) Simulated patients in medical teaching. *Canadian Medical Association Journal*, **98**, 674–678.

Bridges, K. W. and Goldberg, D. P. (1984) Psychiatric illness in patients with neurological disorders: Patients' views on discussion of emotional problems with neurologists. *British Medical Journal*, **289**, 656–658.

Brody, D. S. (1980) Physician recognition of behavioural, psychological and social aspects of medical care. *Archives of Internal Medicine*, **140**, 1286–1289.

Byrne, P. S. and Long, B. F. L. (1976) *Doctors talking to patients*. London: Her Majesty's Stationery Office.

Carroll, J. G., Schwartz, M. W. and Ludwig, S. (1981) An evaluation of simulated patients as instructors: Implications for teaching medical interview skills. *Journal of Medical Education*, **56**, 522–524.

Duffy, D. L., Hamerman, L. and Cohen, A. (1980) Communication skills of house officers: A study in a medical clinic. *Annals of Internal Medicine*, **93**, 354–357.

Fairbairn, S., Maguire, P., Chambers, H. and Sanson-Fisher, R. (1983) The teaching of interviewing skills: Comparison of experienced and novice trainers. *Medical Education*, **17**, 296–299.

Faulkner, A. and Maguire, P. (1984) Teaching ward nurses to monitor cancer patients. *Clinical Oncology*, **10**, 383–389.

Goldberg, D. P., Steele, J. J., Smith, C. and Spivey, L. (1980) Training family doctors to recognise psychiatric illness with increased accuracy. *Lancet*, **2** (8193), 521–523.

Hannay, D. (1980) Teaching interviewing with simulated patients. *Medical Education*, **14**, 246–248.

Helfer, R. E. (1970) An objective comparison of the paediatric interviewing skills of freshmen and senior medical students. *Paediatrics*, **45**, 623–627.

Helfer, R. E., Black, M. A. and Helfer, M. E. (1975) Paediatric interviewing skills taught by non-physician. *American Journal of Diseases in Children*, **129**, 1053–1057.

Hunt, D. D. (1980) 'Bug in the ear' technique for teaching interview skills. *Journal of Medical Education*, **55**, 964–966.

Janek, W., Burra, P. and Leichner, P. (1979) Teaching interviewing skills by encountering patients. *Journal of Medical Education*, **54**, 402–407.

Kagan, N., Schauble, P., Regnikoff, A., Danish, S. J. and Krathwohl, D. R. (1969) Interpersonal process recall. *Journal of Nervous and Mental Disease*, **148**, 365–374.

Kauss, D. R., Robbins, A. S., Abrass, I., Bakaitis, R. F. and Anderson, L. A. (1980) The long term effectiveness of interpersonal skills training in medical school. *Journal of Medical Education*, **55**, 595–601.

Kent, G. G., Clarke, P. and Dalrymple- Smith, D. (1981) The patient is the expert: A technique for teaching interviewing skills. *Medical Education*, **15**, 38–42.

Kirby, R. L. (1983) Running commentary: Recorded simultaneously to enhance video-tape as an aid to learning interviewing skills. *Medical Education*, **17**, 28–30.

Korsch, B. M., Guzzi, E. D. and Francis, V. (1968) Gaps in doctor-patient communication. *Paediatrics*, **12**, 855–871.

Maguire, G. P., Clarke, D. and Jolley, B. (1977) An experimental comparison of three courses in history taking skills for medical students. *Medical Education*, **11**, 175–181.

Maguire, G. P., Julier, D. L., Hawton, K. E. and Bancroft, J. H. J. (1974) Psychiatric morbidity and referral on two general medical wards. *British Medical Journal*, **1**, 268–270.

Maguire, G. P. and Rutter, D. R. (1976) History taking for medical students. I — Deficiencies in performance. *Lancet*, **2** (7895), 556–558.

Maguire, P. (1976) Psychological and social sequelae of mastectomy. In J. Howells (Ed.), *Modern perspectives in psychiatric aspects of surgery*. New York: Brunner/Mazel.

Maguire, P. (1984) How we teach interviewing skills. *Medical Teacher*, **6**, 128–133.

Maguire, P., Fairbairn, S. and Fletcher, C. (1986) Consultation skills of young doctors: I — Benefits of feedback in interviewing as students persist. *British Medical Journal*, **292**, 1573–1576.

Maguire, P., Roe, P., Goldberg, D., Jones, S., Hyde, C. and O'Dowd, T. (1978) The value of feedback in teaching interviewing skills to medical students. *Psychological Medicine*, **8**, 695–704.

Maguire, P., Tait, A., Brooke, M., Thomas, C. and Sellwood, R. (1980) Effect of counselling on the psychiatric morbidity associated with mastectomy. *British Medical Journal*, **281**, 1454–1456.

Marks, J. N., Goldberg, D. P. and Hillier, V. F. (1979) Determinants of the ability of general practitioners to detect psychiatric illness. *Psychiatric Medicine*, **9**, 337–353.

Meadow, R. and Hewitt, C. (1972) Teaching communication skills with the help of actresses and videotape simulation. *British Journal of Medical Education*, **6**, 317–322.

Meier, R. S., Perkowski, L. C. and Wynne, C. S. (1982) A method for training simulated patients. *Journal of Medical Education*, **57**, 535–540.

Moreland, J. R., Ivey, A. E. and Phillips, J. S. (1973) An evaluation of microcounseling as an interviewer training tool. *Journal of Counseling and Clinical Psychology*, **2**, 294–300.

Morrison, A. and Cameron-Jones, M. (1972) A procedure for training for general practice. *British Journal of Medical Education*, **6**, 125–132.

Naftulin, D. H. and Andrew, B. J. (1975) The effects of patient simulations on actors. *Journal of Medical Education*, **50**, 87–89.

Naji, S. A., Fairbairn, S. A., Maguire, P., Goldberg, D. P. and Faragher, E. B. (1986) Training clinical teachers in psychiatry to teach interviewing skills to medical students. *Medical Education*, **20**, 140–147.

Pendleton, D. (1981, May 15) Learning communication skills. *Medical Update*, pp. 1708–1714.

Platt, F. W. and McMath, J. C. (1979) Clinical hypocompetence: The interview. *Annals of Internal Medicine*, **91**, 898–902.

Poole, D. A. and Sanson-Fisher, R. W. (1981) Long term effects of empathy training on the interview skills of medical students. *Journal of Patient Counselling and Health Education*, **2**, 125–129.

Robbins, A. S., Kauss, D. R., Heinrich, R., Abrass, I., Dreyer, J. and Clyman, B. (1979) Interpersonal skills training: Evaluation in an internal medical residency. *Journal of Medical Education*, **54**, 885–891.

Roe, P. (1978) *A comparison of methods for training medical students in interviewing skills.* Unpublished MSc thesis, Manchester University, Manchester.

Rutter, D. R. and Maguire, G. P. (1976) History taking for medical students: Evaluation of a training procedure. *Lancet*, **2** (7895), 558–560.

Sanson-Fisher, R. and Poole, A. D. (1980) Simulated patients and the assessment of medical students' interpersonal skills. *Medical Education*, **14**, 249–253.

Scott, N. C., Donnelly, M. B., Gallagher, R. and Hess, J. W. (1973) Interaction analysis as a method for assessing skill in relating to patients: Studies on validity. *British Journal of Medical Education*, **7**, 174–178.

Stillman, P. L., Sabers, D. L. and Redfield, D. L. (1977) Use of trained mothers to teach interviewing skills to 1st year medical students — A follow up study. *Paediatrics*, **66**, 165–169.

Tanner, L. A. and Silverman, G. (1981) A teachers guide to teaching medical interviewing. *Medical Education*, **15**, 100–105.

Tapia, F. (1972) Teaching medical interviewing: A practical technique. *Journal of Medical Education*, **6**, 133–136.

Thompson, J. A. and Anderson, J. L. (1982) Patient preference and the bedside manner. *Medical Education*, **16**, 17–21.

Verby, J. E., Holden, P. and Davis, R. H. (1979) Peer review of consultations in primary care: The use of audiovisual recordings. *British Medical Journal*, **1**, 1686–1688.

Weiner, S. and Nathanson, M. (1976) Physical examination: Frequently observed errors. *Journal of the American Medical Association*, **236**, 852–855.

Whitehouse, C., Morris, P. and Marks, B. M. (1984) The role of actors in teaching communication. *Medical Education*, **18**, 262–268.

Wright, A. D., Green, I. D., Fleetwood-Walker, P. M., Bishop, J. M., Wishart, E. H. and Swire, H. (1980) Patterns of acquisition of interview skills by medical students, *Lancet*, **2** (8193), 964–966.

7

Innovative Clinical Applications of Social Skills Training

CLIVE R. HOLLIN

As will be clear from the range of applications of SST in this Handbook, the technique has a wide range of usage. Whilst the predominant client groups cover the age span from children to the elderly, including the major clinical disorders and "social problems", the literature is sprinkled with innovative applications of SST. Practitioners or researchers in a number of diverse fields have seen the potential of SST for their own specialist client group and have adapted the training to suit the characteristics of their clients. This, in turn, has led to a variety of methodologies. In some cases, as with spinal cord injury patients, highly sophisticated assessment methods have been devised. Some studies have used refined experimental methodology, others less so. The content of training varies from micro-behaviour skills, to complex aggregations of behaviour, to new uses of the term "social skills" as in one study with anorexic patients. In one case, facial disfigurement, research is only just being reported which suggests the potential for SST.

From literature searches and personal contact the studies below have come to attention: it is not claimed that this list is exhaustive. There may be further applications which even the most diligent search has missed — particularly if papers remain unpublished or are given at conferences and do not find their way into the abstracts. Nevertheless, the studies discussed below stand as testimony to the flexibility of SST and the ingenuity of its practitioners.

Transsexualism and SST

DSM-III, the Diagnostic System of the American Psychiatric Association, identifies transsexualism as a Gender Identity Disorder. The transsexual is an individual who maintains, in the absence of specific stresses or other severe disorders, that their sexual identity is at variance with their biological sex. In other words, they are a man in a woman's body or vice versa. Such gender confusion is frequently associated with anxiety

167

and depression and, as Yardley (1976) notes, treatment traditionally takes one of two forms. Surgery can be used to change the body to that of the preferred sex; or alternatively some therapeutic intervention such as psychotherapy (Green and Money, 1969) can be attempted to assist the individual in accepting their biological sex.

The first attempts at behavioural treatment used aversion therapy methods to try to bring the transsexual to accept their biological sex (Gelder and Marks, 1969; Marks, Gelder and Bancroft, 1970). This treatment approach was not successful in as much as the transsexuals maintained their requests for sex change surgery. Barlow, Reynolds and Agras (1973) also used aversion therapy techniques in the treatment of a 17-year-old male transsexual: however, the innovation they brought to this field was the "modification of gender-specific motor behaviour". Observation of the client showed that he displayed many feminine behaviours which attracted ridicule from his peers, adding to his discomfort and dissatisfaction with life. Barlow, Reynolds and Agras devised a training programme to replace the feminine behaviour with masculine behaviour.

This training took the form of micro-skills teaching, as Barlow, Reynolds and Agras note: "In each session the constellation of appropriate behaviour was broken down and taught piece by piece" (p. 571). The appropriate behaviour was modelled by a male therapist, practised by the client, and then followed with feedback of errors both verbally and by videotape, with praise for successful behaviour also given. Clearly, the major components of SST are being used in this training programme. Evaluation showed that, following baseline assessment, the behaviours of standing, sitting, and walking had all become significantly more masculine. This change was accompanied by the client's self-report that he felt more at ease socially, and was no longer the object of curiosity or ridicule. However, at this stage, his patterns of sexual arousal and fantasy, and his attitudes towards transsexualism remained unchanged.

Barlow, Reynolds and Agras then extended the training to include other micro-skills such as eye contact and voice pitch; and added more complex activities such as conversational skills. This next step was successful in training yet more masculine behaviour, to the client's reported satisfaction — however, he still maintained that "he felt like a girl". Further behavioural treatment using positive rather than negative reinforcement was then conducted and male sexual patterns of arousal and fantasy began to replace those previously found. A 1-year follow-up revealed that the masculine behaviour had been maintained; the client expressed no interest in transsexualism; and had entered a heterosexual relationship.

A long-term follow-up was reported by Barlow, Abel, and Blanchard (1979), over 6 years after completion of treatment. The client's self-reported interest in transsexualism was still extinguished, and he maintained masculine patterns of sexual arousal and fantasy. The trained masculine skills were also maintained, and he reported living a normal male life. Barlow, Abel and Blanchard (1979) also report two further cases of transsexualism, both treated using a combination of skills training and other behavioural techniques. One case was successful in that following the treatment programme the client, a male, adjusted to a satisfactory homosexual relationship. The final case, again a male, was less successful in that whilst masculine skills were satisfactorily trained, the client maintained his interest in transsexualism.

Whilst the work of Barlow and his colleagues was aimed at avoiding transsexualism, Yardley (1976) adopted a quite different approach. Many transsexuals do have surgery to change their biological sex, but they experience difficulty in adjusting both psychologically and socially to their new gender. Yardley's approach was to prepare the transsexual for the change of sex by training the appropriate opposite sex behaviour *before* surgery. Yardley reports a case study in training feminine skills in a male transsexual receiving oestrogen therapy in preparation for complete sex change surgery.

The training techniques were the standard SST methods of instruction, modelling, and feedback, aimed both at microbehaviours such as eye contact, and complex behaviours such as courtship. The skills training was successful in shaping up feminine behaviour as measured by "femininity" and "appropriateness" ratings by independent judges. Genital surgery took place nine months after completion of the skills training, and at almost 1-year follow-up the client expressed satisfaction at the change in sex.

One suggested generalisation of the feminine skills training was that as the level of feminine competence improved, psychometric tests indicated a concomitant improvement in psychological well-being and a stabilising of feminine identity. These changes, in addition to the effects of SST, are thought to have significantly contributed towards successful adjustment following surgery.

In reading these case studies the complexity of the problems facing transsexuals becomes very clear: the decision whether or not to undergo medical surgery; attendant anxiety and depression, at times compounded by drug or alcohol abuse; lack of satisfactory social contact; social curiosity and ridicule; avoidance of talking about oneself with parents and friends; the lack of satisfactory sexual relationships. Given that this state of affairs may have existed for a decade or more the severity of the issue is enormous. The clear emphasis in the Barlow *et al.* studies is the need for several complimentary treatment approaches; whilst in the Yardley study this same need is evident but the weight is more towards a multi-disciplinary approach, with physicians, psychiatrists, and psychologists working in unison. SST in both cases becomes a component in a complex treatment programme, rather than being the specific focus of the entire therapeutic endeavour. Parenthetically, it is also of interest that the specific behavioural changes took place prior to the (satisfactory) cognitive changes. This is particularly noticeable in the Barlow, Reynolds and Agras (1973) study when, after skills training, the previously unsuccessful modification of sexual fantasy and arousal was able to be completed. The morals and politics of the very different uses of SST by Barlow and his co-workers and Yardley opens up a field of debate beyond the scope of this present chapter.

Anorexia Nervosa and SST

The clinical condition of anorexia nervosa is defined by DSM-III as an eating disorder characterised by an intense fear of obesity, disturbance of body image, weight loss of at least 25% of original body weight, and refusal to maintain body weight at a normal level. Anorexia nervosa should be distinguished from bulimia which DSM-III defines as consisting of recurrent binge eating, self-induced vomiting and purging, strict dieting or fasting, and depressed mood (see Schlesier-Stropp, 1984). The aetiology of anorexia nervosa is poorly understood, but most authorities suggest that there are a wide range of causative factors (see Garfinkel and Garner, 1982). Correspondingly, a variety of treatment approaches have been attempted, ranging from pharmacological intervention (e.g. Johanson and Knorr, 1977) to family therapy (e.g. Rosman, Minuchin and Liebman, 1975).

The suggestion that SST might have a role to play in the treatment of anorexia nervosa was first made by Argyle, Trower and Bryant (1974). They summarised the effectiveness of SST — incorporating role-play, modelling and instruction — on a number of patients with a variety of neuroses and personality disorders. One female patient was described as having "anorexia nervosa with depressive features in an immature personality" (p. 65). Unfortunately Argyle *et al.* present very few clinical details of this particular case, only noting that at the completion of training she was judged by her psychiatrist to have improved considerably; and that she thought the SST had been useful and helpful.

Pillay and Crisp (1981) report the only study which has experimentally evaluated the effects of SST with anorexics. The aim of this investigation was to incorporate SST into an established in-patient treatment pro-gramme: the hypothesis being that its inclusion would lead to a greater recovery in terms of increased body weight and decreased social anxiety.

The SST consisted of two phases: the first, whilst the patient was on bed rest, was four weekly sessions of a "word association task" with the aim of encouraging spontaneity and reducing limited verbal responses. This is a highly unusual addition to a SST programme and requires validation as to its usefulness and applicability in training. The second phase, again of four weekly sessions, centred around a "role-playing modelling format" of four social situations — all concerned with initiating conversation — for all the trainees. Ten anorexic patients formed the SST group, and 12 similar individuals were given "non-specific counselling" as a placebo control. The measures taken were of weight and also of social anxiety using psychometric tests.

Pillay and Crisp adopted a data management strategy of *within* group analysis, allowing the changes for each group to be clearly seen, but not directly comparing the difference in change *between* groups. Thus whilst significant changes do occur within both groups on some of the psychometric scales, it is unclear whether the changes are significantly greater in any one group. Body weight increased in mean value for both groups and was maintained at a 1-year follow-up. No statistical analysis of the weight data is recorded but the conclusion is made that SST "does not have an effect on the outcome of anorexia nervosa in terms of body weight" (p. 538).

There are a number of points to be made about the design of this study. The first is that no convincing case had been made for the appropriateness of SST for the anorexic patients. Whilst it is suggested that anorexics are "known to be socially isolated and to have low self-esteem (Crisp, 1970; Pillay and Crisp, 1977)" (p. 533), this was not established for the individuals participating in this study. Secondly, the format of the SST was unusual and limited in scope: no account was made of individual differences in skills ability, or whether some social skill other than "joining in" would be appropriate. Finally, the use of weight as an assessment is a measure of response generalisation; without first establishing a functional relationship between the measure, weight in this instance, and the skills trained, this is of limited value (see the arguments relating to recidivism in Chapter 4 of Volume 1).

Pillay and Crisp conclude that SST may deserve further attention in the treatment of anorexia nervosa, and the findings of Argyle *et al.* would lend support to this contention. Certainly the topic merits further empirical investigation as the studies which exist give only very limited information.

Blindness and SST

Blind children and adolescents face very special problems in the development of their social behaviour. Without the ability to perceive visual details the fund of social activity which provides models for development cannot be utilised; additionally, visual feedback on one's own behaviour cannot be received. Several studies have pointed to the social difficulties of blind children, noting social isolation (Eaglestein, 1975) and delayed social and cognitive development (Warren, 1976) as particular problems. These handicaps can manifest themselves in the failure to learn to attend to social cues (Netlick, 1977), or the development of stereotyped body movements such as rocking (Curtis, Donlong and Tweedie, 1975).

The first published account of SST with a blind child was a single case study reported by Farkas *et al.* (1981). The subject was a 12-year-old blind girl who had been born with congenital bilateral anophthalmia. Her behavioural problems included "excessive body rocking and hand flapping, speaking with distorted intonation, loose associations and talking to inanimate objects" (p. 24). She was seen as severely mentally disturbed by the staff of the institution in which she was a resident.

A SST programme was devised to focus on three particular behaviours — inappropriate addressing, inappropriate motor behaviour, and rocking — and a series of baseline assessments were made. The training was carried out by a trained staff nurse and consisted of a series of standard role-plays and structured conversations relevant to the institutional setting. Verbal feedback was given immediately upon completion of a training sequence. In addition, a system of tactile feedback was used such that after correct behaviour a token, marked in braille to represent that behaviour, was awarded. The tokens could be exchanged for back-up reinforcers later in the same day. Each training session took the form of an initial fifteen minute period in which the role-play, feedback, and reinforcement was completed, followed by a five minute interval, then ten minutes further training. The programme lasted eight weeks and 24 sessions were conducted.

Behavioural measurement was carried out by trained independent observers: there was high inter-observer agreement. Graphical presentation of the data shows significant improvements over training compared with baseline levels. A follow-up over the month after completion of training showed the treatment gains were maintained. Farkas *et al.* noted that members of staff not involved in the training commented on the trainee's "dramatic" change. An interview with her and her parents and teacher after her discharge from the institution indicated that the effects of training had generalised to the natural environment.

A further investigation of SST with blind adolescents was reported by Van Hasselt *et al.* (1983), with the specific aim of training assertive behaviour. Van Hasselt *et al.* note that a previous study by Everhart, Luzader and Tullos (1980) had attempted assertion training with blind people, but had failed to monitor the effects of training in a systematic manner. Using single-case study methodology, as employed by Farkas *et al.* and suggested by Van Hasselt and Hersen (1981), Van Hasselt *et al.*

sought to provide detailed experimental information on the effects of SST to increase assertive behaviour in the blind.

Four totally blind females, aged between 14 and 20 years, took part in the training, which was conducted on an individual basis at a residential summer school for the blind. A baseline assessment utilised a role-play test specifically designed for blind adolescents (Van Hasselt *et al.*, 1981): during this phase each trainee took part in a repeated series of nine role-plays involving assertive behaviour. From the assessment ratings three response components, such as eye gaze or voice tone, were selected for training.

The training phase lasted from three to four weeks, with 5 fifteen to thirty minute sessions per week. In keeping with traditional multiple-baseline methodology, training followed a cumulative pattern: for example, training in gaze was followed by training in posture; followed in turn by training in voice tone with maintained emphasis on gaze and posture. The training was centred on six of the nine role-plays used in assessment, and employed the standard techniques of role-play, verbal feedback and instruction, and rehearsal. On completion of training, evaluation was made of performance on all nine of the original role-plays used in assessment. The three role-plays not used in training therefore provided a test of generalisation.

Graphical representation of the results, as also used by Farkas *et al.*, showed substantial improvement in ratings of the trained behaviours for all trainees. A four week follow-up revealed a slight loss of proficiency in some response components and so four "booster" sessions were added. These extra sessions returned performance to immediate post-training levels, and further follow-ups at eight and ten weeks showed this level was maintained. An identical analysis of performance in the three role-plays not used in training showed very similar patterns of change as for those found in training. This clearly indicates that generalisation of the trained skills across situations had taken place. However, whilst the SST was effective over the period spanned by the study, Van Hasselt *et al.* (1983) did not collect follow-up information in the natural environment. It is unknown, therefore, whether the trainees continued to be more assertive on leaving the residential school.

Several points arise from the two studies reviewed above: the first is that both used female trainees and so it is uncertain whether similar effects would be found with blind males. Secondly, both studies relied on visual inspection of the data to determine significance of change, and whilst this is acceptable within single-case methodology (Hersen and Barlow, 1976) statistical analysis such as time series analysis (Tryon, 1982) would have added additional weight to the findings. Finally, both studies could have used longer follow-up periods to test for generalisation to the natural environment. Nevertheless, the studies illustrate how clear assessment and evaluation can validate the utility of SST.

Diabetes and SST

Insulin dependent diabetes is a serious medical condition, with the additional susceptibility to blindness, strokes, and other physical disorders compounding its severity. However, alongside the medical aspect there is evidence that diabetics experience a number of psychological and social difficulties such as anxiety, depression, and family problems (e.g. Delbridge, 1975; Tavormina *et al.*, 1976). The strict medical regime forced by the diabetic condition — blood glucose monitoring, diet restrictions, insulin administration — means that children with diabetes face potentially difficult social situations with their peers. Gross *et al.* (1981) suggested that an inability to cope with such social demands may contribute towards the development of psychological problems. They further suggested that SST may provide a means to overcome such difficulties, and accordingly designed a programme to produce more effective coping skills in children with diabetes.

The Diabetes Assertiveness Test (DAT) was devised by Gross and Johnson (1981) to provide a measure which focused on the particular social interactions diabetics are likely to face. It is composed of eight social scenes which draw attention to the fact that the person has diabetes. The baseline assessment in the Gross *et al.* (1981) study was three complete presentations of DAT, which were videotaped and subsequently rated for level of eye contact, duration of speech, and appropriateness of verbalisation. On the basis of low ratings on these three behaviours five diabetic children, three girls and two boys aged from 9 to 12 years, were selected for training.

Following baseline assessment, five weeks of SST was conducted at a rate of 2 forty-five minute sessions per week. The training centred around five scenes from the DAT; using modelling, role-play, instruction, feedback, and verbal reinforcement to shape up eye contact and verbal behaviour. Consistent with a multiple-baseline methodology, the behaviours were trained sequentially; eye contact was trained until reliably performed, followed by verbalisation with some emphasis retained on eye contact. Each training session ended with a videotaped role-play of the five scenes used in training. These scenes formed the basis of the evaluation and were later rated for level of behaviour on the trained skills. Finally, upon completion of the training all eight DAT scenes were role-played and recorded: the ratings of the three scenes not included in the programme giving a measure of generalisation. A five week follow-up was carried out, again including all eight DAT scenes to assess maintenance of trained skills and generalisation. During the follow-up period the parents of the diabetic children were asked to practise the five trained scenes with their children.

Analysis of the ratings showed large behavioural gains over the training period compared against baseline levels. These gains were also evident for the untrained scenes, indicating generalisation of training. The improvements were largely maintained at follow-up, for both trained and untrained scenes. An additional *in vivo* test was conducted in a restaurant: each child, unaware that the test was taking place, was pressed by a (primed) waiter to buy a milk-shake, high in sugar content. All five children refused the drink, responding appropriately while doing so.

The training was clearly successful in increasing the coping skills of the diabetic children. However, as Gross *et al.* (1981) point out, only limited generalisation has been assessed: it is unclear whether the improvement would be seen at home without training there involving parents; and it is also unknown whether the changes would be seen in the school environment. However, Gross *et al.* note the further possibility that increased coping ability may improve diabetic control as indicated by various physiological measures (see Delbridge, 1975; Koshi, Ahlas and Kumento, 1976).

Gross *et al.* (1983) sought to expand upon both the findings of Gross *et al.* (1981), and a further study by Johnson, Gross and Wildman (cited in Gross *et al.*, 1983), by including a metabolic measure of diabetic control in the evaluation of SST with diabetic children. It is known that analysis of hemoglobin (Hg) provides an indication of blood glucose levels (Jackson, Hess and England, 1979), with Hg A_1c providing a reliable measure of diabetic control (Gonen *et al.* 1977). Thus Gross *et al.* (1983) selected Hg A_1c as their measure of diabetic control in children participating in SST.

Eleven diabetic children, aged from 9 to 12 years, took part in the study: six children participated in the skills training, the remainder formed a no-treatment control group. The SST design and procedure was very similar to that used by Gross *et al.* (1981); a multiple-baseline design with behavioural rating from the DAT as the dependent measure. The results showed that for the SST group there was an increase in trained behaviours compared against baseline levels. There was also evidence of generalisation to unrehearsed scenes, and a six week follow-up indicated maintenance of the learning. The untrained control group did not change from baseline levels over the duration of the study. A comparison of Hg A_1c levels at baseline and follow-up, using both within-group and between-group analyses, failed to show any significant effects of training on this measure. Thus the poor pre-training levels of diabetic control remained after completion of the programme despite improved coping skills in the SST group. Whilst, as Gross *et al.* (1983) note, SST may not appear to be an effective means of improving diabetic control, it would be unwise to dismiss the possibility on the basis of one study. It is possible that Hg A_1c is not the best index of diabetic control and other measures, such as ketone and free fatty acid, may be more sensitive. The follow-up period was comparatively short: the effects of training may require consolidation through reinforcement from the natural environment before diabetic control is established. Longer follow-up periods would be necessary to answer this point.

From a methodological viewpoint it should be noted that both studies with diabetic children have employed a group design rather than a single-case approach as used, for example, with blind children (Farkas *et al.*, 1981; Van Hasselt *et al.*, 1983). With a group design there is the possibility that whilst the overall group mean increases, this can mask a lack of change, or even negative change, in some individual trainees. A single-case approach may be used in future research to determine if the training effects are universal or mediated by some individual difference.

This application of SST has demonstrated its value in aiding diabetic children to cope more effectively with the social pressures linked to their condition. Given this important contribution, it remains to be established whether SST, either alone or in combination with other interventions, can directly influence diabetic control and decrease the chances of further psychological and social problems in the long-term.

Physical Disability and SST

Advances in the field of medicine have improved both the chances of a normal life span and the degree of physical mobility for those with major physical disabilities such as severe spinal cord injury. However, as Romano (1976) pointed out, as well as physical treatment its often also necessary to assist with psychological and social adjustment. In a brief paper Romano succinctly advanced the case for the role of SST in the psychosocial rehabilitation of the physically handicapped. Dunn and Herman (1982) extended this proposition, distinguishing four types of problem commonly faced by the physically handicapped. The first is *public attitude*: a number of surveys have shown that the non-handicapped generally have unfavourable views of the physically handicapped, and also behave in an anxious manner in social interactions (e.g. Weinberg, 1976). It is possible that this negative evaluation contributes to poor self-image in the disabled (Dixon, 1977). The second common problem is *differential behaviour patterns*. Two studies by Kleck (1966, 1968) have shown that in interactions with a handicapped person, a non-handicapped individual is likely to display a variety of unusual behaviours; for example expressing attitudes at variance with their own beliefs. The effect of this is to create an artificial social environment in which the handicapped person does not experience appropriate social reinforcement and punishment. This, in turn, may precipitate a decrease in social opportunity and normal behaviour for the handicapped person (Kelly *et al.*, 1960). The third class of problem arises with *special social situations* which require a specific type of skilled performance from the handicapped person. Dunn (1977) reported that the three situations which posed the greatest discomfort for those with spinal cord injury were accidental bowel movements in public, leaks in urinary drainage apparatus, and falling from the wheelchair. Finally, the fourth problem is *general assertiveness*. The criticism has been levelled against hospitals that they simplify the problems of being handicapped (Trieschmann, 1980). If the return to the community following hospitalisation is not managed correctly, there is the danger of poor social adjustment unless the handicapped person is able to assert him- or herself in making social contact and putting others at their ease.

Given these special problems faced by the physically handicapped a specific assessment method for social skills ability in this population is clearly required. The Spinal Cord Injury Assertion Questionnaire (SCIAQ) was devised and refined in two unpublished studies conducted by Dunn and his colleagues (cited in Dunn and Herman, 1982). The SCIAQ consists of a series of twenty six potentially sensitive social scenes related to spinal cord injury (e.g. "asking people to move out of your way"; "ask a passer-by for help after you have fallen out of your wheelchair"). Each scene is rated by the handicapped person to indicate how anxious it would make them, and they also note if they would ever allow themselves to be involved in such a situation. Dunn and Herman discuss the SCIAQ in great detail, commenting on its validity, use, and correlation with other objective and subjective measures of social skills.

The detailed assessment work of Dunn and his colleagues has borne fruit in the development of a SST programme for the physically handicapped. Dunn, Van Horn and Herman (1981) compared the effectiveness of three training procedures with spinal cord injury (SCI) patients. The three techniques were: SST focused on managing difficult social situations as detailed in the SCIAQ (Dunn, 1977); a modelling film which simply demonstrated various strategies to deal with the difficult situations; and an SST plus film condition. A control group who completed the assessment measures, without involvement in training, completed the design.

The pre-training assessment included self-report inventories, including the SCIAQ and two assertiveness scales; and a Behavioural Assertiveness Test (BAT), covering role-played scenes both of general assertion and specifically for those in wheelchairs. Performance on the role-played BAT was rated by independent judges. The SST included the techniques of role-play, videotaped feedback, and coaching: there were 8 ninety minute sessions, held at the rate of two per week.

Dunn, Van Horn and Herman conducted a comprehensive statistical analysis of the data and only the principal findings are summarised here. From the BAT a number of dimensions of performance were independently analysed. In terms of *overall assertiveness* the film plus SST group showed the greatest improvement, followed by the SST group; there were no significant changes from pre- to post-training for the film only and control groups on this aspect of performance. For *noncompliance* the greatest improvement was found in the SST group, although improvements were evident in all the other groups. With regard to *requests for new behaviour* the SST group showed the greatest improvement such that at post-training they were rated significantly higher than the film only and control groups. Thus the experimental groups participating in behavioural training — the SST and SST plus film groups — show a clear advantage at post-training over the untrained groups. However, despite the changes following training, separate analyses of the self-report data failed to show any changes from pre- to post-training.

As Dunn, Van Horn and Herman point out, the results of their study raise more questions than they answer. Nevertheless, they are confident enough to comment: "Despite the limitations in the current study, it appears that the major purposes have been fulfilled . . . social skills training is a procedure applicable to the social rehabilitation of male SCI patients . . . groups involving video feedback, modelling, and instructions make significant gains in performance in situations which severely physically handicapped individuals must face in their re-entry into society" (p. 163).

The strength of the work of Dunn and his colleagues is that it begins to offer a way to overcome the problems faced by the physically handicapped in readjusting to a new social role. Alongside this adjustment on an individual level, adjustment must also be made to being "different" from "normal" people. Goffman (1963) used the word "stigma" to describe society's reaction to those it perceives as abnormal or deviant from the accepted norm. While all physically handicapped people may experience this process of stigmatisation, Goffman suggest that the facially disfigured may be especially liable to such social alienation.

The complaints of facially disfigured people that they are looked down on and avoided by society (Andreason and Norris, 1973; MacGregor, 1974) is in accord with Goffman's thesis. The effect of this social alienation is that the facially disfigured person avoids social contact, or exhibits socially unskilled behaviour; in either case reinforcing the stereotype of "abnormal". However, as Rumsey (1983) points out, stereotypes are a two-way phenomena: the way other people behave towards us is to some degree a function of our expectations and behaviour towards them. Thus, if the facially disfigured *expect* to be treated differently and behave accordingly, then the non-disfigured may reciprocate in a manner which confirms the expectation.

Rumsey (1983) set out to investigate this hypothesis using a 2 × 2 factorial experimental design which varied the presence or absence of a large facial birthmark with a high or low level of social skill. The subjects were told that the experimental confederate was a postgraduate student practising interview techniques. The trained confederate performed with a highly socially skilled manner in half the interviews, and with poor social skills in the other half; the presence or absence of the facial disfigurement was balanced across skilled and unskilled conditions. Following the videotaped interview, the interviewees completed a series of rating scales, ostensibly for feedback to the interviewer. A further set of observers viewed the recordings and rated the behaviour of both the interviewer and interviewees: these raters, like the subject-interviewees, were unaware of the experimental manipulations.

Analysis showed that the interviewees' ratings of the interviewer were not influenced by the presence or absence of the facial disfigurement. However, they were strongly affected by the level of social skill; with the high level eliciting more favourable ratings of friendliness, competence, and warmth. The observers, rating from the video recording, were marginally influenced by the disfigurement but much more so by the level of social skill. Similarly they judged the interviewees' behaviour to vary considerably more depending on the interviewer's social skills rather than the presence or absence of the facial disfigurement. Rumsey concludes that the interviewees and the raters: "Were not affected to any great extent by manipulation of the disfigurement variable. The level of social skills used by the interviewer . . . (produced) significantly more favourable impressions" (p. 3).

As Rumsey rightly notes, some caution is necessary in generalising the results of one study to all facially disfigured people. Nonetheless, this study does suggest a potentially fruitful application of SST: the rewarding effects from the use of good social skills may contribute towards dissolving the stigma experienced by many facially disfigured people.

Concluding Remarks

The diverse applications of SST in the studies reviewed here stand as testimony to both the strength of the technique and the creativity of its exponents. The range covered is staggering: assistance with adjustment to a change of sex; help with rehabilitation following the trauma of severe physical injury; and enrichment of the social development of blind and diabetic children. The studies fall prey to the usual experimental and methodological criticisms; the style of training, assessment methods (although in some studies highly appropriate assessment techniques were devised), research design, statistical analysis, measures of generalisation, and so on. However, they all have the common feature that the investigators have seen an application for SST where one would not immediately seem evident. Perhaps the key to this perception comes from a switch in emphasis from a psychopathological approach, where SST is offered as a "cure", to a use more in sympathy with the constructional approach (Goldiamond, 1974) in which the intervention aims to enhance the client's behavioural repertoire. Behavioural training cannot, for example, cure blindness, but as Van Hasselt *et al.* (1983) demonstrated, it can improve the quality of life for blind people. Similarly, it is doubtful whether SST would be satisfactory as the *only* intervention following sex change surgery. When used within the context of a multi-disciplinary treatment programme, SST was seen to play an important role in assisting with post-operative adjustment (Yardley, 1976). Researchers such as Rumsey (1983) are beginning to envisage even more applications for SST. It is heartening that these researchers are adopting a strategy of establishing an empirical case for the use of SST — the work with spinal cord injury patients provides a perfect example — rather than assuming that simply because the client group presents itself training is appropriate With such considered, measured approaches it seems likely that SST will be added to the treatment of yet further diverse populations.

References

Andreason, N. J. C. and Norris, A. S. (1972) Long-term adjustment and adaptation mechanisms in severely burned adults. *Journal of Nervous and Mental Disease*, **154**, 352–362.

Argyle, M., Trower, P. and Bryant, B. (1974) Explorations in the treatment of personality disorders and neuroses by social skills training. *British Journal of Medical Psychology*, **47**, 63–72.

Barlow, D. H., Abel, G. G. and Blanchard, E. B. (1979) Gender identity change in transsexuals: Follow-up and replications. *Archives of General Psychiatry*, **36**, 1001–1007.

Barlow, D. H., Reynolds, E. J. and Agras, W. S. (1973) Gender identity change in a transsexual. *Archives of General Psychiatry*, **28**, 569–576.

Crisp, A. H. (1970) Anorexia nervosa: 'Feeding disorder', 'nervous malnutrition' or 'weight phobia'. *World Review of Nutrition and Dietetics*, **12**, 452–504.

Curtis, W. S., Donlong, E. T. and Tweedie, D. (1975) Adjustment of deaf-blind children. *Education of the Visually Handicapped*, **7**, 21–26.

Delbridge, L. (1975) Educational and psychological factors in the management of diabetes in childhood. *Medical Journal of Australia*, **2**, 737–739.

Dixon, J. K. (1977) Coping with prejudice: Attitudes of handicapped persons towards the handicapped. *Journal of Chronic Diseases*, **30**, 307–322.

Dunn, M. E. (1977) Social discomfort in the patient with SCI. *Archives of Physical Medicine and Rehabilitation*, **58**, 257–260.

Dunn, M. E. and Herman, S. H. (1982) Social skills and physical disability. In: D. M. Doleys, R. L. Meredith and A. R. Ciminero (Eds.), *Behavioral medicine: Assessment and treatment strategies*. New York: Plenum Press.

Dunn, M. E., Van Horn, E. and Herman, S. H. (1981) Social skills and spinal cord injury: A comparison of three training procedures. *Behavior Therapy*, **12**, 153–164.

Eaglestein, A. S. (1975) The social acceptance of blind high school students in an integrated school. *New Outlook for the Blind*, **69**, 447–451.

Everhart, G., Luzader, M. and Tullos, S. (1980) Assertive skills training for the blind. *Journal of Visual Impairment and Blindness*, **84**, 62–65.

Farkas, G. M., Sherick, R. B., Matson, J. C. and Leobig, M. (1981) Social skills training for a blind child through differential reinforcement. *The Behavior Therapist*, **4**, 24–26.

Garfinkel, P. E. and Garner, D. M. (1982) *Anorexia nervosa: A multidimensional approach*. New York: Brunner/Mazel.

Gelder, M. G. and Marks, I. M. (1969) Aversion treatment in transvestism and transsexualism. In: R. Green and J. Money (Eds.), *Transsexualism and sex reassignment*. Baltimore: Johns Hopkins University Press.

Goffman, E. (1963) *Stigma: Notes on the management of spoiled identity*. Englewood Cliffs, New Jersey: Prentice Hall.

Goldiamond, I. (1974) Towards a constructional approach to social problems. *Behaviorism*, **2**, 1–84.

Gonen, B., Rachman, H., Rubenstein, A. H., Tanega, S. P. and Horowitz, D. L. (1977) Hemoglobin A_1c: An indicator of the metabolic control of diabetic patients. *Lancet*, **2**, 734–736.

Green, R. and Money, J. (1969) *Transsexualism and sex reassignment*. Baltimore: Johns Hopkins University Press.

Gross, A. M., Heimann, L., Shapiro, R. and Schultz, R. M. (1983) Children with diabetes: Social skills training and hemoglobin A_1c levels. *Behavior Modification*, **7**, 151–164.

Gross, A. M. and Johnson, W. G. (1981) The diabetes assertiveness test: A measure of social coping skills in adolescent diabetics. *The Diabetes Educator*, **7**, 26–27.

Gross, A. M., Johnson, W. G., Wildman, H. and Mullett, N. (1981) Coping skills training with insulin-dependent pre-adolescent diabetics. *Child Behavior Therapy*, **3**, 141–153.

Hersen, M. and Barlow, D. H. (1976) *Single case experimental designs: Strategies for studying behaviour change*. Oxford: Pergamon Press.

Jackson, R. L., Hess, R. L. and England, J. D. (1979) Hemoglobin A_1c values in children with overt diabetes maintained in varying degrees of control. *Diabetes Care*, **2**, 391–395.

Johanson, A. J. and Knorr, N. J. (1977) L-DOPA as treatment for anorexia nervosa. In: R. A. Vigersky (Ed.), *Anorexia nervosa*. New York: Raven Press.

Kelly, H. H., Hastorf, A. H., Jones, E. E., Thibaut, J. W., and Usdane, M. W. (1960) Some implications of social psychological theory for research on the handicapped. In: L. H. Lofquist (Ed.), *Psychological research and rehabilitation*. Miami: American Psychological Association.

Kleck, R. (1966) Emotional arousal in interactions with stigmatized persons. *Psychological Reports*, **21**, 12–26.

Kleck, R. (1968) Physical stigma and nonverbal cues emitted face-to-face interactions. *Human Relations*, **21**, 19–28.

Koshi, M. L., Ahlas, A. and Kumento, A. (1976) A psychosomatic follow-up study of childhood diabetics. *Acta Paedopsychiatrica*, **42**, 12–26.

MacGregor, F. C. (1974) *Transformation and identity*. New York: Times Book Co.

Marks, I. M., Gelder, M. G. and Bancroft, J. (1970) Sexual deviants two years after electric aversion. *British Journal of Psychiatry*, **117**, 173–185.

Netlick, A. (1977) Programming for consistency in training for deaf-blind in a residential centre. *Education of the Visually Handicapped*, **9**, 41–44.

Pillay, M. and Crisp, A. H. (1977) Some psychological characteristics of patients with anorexia nervosa whose weight has been newly restored. *British Journal of Medical Psychology*, **50**, 375–380.

Pillay, M. and Crisp, A. H. (1981) The impact of social skills training within an established in-patient treatment programme for anorexia nervosa. *British Journal of Psychiatry*, **139**, 533–539.

Romano, M. D. (1976) Social skills training with the newly-handicapped. *Archives of Physical Medicine and Rehabilitation*, **57**, 302–303.

Rosman, B. L., Minuchin, S. and Liebman, R. (1975) Family lunch session: An introduction to family therapy in anorexia nervosa. *American Journal of Orthopsychiatry*, **45**, 846–853.

Rumsey, N. (1983, December) *A social skills approach to improving the quality of social interaction for the facially disfigured.* Paper presented at the London Conference of the British Psychological Society, London.

Schlesier-Stropp, B. (1984) Bulimia: A review of the literature. *Psychological Bulletin*, **95**, 247–257.

Tavormina, J. B., Kastner, L. S., Slater, P. M. and Watts, S. L. (1976) Chronically ill children: A psychologically and emotionally deviant population. *Journal of Abnormal Child Psychology*, **4**, 99–100.

Trieschmann, R. B. (1980) *Spinal cord injuries: Psychological, social, and vocational adjustment.* New York: Pergamon Press.

Tryon, W. W. (1982) A simplified time-series analysis for evaluating treatment interventions. *Journal of Applied Behavior Analysis*, **15**, 423–429.

Van Hasselt, V. B. and Hersen, M. (1981) Applications for single case designs to research with the visually impaired. *Journal of Visual Impairment and Blindness*, **75**, 359–362.

Van Hasselt, V. B., Hersen, M., Kazdin, A. E., Sisson, L. A., Simon, J. and Mastanuono, A. (1981, November). *A behavioral-analytic model for assessing social skills in blind adolescents.* Paper presented at the Annual Convention of the Association for Advancement of Behaviour Therapy, Toronto.

Van Hasselt, V. B., Hersey, M., Kazdin, A. E., Simon, J. and Mastanuono, A. (1983) Training blind adolescents in social skills. *Journal of Visual Impairment and Blindness*, **77**, 199 203.

Warren, T. J. (1976) Blindness and early development: What is known and what needs to be studied. *New Outlook for the Blind*, **70**, 5–16.

Weinberg, N. (1976) Social stereotyping of the physically handicapped. *Rehabilitation Psychology*, **23**, 115–124.

Yardley, K. M. (1976) Training in feminine skills in a male transsexual: A pre-operative procedure. *British Journal of Medical Psychology*, **49**, 329–339.

New Directions

8

Social Skills and the Analysis of Situations and Conversations

MICHAEL ARGYLE

All social behaviour takes place in social situations, and different situations require very different forms of social performance. Examples are parties, committee meetings, interviews, and so on. Some SST clients complain about their difficulties in particular situations, rather than difficulties with social behaviour in general, so that SST for them needs to be focused on those situations. There has been extensive research into the nature and effects of social situations (Furnham and Argyle, 1981a).

Research on person-situation interaction has shown that clinical patients are *more* consistent than non-patients across situations, psychotics more so than neurotics, and that they vary their behaviour more as they recover (Endler, 1973; Mariotto, 1978; Mariotto and Paul, 1975; Moos, 1968). The best interpretation of these findings is probably that patients are being rigid and unresponsive to the different demands of different situations.

Many clinical patients have phobias about particular situations — open spaces, public meetings, air travel — or about specific objects such as spiders, animals, and so on. Anxiety neurosis is now regarded by many psychiatrists as being in many cases a collection of specific phobias rather than generalised anxiety. Schizophrenics, too, are affected by situations. They do not like being supervised at work, being criticised, or being questioned about their problems. Rutter (1976) found that schizophrenics did not avert gaze during discussion of impersonal topics, as compared with non-schizophrenics, although they did avert gaze during interviews.

Most techniques developed to assess social skills involve some form of assessment of behaviour in difficult social situations, either role-play or self-report. Rehm and Marston (1968) developed one of the first role-play tests, the Situation Test — which consists of ten situations requiring some form of heterosexual interaction. Male subjects are informed of the nature of each situation and have to reply to a line of dialogue, said by a female confederate, which is later rated. Twentyman and McFall (1975) devised a similar Social Behavior Situations task which requires lengthy role-playing in six "difficult situations". Freedman *et al.* (1978) conceptualised delinquent behaviour as a manifestation of situation-specific social-behavioural skills deficits. They identified a number of adolescent problem situations and they were able to demonstrate that non-delinquents were rated as more competent in these situations than delinquents.

As Hersen and Bellack (1976) in their review of social skills assessment concluded:

> Rather than providing a single, global definition of social skill, we prefer a situation-specific conception of social skills. The overriding factor is effectiveness of behaviour in social interactions. However, determination of effectiveness depends on the context of the interaction and, given any context, the parameters of the specific situation (p. 512).

Trower, Bryant and Argyle (1978) devised a Social Situations Questionnaire in which clients for SST are first asked to rate their difficulty in coping with 30 situations, and then say how often they had entered each situation, from "every day" to "never". The 30 situations are listed in Table 1a, as well as 15 more difficult situations studied by Furnham and Argyle (1981b) — Table 1b.

Trower *et al.* (1978) suggested a programme for assessment of difficulty in social situations and a method of training. In the assessment the subject is asked to perform in specific situations as well as to complete the Social Situations Questionnaire.

This is to determine the nature of the situations, and the particular skill deficit. Questions are asked about the goals and motivations in these situations, the subjects' planning strategies, their perception of the situation and the nature of their performance.

If some clients need to be taught how to deal with different social situations, they need to be able to classify or label situations, and they need to learn the special skills for each type of situation. One way of finding dimensions of situations is by means of multidimensional scaling, in which subjects indicate how similar a number of situations are to each other, so that the underlying dimensions which they are using can be extracted statistically. Wish and Kaplan (1977) used this method for finding the dimensionality of eight different kinds of social events and eight role relations. They obtained the following dimensions: (1) friendly-hostile; (2) co-operative-competitive; (3) intense-superficial; (4) equal-unequal; (5) informal-formal; (6) task-oriented-not task-oriented. These were not all independent; the first two are correlated, for example.

Although these dimensions are extremely valuable and have appeared in other studies, they do not tell the whole story. Consider the combination of *task-oriented, unequal, friendly, intense*, and *co-operative*. This includes such situations as going to the dentist, being psychoanalysed, saying confession, having a tennis lesson, having a philosophy tutorial, discussing work problems with the boss, and discussing domestic problems with

TABLE 1a. *Social Situations Questionnaire (From Trower et al., 1978)*

Date:	Sex:			Name:...........................	
	No difficulty 0	Slight difficulty 1	Moderate difficulty 2	Great difficulty 3 At the present time	Avoidance if possible 4 This time a year ago
1.	Walking down the street			—	—
2.	Going into shops			—	
3.	Going on public transport...............................			—	—
4.	Going into pubs			—	—
5.	Going to parties			—	—
6.	Mixing with people at work.............................			—	—
7.	Making friends of your own age			—	—
8.	Going out with someone you are sexually attracted to			—	—
9.	Being with a group of the same sex and roughly the same age as you			—	—
10.	Being with a group containing both men and women of roughly the same age as you..........................			—	—
11.	Being with a group of the opposite sex of roughly the same age as you......................................			—	—
12.	Entertaining people in your home, lodgings etc.			—	—
13.	Going into restaurants or cafes			—	—
14.	Going to dances, dance halls or discotheques			—	—
15.	Being with older people			—	—
16.	Being with younger people			—	—
17.	Going into a room full of people			—	—
18.	Meeting strangers...			—	—
19.	Being with people you don't know very well			—	—
20.	Being with friends			—	—
21.	Approaching others — making the first move in starting up a friendship			—	—
22.	Making ordinary decisions affecting others (e.g. what to do together in the evening).....................			—	—
23.	Being with only one other person rather than a group			—	—
24.	Getting to know people in depth			—	—
25.	Taking the initiative in keeping a conversation going..			—	—
26.	Looking at people directly in the eyes..................			—	—
27.	Disagreeing with what other people are saying and putting forward your own views			—	—
28.	People standing or sitting very close to you...........			—	—
29.	Talking about yourself and your feelings in a conversation			—	—
30.	People looking at you.....................................			—	—

TABLE 1b. *Difficult Social Situations (From Furnham and Argyle, 1981b)*

Situations

1. Complaining to a neighbour whom you know well about constant noisy disturbances
2. Taking a person of the opposite sex out for the first time for an evening
3. Going for a job interview
4. Visiting the doctor when unwell
5. Going to close relative's funeral
6. Going round to cheer up a depressed friend who asked you to call
7. Being a host or hostess at a large party (e.g. twenty-first birthday)
8. Give a short formal speech to a group of about fifty people that you don't know
9. Taking an unsatisfactory article back to a shop where you purchased it
10. Going across to introduce yourself to new neighbours
11. Dealing with a difficult and disobedient child
12. Going to a function with many people from a different culture
13. Playing a party game after dinner (charades, musical chairs)
14. Attending a distant relation's wedding ceremony, when you know few people
15. Apologising to a superior for forgetting an important errand

father. (It is difficult to assess them for formality.) If someone has difficulties with one of these situations, as clients for SST often do, then they need to know more than the fact that the situation is task-orientated, unequal, friendly, etc. If we want to understand one of these situations to the point where we can predict or explain the sequence of events in it, we also need to know more. What is it about situations that would be useful to know, and that would provide sufficient information for these purposes?

A clue to the features of the situations which might be found more helpful can be obtained from the situations which SST trainees often report. They are "what are parties *for*?" (i.e. what are the goals?), "what are you supposed to do?" (i.e. what are the rules and repertoire?); candidates at interviews sometimes mistake the goals and think they are there for vocational guidance, or get the rules wrong and think they can ask the questions.

It is useful to take games as models for other social situations. In each case the participants agree to follow certain rules; they pursue certain goals; and only certain moves are recognised as relevant acts. In his analysis of games, Avedon (1971) proposed features like purpose (i.e. how to win), rules, roles of participants, equipment required, and so on.

The list of features of situations that we have been using, and which was developed independently, is as follows:

1. Goal structure
2. Repertoire of elements
3. Rules
4. Sequence of behaviour

5. Concepts
6. Environmental setting
7. Roles
8. Skills and difficulties (Argyle, 1976; Argyle, Furnham and Graham, 1981).

These concepts can incorporate the Wish and Kaplan dimensions; for example co-operative and competitive situations have quite different goal structures.

I believe that common situations are functional in that they enable certain goals to be met, which in turn enable certain needs to be satisfied, and that the features of situations, such as their rules and repertoire, facilitate the reaching of these goals. I turn first to a consideration of the goals of situations.

Goal Structure

The needs, drives, and goals that are satisfied by a situation also form a *structure*; that is, a person may pursue more than one goal, or there may be more than one person there. We shall analyse situations in terms of the relations between two or more goals.

A study was carried out in a school of occupational therapy. Lists of the goals which the girls sought in a number of common social situations were elicited in open-ended interviews, and these were supplemented from earlier lists by Murray (1938) and others. Twenty-one goals were used, including "be accepted by other(s)", "eating/drinking", "convey information to other(s)", "make favourable impression", and so on. Ninety-seven subjects rated the importance of each goal for each person in a number of common situations, including "an interview for a job or course", "a first date", etc. These ratings were subjected to principal components analysis, showing the main groupings of goals for each role and situation. There were thus two criteria for deciding that a goal was relevant for a given role and situation — the emergence of a principal component, and the average relevance score. In most cases there were three such main goals: for example, in the case of a nurse and patient encounter the following goals were most relevant.

nurse	*patient*
mutual acceptance	mutual acceptance
take care of other	obtaining information
look after self	own well-being

In a second study we studied "goal structure" — degree of conflict or instrumentality between the goals found in the first study. Thirty-six further subjects rated the degree of conflict v. compatibility of pairs of goals on 5-point scales, and also the direction of instrumentality and interference. In the nurse-patient encounter there is a small amount of conflict (4.16 on the 1–5 scale) between well-being of nurse and patient. In the complaint situation there is a lot of conflict, especially over dominance; if a complainer concentrated on persuasion rather than dominance they might be more successful (see Graham, Argyle and Furnham, 1980).

Two studies of the choice of situations were also conducted. Furnham (1981) found that different leisure activities were chosen as a function of personality. Extroverts chose leisure activities involving social interaction and physical pursuits, while introverted neurotics did not engage much in reading or competitive indoor games perhaps because they are too

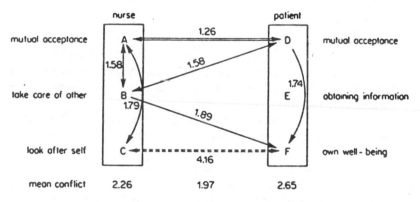

Fig. 1. Nurse-Patient. (From Graham, Argyle and Furnham, 1980).

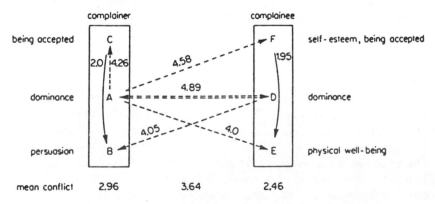

Fig. 2. Complaint. (From Graham, Argyle and Furnham, 1980).

stimulating. Extroverts chose stimulating, active and unusual situations, while introverts and neurotics avoided them. Stressful social situations were avoided by introverts, though not by neurotics. In the second study Argyle and Furnham (1982) studied choice of situations as a function of relationship with others. It was found that each relationship was associated with a characteristic range of situations, and that situations chosen varied with relationship domain (family, friends, work), intimacy, and status equality or difference. Examples of typical situations and activities are given in Table 2.

It can be seen that there is a characteristic range of situations for each relationship. It follows that training for a particular relationship should focus on performance in the relevant situations.

Rules

Continuing the analogy between social situations and games, I want to propose that all social situations are rule governed. There could not be a game between a team following the rules of, say hockey, and a team following the rules of rugby football, or between someone playing chess and someone playing tennis. Some of the rules can be described in terms of repertoire; they are rules about which moves are allowed and which are not. If a rule is broken, the game is usually stopped; and further rules prescribe what sanctions shall be imposed — a free kick, etc. Even the most fiercely competitive and aggressive games can only take place if both sides abide by the rules, of boxing or wrestling for example. Rules are developed gradually as cultural products, as ways of handling certain situations; they can be changed, but changes are slow. The rules have to be learned, by children as part of their socialisation, by new members of organisations, and by people from other cultures. We can define a rule in terms of shared beliefs — that certain behaviours are appropriate or inappropriate in a given situation.

The rules of social situations may be discovered through the observation of behaviour, but it is very difficult to infer rules unless regular sanctions are used, as in games. Rules may also be ascertained through reports by participants.

Our procedure has been to take formal situations, in this case games, as models for less formal situations governed by rules (Harré and Secord, 1972). But are less formal situations governed by rules at all? Clearly some situations are more rule bound than others. Price and Bouffard (1974) asked subjects to rate the appropriateness of 15 kinds of behaviour in 15 situations. It was found that the situations varied greatly in "constraint" (i.e. the number of things not permitted). At one extreme were church services and job interviews; at the other were being in one's own room or

TABLE 2. *Situations/activities Most Chosen for Certain Relationships (Ratios to Mean Frequency for all Relationships) (From Argyle and Furnham, 1982)*

Spouse (mean ratio 1.64)		Work colleagues, liked, same status (mean ratio 1.11)		Friend, similar age (mean ratio 1.26)	
Situations above this ratio:		*Situations above this ratio:*		*Situations above this ratio:*	
2.61	Watch TV	2.11	Attend lecture	2.00	Dancing
2.48	Do domestic jobs together	1.56	Work together on joint task	1.67	Tennis
2.31	Play chess or other indoor games	1.55	Together in a committee	1.63	Sherry party
2.28	Go for a walk	1.50	Morning coffee, tea	1.63	Joint leisure
2.15	Go shopping	1.35	Casual chat, telling jokes	1.60	Pub
2.03	Play tennis, squash	1.31	One helps the other	1.52	Intimate conversation
1.93	Informal meal together			1.50	Walk
1.92	Intimate conversation				
1.84	Have argument, disagreement				

in a park. Even apparently disorderly situations are governed by rules. Marsh, Rosser and Harré (1978) found that most football hooligans followed informal rules, for example about not injuring opposing fans. Campbell (1980) found that fighting among women was also governed by agreed rules (Table 3).

It must be emphasised that there is play within the rules. Just as the playing of football depends on individual and joint skills and strategies within the framework of the rules, the same is true of behaviour in social situations.

Rules are developed so that the goals of situations can be attained. Some of these are common to many different situations, such as:

1. Maintaining communication — rules about turn-taking, the use of common language.
2. Preventing withdrawal — rules about equity, division of rewards.
3. Preventing aggression — rules about restraint of violence by rules of ritual aggression, e.g., among football hooligans.
4. Co-ordinating behaviour — driving on the same side of the road, having morning coffee at the same time.
5. Achieving co-operation — keeping quiet at concerts.

When the goal structure of specific situations is examined, it is evident that more than one set of rules will do the job. For example, buying and selling can be done by barter, bargaining, auction sale, raffle, or in

TABLE 3. *Rules for Fighting Among Females*

1.	Should not use a bottle to hit the other person schoolgirls 85% (borstal girls 58%)
2.	Should not ask friends to call the police borstal girls 85%
3.	Should not use a handbag to hit the other person 69%
4.	Should not use a knife on the other person schoolgirls 89% (borstal girls 52%)
5.	Should not report it to the police later 86%
6.	Should not ask friends to join in 81%
7.	Should not tell the school later 85%
8.	It is OK to kick the other person borstal girls 78%
9.	It is OK to slap the other person prison women 85%
10.	It is OK to punch the other person borstal girls 90%

Survey of 251 schoolgirls, borstal girls and prison women, from Campbell (1980).

fixed-price shops; the latter can be further divided into supermarkets and personal selling. The goal of taking open-air exercise with a ball in a group of people can be met in a larger number of ways. Here the rules represent not so much a limited set of logical alternatives as in the case of selling but more a set of elaborate cultural constructions. The same could be said of some social situations like dinner parties, weddings, and religious ceremonies.

Mann (1969) carried out a field study showing the emergence of rules as a function of goals. The queues for Australian football games last for over twenty-four hours. Rules have developed about how much time out is allowed (two to three hours at a time), staking claims by property (wooden boxes), and turn-taking in groups. Queue jumpers are rarely attacked but simply booed. They are kept out by the closeness of the queue. This is an example of the emergence and negotiation of local rules modifying more general cultural rules or deciding how they should be applied.

A Study of the Rules of Different Situations

Two studies were carried out by Argyle *et al.* (1979). In each, a list of possible rules was obtained by pilot interviews, 124 rules being used in one case, 20 in the other. Samples of subjects were asked to rate the applicability of each rule to each of 25 and 8 situations, respectively. It was found that subjects could rate whether or not they considered that a rule applied to a situation. There was a greatly above chance degree of agreement on which rules applied. There were a number of rules which were almost universal (e.g. should be friendly, should not try to make others feel small). Some rules were specific to one or two situations (e.g. should dress smartly — wedding). Cluster analysis produced clusters both of rules and situations and showed the cluster of rules for each cluster of situations. Some situations had far more rules on which subjects agreed than others (e.g. a tutorial versus a conversation with boy or girl friend), and some of the rules could be given a functional interpretation (e.g. at a tutorial "don't pretend to understand when you don't"). Others guarded against situational temptations (e.g. "don't touch" at a first date) or helped with difficulties common in a situation ("don't outstay your welcome" when visiting a friend in a college room). The cluster analysis for rules is shown in Fig. 3. The cluster of universal rules appears at the top. Rules for sherry parties and similar polite social events appear at the bottom.

The Repertoire of Elements

Early research on behaviour in groups led to sets of categories such as those of Bales (1950) which were believed to be applicable to all kinds of

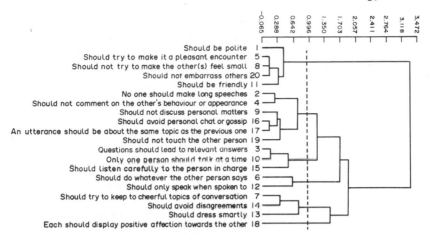

F<small>IG</small>. 3. Clusters of Rules. (From Argyle *et al.*, 1979).

behaviour. In fact, later research on different social settings has produced quite different sets of categories for behaviour in the classroom (Flanders, 1971), doctor-patient interaction (Byrne and Long, 1976), children at play (Blurton-Jones, 1972), and so on. The categories of behaviour that appear to be useful for studying behaviour in different situations are very different.

The hypothesis I want to develop is that each basic kind of situation has a characteristic repertoire of elements. To some extent these elements follow from, and could be deduced from, the goals of the situations; the elements are the moves that are needed to attain the goals. Thus, problem-solving requires moves like "makes suggestion", "asks questions", "disagrees", and so on. The repertoire is the product of cultural development in the course of which different ways of reaching the goals are worked out. This is reflected also in the emergence of different rule systems. Thus buying and selling can be done by auction sale with its special rules and limited number of moves by the buyers, who can only bid or not bid.

A further part of the hypothesis is that the "semiotic structure" of the repertoire is characteristic of the situation. What I mean by semiotic structure is the way certain acts are perceived and responded to as equivalent or similar, while others, perhaps equally similar in physical terms, are sharply contrasted. The hypothesis is obviously true in the case of games, where small differences in the way a ball is hit or thrown or the point at which it lands, make a great difference.

There are also situational differences in repertoire at the level of speech style or linguistic code. Immigrants and other bilinguals may speak different languages at home and at work or school. There are often "high" and "low" forms of speech used on formal and informal occasions. The high version is more carefully planned and has more nouns, adjectives and prepositions and fewer verbs, adverbs and pronouns (Brown and Fraser, 1979). Different vocabularies are used for different topics, especially technical topics. Sometimes these are designed to remove emotional associations as in nursing and sometimes to prevent outsiders from understanding, as in criminal argots. The meaning of words varies considerably between situations. Grammar takes simpler alternative forms in low versions of a language and in dialects like Black English. Accent moves towards upper class pronunciation in formal situations. People speak louder when farther apart and when excited (Bell, 1976; Dittmar, 1976).

Two studies have been carried out in which the repertoires of different situations were compared directly. Graham et al. (1981) studied the repertoire, as perceived by participants, in the following situations: (1) an evening at home; (2) visiting the doctor; (3) a sporting occasion with someone of the same sex; (4) a first date. Interviews were held with a sample of members of the Oxford Psychology Department subject panel, who were female, married, and under the age of 35. Elements of three kinds were elicited: (1) activities; (2) types of utterance; and (3) feelings. A total of 194 elements was obtained for the four situations. In a second stage, a further sample of 10 subjects from the same subculture were asked to check the items that they considered normal and typical for each situation. There was no obvious cut-off, and we accepted all items that 40% of the sample agreed to, giving 91, 65, 76 and 91 items, respectively, for the four situations. The greatest differences between situations were for activities (e.g. at the doctor's). A substantial proportion of the conversation and feeling elements were common to all four situations though there were also items unique to situations (e.g. "ask if disease is serious", and "hope treatment will work").

Duncan (1969) had contrasted experimental and structural approaches to social psychology. The following study combined both methods. Argyle, Graham and Kreckel (1982) studied the way in which elements of behaviour were grouped and contrasted in two situations. The situations were a young man and a young woman, on a date and at work in an office. Twenty-six elements of behaviour were used that could occur equally in either situation. Twenty subjects rated each element on ten rating scales, regarding each element as if it has been directed to them by the person of the other sex.

The data were analysed by hierarchical cluster analysis. As predicted, there was a very clear separation of task and personal issues in the work situation but not in the date. For example, questions about work and private life fell into distant clusters for work but were seen as very similar for the date. Although the main division for both situations was between positive and negative, in the work situation there were also work and social clusters.

Roles

Most situations contain a number of different roles, that is, there are positions for which there are different patterns of behaviour and different rules. The game analogy shows that in some games, like cricket, there are a number of different roles, but it does not show how these roles have come about. Roles are usually discussed in relation to social organisations, which have roles like doctor, nurse, patient, etc. Here we are concerned with roles in social situations, though these may be part of organisational roles. I also want to extend the idea of role to include informal roles, i.e. distinctive patterns of behaviour that occur in the absence of independently defined social positions.

I suggest that situational roles come about for four main reasons:

Different Goals

When two people are drawn to a situation to pursue different goals, their roles will be different. Usually these goals will be at least partly complementary and co-operative, and the joint behaviour satisfies the different goals. Examples are buying and selling, teaching and learning, doctor and patient.

Division of Labour

When there is a joint task to be done, there is often division of labour. In a restaurant, waitresses, cooks, barman and cashier divide up the work. Different industrial workers and their equipment are linked in "socio-technical systems". As organisations become larger, the more complex is the division of labour, and the more complex the possible situational role structure.

Social Control and Leadership

One individual may have the power to reward or punish others in a situation. Teachers and interviewers, for example, have such power. "Equal-unequal" was one of Wish and Kaplan's dimensions of situations. How do such differences of power come about? A group of four can function quite well without a leader. Larger groups progressively need a formal, an informal leader, and then two or more levels of leadership.

There is a rather crucial point at which the position of leader (or chairman) is established, and someone is formally appointed to this position. There is evidence that hierarchical role differentiation is functional. It reduces conflict, decisions can be made quickly, and the most skilled at the task have more influence over decisions.

Informal Roles

Informal roles are different. Because of the existence of different personalities in a situation, different people may react to it in different ways. However, the nature of the situation creates a limited and characteristic set of opportunities of this kind. In many groups there is a "socio-emotional" leader — who looks after the social as opposed to the task aspects of the situation. In juries and some work groups there is often a "leader of the opposition" (Argyle, 1969). Mann *et al.* (1967) found some interesting roles that often appeared in the Harvard variety of T-group, including "distressed females" and "sexual scapegoat" — a male who had doubts about his masculinity and invited the group to study him.

Marsh *et al.* (1978) report on the roles that they found among football fans at British football grounds. These are: (1) rowdies, aged 12–17 years, who make the most noise, produce the most violent displays of aggression, and wear the most spectacular costumes; (2) town boys, aged 17–25 years, who have graduated from being rowdies and are quieter and normally dressed (they are deferred to by boys in the other roles); (3) novices, younger than the rowdies, set apart from them, and keen to join them; (4) part-time supporters, a varied group not so fully involved in aggressive displays and despised by the others; (5) "nutters", extremely aggressive boys, who often behave in a crazy way and break the rules accepted by the majority of fans.

Concepts

In order to deal with people, individuals use personal constructs (Kelly, 1955). Individuals vary in the complexity of their constructs, using a larger or smaller number of independent variables. They use salient dimensions reflecting their main preoccupation — with race, class, intelligence, sexual attractiveness, and so on. The links between their constructs constitute "implicit personality theories", about how constructs are related to one another (e.g. race and intelligence). We should expect that people would be more socially competent in situations: (1) if they are cognitively complex (i.e. use a greater number of independent construct dimensions), and (2) if their constructs are relevant to the situations in question. It is familiar in repertory grid research that constructs have a limited "range of convenience"; for example, false teeth cannot be rated as *religious* or *atheist* (Bannister and Mair, 1968). Similarly, small children cannot be rated as *radical* or *conservative*, and it would usually be pointless to rate members of a psychology conference as good or bad at croquet. Research on intergroup attitudes has shown that traits become salient to a group when these distinguish the group from other groups and can be used to evaluate the group favourably (Tajfel, 1970). For example, South African Hindus emphasise their spiritual superiority (Mann, 1963).

In order to deal with complex stimuli or problems or to perform skills it is necessary to possess the relevant concepts. In order to play cricket it is necessary to be familiar with such concepts as "out", "declare", "no-ball", and "l.b.w.". In addition, the higher levels of skill may depend on the acquisition of additional concepts. In chess, for example, it soon becomes necessary to know about "check by discovery", "fork", and so on. These new concepts may refer to more complex aspects of the state of the game or to larger units of performance. In most skills the more skilled performer is able to run off larger strings of performance automatically, and these will be conceptualised. Committee meetings require the mastery of a number of concepts like "straw vote", "casting vote", "nem con", "unanimous", "abstain", and so on. The concepts for everyday social interaction have not so far been much studied, but it is known that there are interesting cultural differences (Benedict, 1935).

Forgas, Argyle and Ginsburg (1980) studied a group of 14 research psychologists. Each person completed a set of 36 rating scales to describe the behaviour of each person, including the rater, in four situations — morning coffee, going to the pub, seminars, and parties at the home of the senior member of the group. The ratings were analysed by multidimensional scaling, to find the underlying dimensions being used. In the social situations there were two dimensions — extraversion and evaluation (as an enjoyable companion). In the seminar situation, however, there were three quite different dimensions — dominance, supportiveness and creativity.

Argyle *et al.* (1981) carried out a study with a group of housewives and a group of students, who were asked to rate the relevance of 36 bipolar constructs in four situations and for seven target groups. Factor analyses showed that the constructs produced rather different factors in each situation. However, there was a friendly-extraversion factor in each situation, which was rated as highly relevant. Work-related constructs, like industrious, competent, and dependable, were rated as much more relevant in work situations than in social ones. Different constructs were found relevant for different target groups. For example, the relevant scales for children were judged to be *well-behaved* and *noisy*, while for professional people the most relevant scales were *competence* and *high-status*. It appeared that the most relevant scales were those that reflected the nature of social interaction with different target groups.

Physical Environment

Barker and Wright (1954) defined their "behaviour settings" as combinations of "standing patterns of behaviour" (i.e. rules, roles and repertoire, and environmental setting). We, too, want to emphasise the physical setting as an important feature of situations. The environment affects behaviour, as is shown by studies of the effects of overcrowding for example. The environment is partly created for purposes of interaction, by architects, planners, and anyone who furnishes, decorates, or merely arranges a room. Someone who, for example, arranges the furniture in a room, does so in the expectation that this will affect social interaction in some way; therefore we can concentrate on environment as a cause of behaviour.

Several aspects of physical environment have been shown to influence behaviour:

1. *Proximity* produces greater intimacy, or discomfort when closer than a certain distance, and progressive aversion of gaze.
2. *Crowding* produces high arousal, discomfort, aggressive behaviour in males, laughter (tension release), withdrawal from social contact, and, if prolonged, emotional disturbance.
3. *Orientation*. Side-by-side creates a more co-operative and friendly relationship; facing opposite creates an atmosphere of competition and conflict unless two people are eating a meal.

However, environments affect behaviour in another way via the perception of the meaning of the setting.

1. *Furniture arrangement* produces various combinations of the factors above, together with creation of private spaces. Desks can be placed to dominate the room, chairs placed together by a fire suggest friendly chat. Sofas of different designs suggest varying degrees of intimacy.
2. *Colour and decoration*. Colours affect emotional state — red and yellow for warmth and cheerfulness, dark blue and brown for gloom. The nature of the furnishings can suggest interrogation, romance, office work, or important decision-making. People seen in a pretty room are liked more than the same people seen in an ugly room.
3. *Equipment*. In many situations special equipment in needed, which extends the range' of social behaviour possible. These might include blackboard and chalk, pointer, and overhead projector, or bottles of drink and glasses, or various toys and games. Some of these features of environment can be looked at as "behavioural residues": the setting indicates what is usually done there.

The physical environment is of particular interest in the analysis of situations as this is the easiest part of situations to change. Sommer (1969) was able to increase the amount of interaction among the inmates of an old people's home by moving the chairs into circles round coffee tables. Harold Cohen found that fighting in a prison mainly took place at the corners of corridors and was started by inmates bumping into one another. He reduced the amount of fighting by rounding off the corners so that people could see each other coming. A number of co-operative toys are available that, like see-saw and table tennis, require two players, thus reducing one major form of conflict between pairs of children.

Skills and Difficulties

Every social situation presents certain difficulties, and needs certain social skills in order to deal with it. The same is true of games. Polo, high diving and pole vaulting, each present obvious difficulties and require special skills. They also create some degree of anxiety that must be controlled. There are a number of general skills that are required — horse riding, swimming, hitting balls, etc. The same is probably true of social skills (Argyle, 1969).

Social competence can be assessed by measures of effectiveness (e.g. goods sold by a salesperson), observation of role-playing, ratings in real-life situations, tests of social competence, and various kinds of self-rating. Self-reports show primarily how comfortable versus how anxious a person feels in a situation, which is not quite the same as his effectiveness (Argyle, 1981).

There are a number of studies of the situations which people find difficult or uncomfortable. The factors or clusters that are obtained vary with the range of situations studied and the statistical procedures used. The common areas of difficulty are as follows: (1) assertive situations (e.g. having to stand up for your rights); (2) performing in public; (3) conflict, dealing with hostile people; (4) intimate situations, especially with the opposite sex; (5) meeting strangers; (6) dealing with people in authority; (7) fear of disapproval, criticism, making mistakes, looking foolish (Richardson and Tasto, 1976; Stratton and Moore, 1977).

Furnham and Argyle (1981b) carried out cluster analyses of difficult situations with a number of different but mainly young populations, and the most common clusters were as shown in Table 4.

Our previous analysis can help us account for these difficulties and also suggest the skills that would solve the problem. We showed the goal structure for complaining, with various conflicts. The solution might be to avoid dominance and to increase the interpersonal rewards provided. Difficulties with strangers (i.e. making friends) and with the opposite sex

TABLE 4. *Difficult Social Situation Clusters (From Furnham and Argyle, 1981b)*

Assertiveness
  1.   Complaining to a neighbour about noisy disturbance
  9.   Taking an unsatisfactory article back to a shop

Intimacy
  2.   Taking a person of the opposite sex out for the first time
  4.   Visiting a doctor when unwell

Counselling
  6.   Going round to cheer up a depressed friend
  5.   Going to a close relative's funeral

Public performance
  8.   Give short speech
  7.   Being host at a large party
  3.   Going for a job interview

Parties etc
  13.   Going to a function with many people from a different culture
  14.   Attending a wedding

are very common among candidates for SST. The trouble is that they have failed to learn certain basic social skills, such as rewarding behaviours, non-verbal communication and sustaining conversation (Trower *et al.*, 1978).

There are theoretical grounds for expecting other forms of social difficulty that did not appear in the studies cited earlier, perhaps because they were not included in the lists of situations studied. *Unfamiliar situations* where the rules, goals or concepts are unknown is an example of these and include visiting a foreign country, joining a new organization, first visits to an encounter group or a psychoanalyst. *Complex situations* where a number of different people have to be attended to at once, several different goals pursued, and the like, were also excluded.

Situationally Focused SST

The analysis of situations makes it possible to carry out SST which is focused in those situations which are found most difficult. A group of clients is formed, who all have difficulties with, say, parties. The first step is to discuss the main features of the situation — goals, rules, etc., including the main sources of difficulty, and the social skills needed to deal with them. Sometimes this is done didactically, drawing partly on published findings, and partly on the experience of the trainers. In the course of the training session it is possible to arrive at an agreed list of the main goals, rules and repertoire, the main difficulties and how they can be tackled. This is then followed by role-playing of the situation, to train clients in these skills.

Situation-focused SST contains a strong educational component. Research on training for inter-cultural skills using the Culture Assimilator has shown that a purely instructional approach can be successful here (Brislin and Pederson, 1976). It is necessary to *understand* why situations are difficult, but it may also be necessary to master the skills needed for these situations.

Marital therapy can also profit from situational analysis. The first step is to discover the situations in which trouble occurs. There might be the husband coming home from work and not speaking to his wife, disagreements over finance, or repeated rows of a standard pattern. The next stage could be an analysis of the difficult situation, followed by suggestions of alternative ways of dealing with it. This could include treatment of SST for one partner; for example the "sleeping husband syndrome" can be treated by a token reward system, in which he gets a token for each conversation, and three tokens can be exhanged for various physical rewards (Jacobson and Martin, 1976).

Similar methods have been developed for dealing with alcoholism, Sanchez-Craig (1979) has developed a form of treatment based on situational analysis. Patients keep a diary and fill in questionnaires to identify the problem situations in which they drank too much. They then rehearse self-statements designed to inhibit drinking, and they consider the consequences of drinking in these situations. They decide on rules, e.g. "don't drink alone", "don't go pub-crawling with friends", "drink only in the company of people I enjoy". They also decide on rules about the amount of drinking, e.g. a glass of sherry before a meal and one glass of wine with it. No follow-up results are available yet for this form of treatment.

Obesity can be tackled by situational management; treatment consists of identifying and controlling the environmental stimuli that lead to overeating. This includes keeping food out of sight in the house, for example in opaque containers, and taking serving dishes off the table. A number of useful rules can be introduced, such as only eating at a designated eating place, not doing anything else while eating, such as watching TV, not buying "junk food", and only shopping on a full stomach. Part of the aim is to break behaviour sequences that lead to overeating, such as; "watching a long TV show — feeling bored — feeling sleepy — arguing with spouse — getting out of easy chair — entering the kitchen — opening the refrigerator — eating cheesecake — feeling guilty — wanting more cheesecake" (Ferguson, 1975). An experimental study of Chapman and Jeffrey (1980) showed that situational management produced an average weight loss of 4 pounds after eight weekly sessions; those who were in addition taught the setting of goals lost 7½ pounds.

Conclusions

Early research on social interaction was one of the origins of SST. However research in social psychology has subsequently opened up a number of new areas which are highly relevant to SST. One of these is the analysis of social situations, which is important since many SST clients need to master fairly specific situations. Situation-focused SST includes a strong cognitive element — to understand the rules, goals and roles of each situation. It also includes skill-learning — mastering the elements of the repertoire and the special sequences of social behaviour involved.

Conversations

If situations provide the context of social interaction, conversation provides the means, and is obviously of equal importance from the point of view of SST. Like situations, conversations are structured, in ways both isomorphic with and distinctive from the situations in which they take place. There is now overwhelming evidence of the sequential organisation of discourse, and current research is interested in the notion of a syntax or underlying "grammar" of discourse (Clarke, 1983). Good (Chapter 9) reviews some of the leading models of conversation analysis. In the remainder of this chapter we will highlight some features with more immediate practical implications for SST.

Social Skills and Conversation Sequences

We turn now to the performance of sequences of interaction by individuals, and to the nature of the social skills required. (cf. Clarke and Argyle, 1982).

Adjacency pairs, two-step sequences

Adjacency pairs play an important, though limited role in the generation of interaction sequences. It would be difficult to take part in a conversation without knowing that questions normally lead to answers. These adjacency pairs are not necessarily universal to all situations. For example, a question will only lead to a relevant answer if it is suitable in terms of the role relationship of those concerned and the situation. There is, however, a general rule that an utterance should be relevant to the one before it, and this is often taken into account in decoding utterance (Grice, 1975). There is also a rule that a speaker should take for granted, i.e. not repeat, knowledge that is shared by the listener, and he should add something new to it: "The new is nested in the old" (Rommetveit, 1974). When a social psychologist looks at adjacency pairs, it is evident that several different principles are involved: (a) The speech act types are related in terms of rules of discourse, whereby a question leads to an answer rather than a question, and a joke leads to a laugh rather than an apology — though a very bad joke could perhaps lead to a farewell or sympathy; (b) The meanings of successive utterances are linked — as described by Grice's maxim of relevance; (c) Some two-step links are based on principles of social behaviour, like reinforcement, response-matching or equilibrium maintenance, these are not rules, but are more like empirical generalisations or laws; (d) Some two-step links are based on the rules of particular situations, like auction sales, card games, committee meetings, etc.

However, we need to go beyond two-step sequences to explore some other principles of organisation.

Cycles of interaction

Some Markov chains suggest the existence of cycles of interaction, as when A usually leads to B, B to C, and C to A. Dawkins (1976) devised a way of locating such repeated cycles with his "fly music machine", in which audible tones coded individual units of behaviour, and repeating patterns and variations emerged as recognisable "melodies".

The selection interview sequence may contain more than one level of repeated cycle. There may be repeated cycles in which the interviewer deals with a series of topics — school career, college career, etc. And there may be repeated cycles within each of these topics consisting typically of an open-ended question and a number of follow-up questions.

Flanders (1970) found that there are repeated cycles of this kind in the classroom. He maintains that the skills of teaching consist partly of the ability to control these cycles, and to shift from one to another. Thus the teacher might start with a short cycle; Lecture (by teacher) — Question (by teacher) — Answer (by pupil). She could then shift to a longer cycle which included more pupil participation and initiative by stimulating and reinforcing such move on the part of pupils. However the actual questions, answers, etc. are of course not repeated, and it is misleading to describe lessons as repeated cycles. What is happening is a progressive build-up of ideas and information as the lesson proceeds. The cycles do not carry on indefinitely, and stop when the teacher has gone as far as she had planned with a particular topic.

There is another kind of repeated cycle in marital squabbles. Cronen (personal communication) found that many married couples had rows which took a standard form, and that this often involved a cycle of increasing antagonism or recrimination.

Episodes

Several investigations of behaviour in the classroom have recognised these repeated cycles as a natural larger unit of analysis. A still larger unit of analysis is the period of cycles which ends when some pedagogical goal has been attained. Smith *et al.* (1967) defined a "venture" as "a segment of discourse consisting of a set of utterances dealing with a single topic and having a single overarching content objective". While in a sense there are repeated cycles, there is also a continuous build-up in the complexity of the material discussed.

These two levels of larger units have been found in other social situations. We are concerned in this section with the larger units, which we shall call an "episode". In doctor-patient encounters, for example, it has been suggested that there are six episodes, in a fixed order, though some may be omitted:

1. Relating to the patient
2. Discussing the reason for the patient's attendance
3. Conducting a verbal or physical examination or both
4. Consideration of the patient's condition
5. Detailing treatment or further investigation
6. Terminating (Byrne and Long, 1976).

An episode may be defined as a segment of a social encounter which is characterised by some internal homogeneity, such as pursuit of a particular goal, a particular activity, topic, conversation or mood, a particular spatial location, or individuals taking particular roles. Episodes may be identified by the investigator, or a sample of judges may be used to determine the episode boundaries.

Repeated cycles and episodes are found in the play of young children. Repeated cycles are a feature of early mother-infant interaction, as in "peek-a-boo" games (Bruner, 1975). Episodes are found in the play of 3–5 year-olds, whose games consist of complete episodes of "going shopping", "going to the doctor", etc. (Garvey, 1977).

We have conducted studies of episode structure. The beginnings of a number of situations were briefly introduced, and subjects asked to write a sketch of how the situation might develop. They were then asked to parse their scripts into main episodes, and then to parse the episodes into sub-episodes. There was considerable agreement on the main episodes, and these were described in fewer words than the sub-episodes. There was considerable agreement on the phase sequence for each situation. For example when a wife calls on a new neighbour, it was agreed that the following episodes would occur: (a) greeting; (b) visitor admires house; (c) other provides coffee, etc.; (d) exchange of information about jobs, husbands, interests, etc.; (e) arrange to meet again and introduce husbands; (f) parting.

We suggest that social encounters usually have a five-episode structure:
1. Greeting
2. Establishing the relationship, clarifying roles
3. The task
4. Re-establishing the relationship
5. Parting.

The task, episode 3, in turn often has several episodes, which come in a fixed order, as in the doctor-patient case described above. What is the "task" in encounters which are primarily social occasions? It appears to be a combination of eating and drinking combined with exchange of information, though there may also be pseudo-tasks like dancing and playing games.

Rules

Conversations differ in their rules, depending on the situation. This is most obviously true of games, and of formal situations like rituals and ceremonies, but it is also true of less formal situations. Schank and Abelson (1977) have given an account of this in terms of the knowledge a person would need to have, or how a computer would need to be programmed to cope with common social situations, like going to a restaurant. It needs a certain body of knowledge to understand stories like the following.
1. John went to a restaurant. He ordered a hamburger. It was cold when the waitress brought it. He left her a very small tip.
2. Willa was hungry. She took out the Michelin guide.

Schank and Abelson say that we know the "scripts" for these situations, i.e. have organised knowledge about the situation.

Their central concept is the *script*: the restaurant script for example described the sequence of events at a restaurant for the four main episodes — enter, order, eat and exit. Scripts incorporate the kind of features we have been considering: *goals* and the relations between them; *plans* — knowledge of the sequence of elements which will realise the goals; *elements* of behaviour, e.g. order, eat, pay, leave, tip; roles, e.g. of waiter and diner; and *physical equipment* — menu, food. The *rules* are implicit in the scripts, especially role scripts. And there are "interpersonal themes" which are scripts for love, father-son interaction; etc. This scheme does not include the skills or difficulties of situations, but it does formalise much of the conceptual knowledge needed in a situation.

The way in which one utterance or other element would follow another depends on the properties of the situation. Thus the significance of "Can I pay the bill?" would be quite different and lead to different answers if addressed to (a) a waiter, (b) another diner, (c) a bank manager. The same applies to the sequence of events in a game of cricket; it is necessary to understand the game to know what will happen next after (a) six balls have been bowled, (b) ten men are out, (c) the ball reaches the boundary, etc.

Sequences also depend on the role-relations between people, as the paying the bill example showed. Victorian parents liked their children to be "seen and not heard", which is one kind of discourse (Fishman, 1972). Wittgenstein (1953) thought that the conversation between a builder and his assistant would consist solely of directions from the builder. With more enlightened skills of supervision, the builder would ask the assistant for his suggestions, listen to his ideas, and ask how he was getting on. The motives of the builder here are more complex — he wants to tell the assistant what to do, but he also wants to motivate him, make use of his skills and knowledge, and keep him happy (Argyle 1972).

The Motor Skills Model

We need a model of social behaviour to see how these principles operate in social interaction. One such is the social skills model. This model, described elsewhere in this Handbook, draws attention to a number of analogies between social performance and the performance of motor skills like driving a car. In each case the performer is pursuing certain goals, makes continuous responses to feedback, and emits hierarchically organised motor responses. The model has been heuristically very useful in drawing attention to the importance of feedback, and hence to gaze; it also suggests a number of different ways in which social performance can fail, and suggests the training procedures that may be effective, through analogy with motor skills training.

The model emphasises the motivation, goals and plans of interactors. It is postulated that every interactor is trying to achieve some goal, which may be linked to more basic motivational systems. Goals have sub-goals and patterns of response are directed towards goals and sub-goals, and have a hierarchical structure — large units of behaviour are composed of smaller ones, and at the lowest levels these are habitual and automatic.

The social skills model also emphasises feedback processes. Feedback requires perception, looking at and listening to the other person. It requires the ability to take the appropriate corrective action, referred to as "translation" in the model. And it depends on a number of two-step sequences of social behaviour whereby certain social acts have reliable effects on certain others. The operation of this model depends on the performer's knowledge of which moves on his part will produce certain responses in the other.

However there are several important differences between social behaviour and motor skills.

1. *Rules*. The moves which interactors may make are governed by rules as described above — they must respond properly to what has gone before. Similarly, rules govern the other's responses and can be used to influence his behaviour, e.g. questions lead to answers.
2. *Taking the role of the other*. It is important to perceive accurately the reactions of others. It is also necessary to perceive the perceptions of others, i.e. to take account of their point of view. This appears to be a cognitive ability which develops with age (Flavell, 1968), but which may fail to develop properly. Those who are able to do this have been found to be more effective at a number of social tasks, and more altruistic. Meldman (1967) found that psychiatric patients are more egocentric, i.e. talked about themselves more, than controls, and it has been our experience that socially unskilled patients have great difficulty in taking the role of the other.
3. *The independent initiative of others*. Other interactors are pursuing their goals, reacting to feedback and so on as well. We shall discuss below ways of analysing the resulting sequences of interaction. The social skills model fits best in cases of "asymmetrical contingency", i.e. interviewing, teaching, etc., where one person is effectively in charge. In such cases it is possible to compare the social skills used by effective and less effective performers.

Sequences in Different Situations

Some features of conversation sequences may be universal, for example people take turns to speak. In this section we shall explore the extent to which the differences can be explained in terms of the goals or other features of situations.

Reacting and Initiating

Jones and Gerard (1967) suggested that there are four different kinds of dyadic encounter, in terms of who is reacting to whom.

Pseudo-contingency. Here neither interactor is reacting to the other, except as regards timing. Examples are people acting in a play, or enacting a ritual, like greeting and saying farewell. Greetings and farewells are a little different, in that there is some variation and interaction. Such formal sequences are taken by Harré and Secord (1972) and Goffman (1971) as a model for other situations; our view is that they lack some of the key properties of other kinds of sequence. In pseudo-contingencies the sequence is totally predictable from the rules; there is no variation within the rules, except in style.

Reactive contingency. Here each person reacts to the last move by the other. Examples are rambling conversations. The sequence is limited by the universal rules of all social behaviour, and the particular rules of situation, which will allow only certain kinds of utterances, for example, and certain sequences. Thus a conversation in a pub is somewhat different from a conversation at a polite dinner party. In either case the sequence could be described, and to a limited extent predicted by the rules governing which sequences are allowable, as sensible sequences of social behaviour and the probabilities (in each situation) that the allowable move will be made.

Asymmetrical contingency. Here only one person has a plan, while the others are mainly reacting to what he does. Examples are teaching and interviewing. However the person being interviewed does have some initiative; he gives long or shorter replies, he may pursue his own plan, e.g. to impress the interviewer, and he may ask questions.

Mutual contingency. Here each interactor is pursuing his own goals, is reacting to the moves made by the other, and neither is in charge of the situation. Examples are negotiation and serious discussion. There are no sharp dividing lines between this kind of encounter and asymmetrical (where the subordinate person has some initiative) and reactive contingency (where neither person is pursuing a particular goal) (see Argyle, 1979).

Sequence and Social Competence

Social competence requires not only the skilled use of certain utterances, but also the ability to produce them at the right point in the sequence, and to produce a number of related utterances in sequence.

The analysis of skilled performance

The usual method of discovering the most effective social skills is to compare the performance of samples of effective and ineffective practitioners — defined in terms of some objective index of success. The difference may lie in the use of particular kinds of utterance: successful teachers make more use of praise, illustrative examples, developing pupils' ideas, and structuring, and they are warm and enthusiastic (Rosenshine, 1971).

A socially skilled person is someone who is able to realise his goals in social situations. A skilled teacher teaches his pupils more, a skilled therapist's patients recover, and so on. For such professional social skills the goals are fairly obvious, though there may be more than one goal present. In everyday situations it is less clear what the goals are. Graham, Argyle and Furnham (1980) asked samples of people to rate lists of goals for their relevance in different situations, and extracted factors of highest relevance. There were usually three such factors: (a) social acceptance, making friends, etc.; (b) eating drinking and other bodily needs; (c) task goals specific to the situation.

There is considerable skill in the construction of single utterances. Bates (1976) found that Italian children aged 2 would say the equivalent of "I want a sweet", but by 6 years could add "please", rephrase it as a request, without question intonation, as a conditional ("I would like"), use formal pronouns in addressing the other. Adult polite speech goes a long way beyond this, as in "If you're passing the letter box could you post this letter for me", for which it might be hard to provide grammatical rules. Being polite cannot entirely be reduced to the gammar of the sentences however; how polite is "Please could you tell me why you gave us such a terrible lecture this evening?" Giving orders or instructions needs skill: "Do X" does not get things done, in most settings, even when the speaker has the power to command. Orders are usually disguised as suggestions, or even questions.

There is an important non-verbal component in skilled utterances. The amount of warmth, directiveness, or questioning is shown by the tone of voice and pitch pattern. Elaboration and comments on the utterance are provided by special ways of delivering words or phrases — in special accents, volume, pitch, etc., which Fonagy (1971) has called "double-coding".

What is usually regarded as "tact" requires more social skill. Tact could be defined as the production of socially effective utterances in difficult situations; these are usually utterances which influence others in a desired way, without upsetting them or others present. How do you congratulate the winner without upsetting the loser? What do you say to a child who has just been expelled from school? This is clearly an area of social skills where the skill consists in finding the right verbal message; again it seems to have little to do with grammar. McPhail (1967) presented teenagers with written descriptions of a variety of difficult social situations and asked them what they would say. The younger ones opted for boldly directed, often aggressive, utterances, but the older ones preferred more skilled, indeed "tactful" remarks.

Similar considerations apply to professional social skills. A selection interviewer may want to assess candidates in terms of adjustment, authoritarianism, judgement, motivation, social competence, etc. He needs to ask the best questions to produce useful information in these areas. Asking "Are you neurotic?", for example, wouldn't be very useful. The usual approach is to explore the candidate's performance in past situations which called for judgement, hard work, stability, etc. Tactful skills are required to explore areas of failure, or to find out the truth where a candidate is concealing it. A skilled interviewer can control the length of the other's replies by using open-ended or closed questions, by the amount of head-nodding and other reinforcement given while the other answers, and by the use of interruptions.

Skilled sequences

Complex professional skills require the construction of quite elaborate sequences. Here are some of the points we have made about teaching:

1. A teacher should follow the statement of a principle by an example
2. He should be able to establish certain cycles of interaction, such as lecture — question — answer — comment
3. He should use a series of cycles to build on educational episodes, intended to teach a certain body of knowledge
4. He should be responsive to feedback, and modify his style of behaviour when necessary.

Sometimes the performer needs to make two related utterances, separated by the other's response to the first utterance. An example is the use of a follow-up question, in a social survey interview, as illustrated above in discussing the independent initiative of others. In persuasion the first move is to establish that the other person has some goal or need; the second step is to suggest a way of satisfying this need — in a way that is advantageous to the persuader. An ingratiator starts by flattering, agreeing with, or otherwise strengthening his rewards for the others; this is followed by a request for a favour (Jones, 1964).

Longer sequences are used in a selection interview. The sequence follows a plan made beforehand by the interviewer. The episode usually follows a chronological order, the sequence within episodes consists of an initial open-ended question and a number of more sharply focused follow-up questions. Making friends with someone involves a sequence over a longer time scale. There is a gradual increase in self-disclosure, carefully timed, and reciprocated by the other.

General Conclusion

Many people are lacking in social skills — they can't make friends, they suffer acute social anxiety, they can't cope with certain social situations. They are lacking in assertiveness, they can't establish relationships with the opposite sex, and so on. About 7–10% of the normal population are quite seriously handicapped in this way, 25–30% of neurotics and virtually all psychotics are socially inadequate (Argyle, 1980).

This may be due to failure of several kinds. Socially inadequate neurotic

patients are usually very poor conversationalists, and we have observed a number of characteristic types of failure:
1. Failure to make non-verbal responses and feedback (head-nods, smiles, "uh huh" noises) as a listener.
2. Failure to pursue any persistent plan, producing only passive responses.
3. Attempts to make conversation by producing unwanted information ("I went to Weston-super-Mare last year").
4. Failure to make a proactive move after replying to a question ("Where do you come from?", "Swansea . . ." — end of conversation).

In order to identify these forms of failure, it is necessary to understand the structure of normal conversation. It is then possible to train people in how to do it. The general procedure is instruction and demonstration followed by role-playing and play back of tape or videotape recordings. Sometimes special exercises are used. For example, lack of persistent planning can be tackled by practice at a simple skill, like interviewing, where the performer is in charge. He is asked to make notes beforehand, and plan the whole session. Failure to make non-verbal responses can be dealt with by playing back video-recordings (Trower, Bryant and Argyle, 1978).

People with social skills problems often have difficulty with particular social situations as we have seen — parties, dates, interviews, etc. This is often because they have failed to understand the situation, for example thinking that an interview is an occasion for vocational guidance, that a date is a kind of philosophy tutorial, or bidding less than the last person at an auction sale. In some cases they lack the special skills needed for the situation. The training consists partly of working through the main features of the situation with the trainee — the goals, conflicts between them, the main rules, the roles, the repertoire of verbal and non-verbal elements, the special difficulties, and the skills needed. This is followed by training in skills needed in the situation (Argyle *et al.*, 1981). Situations which have been the object of workshop training include parties, dating, assertiveness situations and making friends.

A great deal of detailed information has now accumulated about people's habits and practices in the organisation of interpersonal encounters. How far are these principles of sequence universal to all situations, or to all cultures? Some two-step links are very common, though not universal, like question-answer, request-comply or refuse, joke-laugh, etc. The four-step goal-directed sequence is probably universal, though the actual goals and sequences vary. Similarly the details of repeated cycles vary between situations. We suggested earlier that encounters have a basic five-episode structure, though episode three, the task, divides up into a series of sub-episodes specific to each task.

Some of these principles of sequence are clearly functional in relation to situational goals. In our study of doctor-patient interaction we found that one of the main goals of patients is "seek help, advice, reassurance", and that a common two-step sequence is "ask if disease is serious — reassure that illness/disease is not serious". Four-step goal-directed sequences are clearly functional. Cycles of the type "lecture — asks question — answer — comment" (in the classroom) are processes of social interaction which have been found to be successful, in this case in attaining the goal of teaching. Rules governing the order of events have presumably emerged, like other rules, because they help in goal attainment. Episodes are often ordered — e.g. the six doctor-patient episodes — because tasks have to be done in a particular order.

All in all the state of the art seems to be that interest in conversation structure is growing, and a number of recurring constructions have been found and described already, so that many conversation types can be viewed in terms of their middle-sized building blocks. What remains is to find the overall structuring principles that govern the global levels of conversation structure, if indeed such principles and such patterns exist.

References

Argyle, M. (1969) *Social interaction*. London: Methuen.

Argyle, M. (1972) *The social psychology of work*. London: Allen Lane.

Argyle, M. (1976) Personality and social behaviour. In: R. Harré (Ed.), *Personality*. Oxford: Blackwell.

Argyle, M. (1979) Sequences of social behaviour as a function of the situation. In: G. P. Ginsburg (Ed.), *Emerging strategies in social psychology*. London: Wiley.

Argyle, M. (1980) Interaction skills and social competence. *In* M. P. Feldman and J. Orford (eds.) *The Social Psychology of psychological problems*. Chichester: Wiley.

Argyle, M. (1981) Interaction skills and competence. In: M. P. Feldman and J. Orford (Eds.), *The social psychology of psychological problems*. Chichester: Wiley.

Argyle, M., Forgas, J. P., Ginsburg, G. and Campbell, A. (1981) Personality constructs in relation to situations. In: M. Argyle, A. Furnham and J. A. Graham (Eds.), *Social situations*. Cambridge: Cambridge University Press.

Argyle, M. and Furnham, A. (1982) The ecology of relationships: Choice of situations as a function of relationships. *British Journal of Social Psychology*, **21**, 259–262.

Argyle, M., Furnham, A. and Graham, J. A. (1981) *Social situations*. Cambridge: Cambridge University Press.

Argyle, M., Graham, J. A., Campbell, A. and White, P. (1979) The rules of different situations. *New Zealand Psychologist*, **8**, 13–22.

Argyle, M., Graham, J. A. and Kreckel, M. (1982) The structure of behavioural elements in social and work situations. In: M. R. Key (Ed.), *Nonverbal communication today: Current research*. The Hague: Mouton.

Avedon, E. M. (1971) The structural elements of games. In: E. M. Avedon and B. Sutton-Smith (Eds.), *The study of games*. New York: Wiley.

Bales, R. F. (1950) *Interaction process analysis*. Cambridge, Mass.: Addison-Wesley.

Bannister, D. and Mair, J. M. M. (1968) *The evaluation of personal constructs*. New York: Academic Press.

Barker, R. G. and Wright, H. F. (1954) *Midwest and its children: The psychological ecology of an American town*. Evanston, Illinois: Row, Peterson.

Bates, E. (1976) *Language and context: The acquisition of pragmatics.* New York: Academic Press.

Bell, R. T. (1976) *Sociolinguistics.* London: Batsford.

Benedict, R. (1935) *Patterns of culture.* London: Routledge and Kegan Paul.

Blurton-Jones, N. (Ed.) (1972) *Ethological studies of child behaviour.* London: Cambridge University Press.

Brislin, R. W. and Pederson, P. (1976) *Cross-cultural orientation programs.* New York: Gardner Press.

Brown, P. and Fraser, C. (1979) Speech as a marker of situations. In: K. Scherer and H. Giles (Eds.), *Social marks of speech.* Cambridge: Cambridge University Press.

Bruner, J. S. (1975) The ontogenesis of speech acts. *Journal of Child Language*, **2**, 1–19.

Byrne, P. S. and Long, B. E. L. (1976) *Doctors talking to patients.* London: HMSO.

Campbell, A. (1980) *Female delinquency in social context.* Oxford: Blackwell.

Chapman, S. L. and Jeffrey, D. B. (1980) Situational management, standard setting, and self-reward in a behavior modification weight loss program. *Journal of Consulting and Clinical Psychology*, **46**, 1588–9.

Clarke, D. D. (1983) *Language and action.* Oxford: Pergamon.

Clarke, D. D. and Argyle, M. (1982) Conversation sequences. In: C. Fraser and K. Scherer (Eds.), *Advances in the social psychology of language.* Cambridge: Cambridge University Press.

Dawkins, R. (1976) Hierarchical organisation: A candidate principle for ethology. In: P. P. G. Bateson and R. A. Hinde (Eds.), *Growing points in ethology.* Cambridge: Cambridge University Press.

Dittmar, M. (1976) *Sociolinguistics.* London: Arnold.

Duncan, S. (1969) Non-verbal communication. *Psychological Bulletin*, **72**, 118–137.

Endler, N. (1973) The person versus the situation — a pseudo issue? A response to Alker. *Journal of Personality*, **41**, 287–303.

Ferguson, J. M. (1975) *Learning to eat: Behavior modification for weight control.* New York: Hawthorn Books.

Fishman, J. A. (1972) *The sociology of language.* Rowley, Massachusetts: Newbury House.

Flanders, N. A. (1970) *Analyzing teaching behavior.* Reading Massachusetts: Addison-Wesley.

Flavell, J. H. (1968) *The development of role-taking and communication skills in children.* New York: Wiley.

Fonagy, I. (1971) Double coding in speech. *Semiotica*, **3**, 189–222.

Forgas, J. P., Argyle, M. and Ginsberg, G. P. (1980) Person perception as a function of the interaction episode: The fluctuating stucture of an academic group. *Journal of Social Psychology*, **109**, 207–222.

Freedman, B., Rosenthal, L., Donahue, C., Schlundt, D. and McFall, R. (1978) A social-behavioral analysis of skill deficits in delinquent and nondelinquent adolescent boys. *Journal of Consulting and Clinical Psychology*, **46**, 148–162.

Furnham, A. (1981) Personality and activity preference. *British Journal of Social Psychology*, **20**, 57–68.

Furnham, A. and Argyle, M. (Eds.) (1981a) *The psychology of social situations.* Oxford: Pergamon.

Furnham, A. and Argyle, M. (1981b) Responses of four groups to difficult social situations. In: M. Argyle, A. Furnham and J. A. Graham (Eds.), *Social situations.* Cambridge: Cambridge University Press.

Garvey, C. (1977) *Play.* London: Fontana and Open Books.

Goffman, E. (1971) *Relations in public.* London: Allen Lane.

Graham, J. A., Argyle, M., Clarke, D. D. and Maxwell, G. (1981) The sequential structure of social episodes. *Semiotica*, **35**, 1–27.

Graham, J. A., Argyle, M. and Furnham, A. (1980) The goal structure of situations. *European Journal of Social Psychology*, **10**, 345–366.

Grice, H. P. (1975) Logic and conversation. In: P. Cole and J. L. Morgan (eds). *Syntax and semantics, vol. 3. Speech acts.* New York: Academic Press.

Harré, R. and Secord, P. F. (1972) *The explanation of social behaviour.* Oxford: Blackwell.

Hersen, M. and Bellack, A. S. (1976) Social skills training for chronic psychiatric patients: A two year follow-up. *Comprehensive Psychiatry*, **17**, 559–580.
Jacobson, N. S. and Martin, B. (1976) Behavioral marriage therapy: Current status. *Psychological Bulletin*, **83**, 540–56.
Jones, E. E. (1964) *Ingratiation: A social psychological analysis*. New York: Appleton-Century-Crofts.
Jones, E. E. and Gerard, H. B. (1967) *Foundations of social psychology*. New York: Wiley.
Kelly, G. A. (1955) *The psychology of personal constructs*. New York: Norton.
Mann, J. W. (1963) Rivals of different rank. *Journal of Social Psychology*, **61**, 11–28.
Mann, L. (1969) The social psychology of waiting lines. *American Scientist*, **58**, 390–398.
Mann, R. D, Gibbard, G. S. and Hartman, J. J. (1967) *Interpersonal styles and group development*. New York: Wiley.
Mariotto, M. J. (1978) Interaction of person and situation effects for chronic mental patients: A two year follow-up. *Journal of Abnormal Psychology*, **87**, 676–679.
Mariotto, M. J. and Paul, G. F. (1975) Persons versus situations in the real-life functioning of chronically institutionalised mental patients. *Journal of Abnormal Psychology*, **85**, 483–493.
Marsh, P., Rosser, E. and Harré, R. (1978). *The rules of disorder*. London: Routledge & Kegan Paul.
McPhail, P. (1967) The development of social skill in adolescents. Unpublished MS cited in M. Argyle (1969) *Social interaction*. London: Methuen.
Meldman, M. J. (1976) Verbal behavior analysis of self-hyperattentionism. *Diseases of the Nervous System*, **28**, 469–473.
Moos, R. H. (1968) Situational analysis of a therapeutic community milieu. *Journal of Abnormal Psychology*, **83**, 49–61.
Murray, H. A. (1938) *Explorations in personality*. New York: Oxford University Press.
Price, R. H. and Bouffard, D. L. (1974) Behavioral appropriateness and situational constraint as dimensions of social behavior. *Journal of Personality and Social Psychology*, **30**, 579–586.
Rehm, L. P. and Marston, A. R. (1968) Reduction of social anxiety through modification of self-reinforcement: An instigation therapy technique. *Journal of Consulting and Clinical Psychology*, **32**, 565–574.
Richardson, F. C. and Tasto, D. L. (1976) Development and factor analysis of a social anxiety inventory. *Behavior Therapy*, **7**, 453–462.
Rommetveit, R. (1974) *On message structure: A conceptual framework for the study of language and communication*. Chichester: Wiley.
Rosenshine, B. (1971) *Teaching behaviours and student achievement*. Slough: NFER.
Rutter, D. R. (1976) Visual interaction in recently admitted and chronic long-stay schizophrenic patients. *British Journal of Social and Clinical Psychology*, **15**, 295–303.
Sanchez-Craig, M. (1979) Reappraisal therapy: A self-control strategy for abstinence and controlled drinking. Unpublished paper, Addiction Research Foundation, Toronto.
Schank, R. E. and Abelson, R. P. (1977) *Scripts, plans, goals and understanding*. Hillsdale, New Jersey: Erlbaum.
Sommer, R. (1969) *Personal space*. Englewood Cliffs, New Jersey: Prentice-Hall.
Smith, B. O., Meux, M. O., Coombs, J., Nuthall, G. A. and Precians, R. (1967) *Studies of the strategies of teaching*. Urbana, Illinois: Bureau of Educational Research, University of Illinois.
Stratton, T. T. and Moore, C. L. (1977) Application of the robust factor concept to the fear survey schedule. *Journal of Behavior Therapy and Experimental Psychiatry*, **8**, 229–35.
Tajfel, H. (1970) Experiments in intergroup discrimination. *Scientific American*, **223**, 96–102.
Trower, P., Bryant, B. and Argyle, M. (1978) *Social skills and mental health*. London: Methuen.
Twentyman, C. and McFall, R. (1975) Behavioral training in social skills in shy males. *Journal of Consulting and Clinical Psychology*, **43**. 384–395.
Wish, M. and Kaplan, S. J. (1977) Toward an implicit theory of interpersonal communication. *Sociometry*, **40**, 234–246.
Wittgenstein, L. (1953) *Philosophical investigations*. Oxford: Blackwell.

9

Social Skills and the Analysis of Conversation

DAVID GOOD

In the past two decades, there has been a significant growth of interest in the form and content of everyday conversation in a number of academic disciplines. This chapter will examine this growth focusing on two areas which have employed radically different research perspectives, that is Speech Act Theory and Conversational Analysis. The essence of this difference lies in the extent to which an investigator's own intuitions about the conversational world are exploited in the research process. For the former, they constitute the primary data in what is essentially the description of different utterance categories. For the latter, they are ignored as far as is practically possible with preference being given to inductive generalisations based on the scrutiny of a large body of actually recorded conversations.

Despite this difference, however, both approaches are compatible with the proposals of Trower and others (see Trower, 1984) on the directions that SST research should take. Amongst other things, they argue for a shift of emphasis from the quantitative parametric analysis of social skills to analyses that examine the structure and organisation of such skills. That is, a shift to an analytic focus which this work already employs.

This focus means that many parts of the research literature in this area will not be discussed. Good overviews of these areas can, however, be found in Coulthard (1977), Hudson (1980), Brown and Yule (1983), and Levinson (1983). Coulthard (1984) has also reviewed the work of the English Language Research group at Birmingham University with the expressed needs of SST in mind.

Speech Act Theory

The Background

Speech Act Theory dates to Austin's analysis of sentences such as (1)–(4) to which his philosophical contemporaries paid little attention because they were not of interest to truth based theories of meaning (see Austin, 1962). Initially, such sentences would not appear to be of interest to any kind of social scientist either, but the extension of Austin's account to all utterances has revealed a large number of important issues relevant to the understanding of utterance production and comprehension.

(1)   I bet you sixpence it will rain tomorrow.
(2)   I name this ship the Queen Elizabeth the Second.
(3)   I give and bequeath my watch to my brother.
(4)   I find him not guilty.

His first observation was that these sentences acquire their meaning and significance not by referring to states of affairs, but by actually bringing them into being. For example, the speaker of (1) is not just referring to some bet or other, but is *creating* a bet through the act of uttering (1). Likewise in uttering (2), the launcher produces a state of affairs in which that Cunard liner could be referred to as the Queen Elizabeth the Second, and the occasion of its naming could be referred to as a launching.[1] As a consequence Austin claimed that to understand sentences such as (1)–(4) it is necessary to understand how they function as these kinds of social linguistic acts, or speech acts as they have become known, with these kinds of institutional or conventional consequences.

Having established his argument for cases like (1)–(4), he then went on to claim that in fact all utterances, except perhaps recitations, screams of pain, and so on are used as speech acts of one sort or another in much the same way as (1)–(4). That is, language is not simply used in the uttering of true or false sentences, it is also used in the *making* of events, as in the making of requests, promises, compliments and apologies, the issuing of warnings, the raising of questions and complaints, and so on. Consequently, analysing language entails analysing the social conduct and conventions which these various acts represent. In his own analysis, Austin proposed that most utterances accomplish three basic kinds of act (to be defined below) — the locutionary, the illocutionary, and the perlocutionary; and it is the second of these which has been of greatest interest in subsequent work in the social sciences.

In Austin's view, an illocutionary act is the linguistic act which is accomplished *in* saying something, and it reflects the force with which something is said. To know which illocutionary act an utterance is achieving, it is necessary to know how an utterance is being used. In some cases it seems fairly straightforward which illocutionary act is being accomplished as for example in (1), which is a bet, but in some cases it is not, as in (5) below, which can be heard as a threat in the appropriate circumstances, as a promise in others, as a warning in yet others, and so on.

[1]In other words, these are not only verbal utterances, but social *acts* which literally do things, create new events, and do not simply refer to other events.

(5)   I'll be there.

Simply defining an illocutionary act as the way a sentence is being used is inadequate though, because utterances are used in many ways other than performing illocutionary acts. However, the important feature of illocutionary acts is their conventional nature, and Austin pointed out that this is reflected in the availability of explicit conventional forms for their accomplishment. For example, in uttering (6) I might be said to be using the sentence to urge you to sell your stocks and shares, and also to be using it to persuade you to do so. However, whereas the former use can be made explicit as in (7), the latter cannot, as is shown by (8). Therefore persuading is not an illocutionary act.

(6)   Sell now!

(7)   I urge you to sell your shares.

(8)   I persuade you to sell your shares.

Persuading is nevertheless a kind of linguistic and social act, but in contrast to an illocution it is the act which is achieved *by* the saying of something.[2] This is what Austin referred to as a perlocution. It is essentially defined by the effects or consequences of an utterance, whether these effects are intended by the speaker or not. For example, in saying (6) I may well intend and achieve the outcome proposed by (8), but unlike the illocutionary component it cannot be guaranteed in the same way. It is also possible that I will convince you not to sell, that I am an idiot who does not know the stock market, that I am a deceitful character who is persuading you to sell unwisely so that I might profit, and many other things. Consequently, I would have accomplished the perlocutionary acts of convincing you not to sell, of convincing you that I am an idiot, etc.

All illocutionary act cannot be performed in the absence of some content. If one is going to make a request, for example, it has to be a request for something. Examples (9)–(12) can all be heard as having the illocutionary force of a request, but they are requests to do different things, and they are therefore different speech acts. This distinction between an illocutionary act and the associated content in any particular speech act is usually represented in the general form of (13). F is referred to as an illocutionary force indicating device or IFID, and p is a propositional content. In the case of (9), the corresponding representation will be something like (14).

(9)   Will you get me a clean towel?

(10)   Can I have three white coffees?

(11)   Are there any copies of the *Guardian* left?

(12)   Have you got a light?

(13)   F(p)

---

[2] i.e. the consequences, which are by no means entirely predictable.

(14) REQUEST (Hearer to give speaker a clean towel).

Since Austin's day a variety of issues have been pursued in the speech act literature, but the one which will probably be of greatest use to SST lies at the very heart of speech act theory. This is the question of how any member of a speech community knows which speech act an utterance is achieving. In terms of psychological processes, this is the problem of how the surface form of an utterance is mapped on to an underlying form which has the characteristics of (13). This mapping problem has its most interesting reflexes for those utterances known as indirect speech acts.

Indirect Speech Acts (ISA)

Initially, a clear appreciation that any problem exists with ISAs is often hard to obtain, since many of the utterances so classified, and discussed at length in the literature, can seem quite unambiguous as to their function. For example, (15)–(19) are described as indirect requests, yet it seems hard to imagine that meal-time speakers of these sentences could possibly intend anything else than a request for the hearer to pass the salt to the speaker.

(15) Can you pass me the salt?
(16) Is there any salt?
(17) Can you reach the salt?
(18) Is the salt near you?
(19) Can I have the salt?

It is precisely this certainty, though, which is the object of interest since it is clear, as Austin himself argued, that there are very few, if any, form-function correspondences between sentences and the illocutionary acts they can achieve. That is, there are rarely any simple surface markers in an utterance which undeniably mark an utterance as achieving a particular speech act.[3] Therefore, the sense of certainty must arise from an inference based on the information provided by the utterance, and our understanding of the social situation in which that utterance has occurred. If there are only a very limited number of possible interpretations and contexts for an utterance, as in (15)–(19), this inference may seem relatively trivial, but for other utterances, as we shall see, this is not so. Trivial or not though, this inferential capacity is critical for both producing and interpreting socially appropriate utterances, and thus skilled social performances.

[3]For this reason the term Indirect Speech Act might almost seem a misnomer because if these correspondences do not exist, then the contrasting Direct Speech Act is quite possibly undefinable. This problem has yet to be solved satisfactorily, and at present the definition hinges upon the intuition that cases like (15)–(19) are questions before they are anything else, and that therefore a request reading must be secondary or indirect.

The study of ISA began in linguistics with the work of Gordon and Lakoff (1971) and Heringer (1972), and subsequently the topic interested sociolinguists (e.g. Labov, 1972), psychologists (e.g. Clark and Lucy, 1975) and Artificial Intelligence researchers (e.g. Power, 1979). Much of this literature has restricted itself to the study of indirect requests, and therefore any claims about the full range of illocutionary acts must be treated with caution. Nevertheless, requests provide an interesting exploration of the issue, and their treatment makes important suggestions for how other illocutionary acts might be handled.

The basis of this work lies in Austin's remarks on the many ways an illocutionary act can fail, or, in his terms, be infelicitous. For example, in naming a ship, I may utter the words "I name this ship the Joe Stalin" and smash a bottle of champagne on the bows of some ship, but if I am not the official launcher, or I have incorrectly named it, or I have got the wrong ship then, it will not be said to have been named or launched. Similarly, an apology will not be taken as genuine unless it is believed that the speaker is contrite, a promise will not be believed unless the speaker is able to fulfil it, a request will not be recognised unless the hearer believes the speaker desires the particular outcome, and so on. These remarks were elaborated by Searle (1969) into what are now known as the felicity conditions for an illocutionary act. Essentially, the felicity conditions for an illocutionary act specify the states of affairs which have to obtain if that act is to be successfully performed. His account of these conditions for requests is given in (20), from Searle (1969) (p. 66).

(20) Propositional Content   Future act A of H.

    Preparatory   1.   H is able to do A. S believes H is able to do A.
                       2.   It is not obvious to both H and S that H will do A in the normal course of events of his own accord.

    Sincerity   S wants H to do A.

    Essential   Counts as an attempt to get H to do A.

In this form, these conditions appear distant from actual conversation, but they capture the essential contextual requirements which the speaker and hearer must understand to be satisfied if a request is to go through. If they are not satisfied, a request will fail. For example, if I utter (21) under most normal circumstances, it is not heard as a possible request because most ordinary hearers are not able to climb the Empire State Building, and therefore part 1 of the preparatory condition fails. However, if the addressee is Superman, and (21) follows (22) then the condition can be satisfied, and a request can be heard. More mundanely, if I utter any of (15)–(19) when the hearer is already passing the salt, then the utterance sounds more like a complaint than a request.

(21) Can you climb the Empire State Building?
(22) Spiderman, I'd like you to climb the Chrysler Building and Wonder Woman, could you climb the World Trade Towers, and Superman, —

These conditions are interesting in their own right as observations on our knowledge of conversational situations, but their importance for the analysis of ISA lies in the way they relate to those utterances which can serve as an indirect request.

There are several versions of this relationship, but its essential form is given by Forman (1974) in what he refers to as "The Speaker Knows Best Principle". This is that to achieve a request a speaker may question a hearer based felicity condition or assert a hearer based one. For example, (23) can work as a request because it questions the hearer based first part of preparatory condition, but the corresponding assertion (24) can not. Generally, it can be shown that all utterances which can be linked to the felicity conditions in this way can function as requests, and those which cannot be so linked cannot so function (see Searle, 1975, for a number of examples).

(23) Can you give me a light?
(24) You can give me a light.

The recognition of this relationship has lead a number of writers (e.g. Clark, 1978; Searle, 1975) to argue that the felicity conditions are an important part of the process whereby hearers recognise the illocutionary intent of an utterance. Essentially, they propose that on hearing an utterance, the hearer will attempt to see if its literal surface meaning simply describes its illocutionary intent. So, for example, on hearing (23) the hearer will first estimate if the speaker is simply attempting to discover something about the hearer's light-giving abilties. If, as a result of this estimation the hearer concludes that this is not the speaker's prime interest, there will then be an attempt to discern the likely intent by relating this surface meaning to the felicity conditions for various different kinds of speech act. In (23), the utterance is a question about the hearer's abilities, and can therefore be related to a request via the preparatory condition. Consequently, it is inferred that a request is intended, and more specifically that the utterance is a request for a light.

This account can be plausibly extended to most if not all utterances which function as requests, thereby supporting the basic claim that the felicity conditions provide the route for illocutionary uptake. These extensions are not unproblematic, but the resolution of the difficulties encountered offers a recasting of the felicity conditions which provides some interesting links to other areas of sociolinguistic and psychological research.

The first problem concerns the relationship between an utterance, and the felicity condition to which it supposedly corresponds. For many utterances, e.g. (15), (17) and (19), this is a relatively simple matter. They link to the preparatory condition for a request, and the "Can you", in being about ability, specifies how the link is made. However, many utterances do not address these conditions so directly, and they are, so to speak, indirect ISAs. For example, many requests deal with the preconditions for the ability to fulfil the request rather than mentioning the ability directly. Examples (16) and (18) are of this type, and while the link to the preparatory condition is intuitively simple, it is not provided by the utterance in the same way as it is in (15), (17) and (19). It has to be provided by the hearer's understanding of the utterance in the particular context, and the felicity conditions as they stand say nothing about the provision.

The second relates to the first in that it is also about the link from utterance to felicity condition. All the felicity conditions contain direct reference to the propositional content condition. Therefore, which condition is being addressed can only be ascertained when a value for the propositional content condition (which is essentially the value of "p" as in (13) for the indirect act) has been established. In many cases, e.g. (9) and (15), this value is directly given in the surface form of the utterance. In many others, e.g. (16) and (17), it is not. Consequently, the hearer must be able to produce at least a candidate value for "p" before proceeding to infer the illocutionary force of an utterance. Again this is an ability extra to the felicity conditions as they currently stand.

A third and final problem which is not simply raised by these extensions concerns the felicity conditions themselves. They represent observations on our intuitions as to successful and unsuccessful requests, but by themselves they do not constitute an explanation of those observations. One might validly ask, why those conditions and not others, and what is their relationship to one another?

The solution to these problems probably lies in proposals which have their origins in computational studies of natural language comprehension. The suggestion there is that a key element in the comprehension of requests and many other utterances, is our ability to construct plans of action for achieving certain goals, and to recognise such plans and goals in the actions of other people (Allen, 1983; Schmidt, Sridharan and Goodson, 1978). These plan construction abilities have received a great deal of attention in the Artificial Intelligence literature, and there are now some well understood principles for the creation of appropriate algorithms.

Under this view, most of the felicity conditions are recast as elements of plans for achieving particular goals. The structural principles of these plans describes the relationship between the felicity conditions, and provides a principled route for their expansion as and when the conditions demand.

For example, any plan construction algorithm must include principles for checking that various preconditions for action are satisfied. In turn, these preconditions will presume the satisfaction of other preconditions, and so on. If somebody is to pass salt to me at the dinner table, then they must be able to do so, and in turn that ability will have various sub-components such as the nearness of the salt, their ability to reach it, and the like. This is what the preparatory condition is about, but in these terms there is a principled basis for its expansion, and thus a way of dealing with those utterances which were nominated as indirect ISAs.

This recasting resolves the first and third of the problems mentioned above, but the second one remains although in a different form. The propositional content becomes a statement of the goal to which the plan is oriented, and although there is a structured basis for the relationship between this goal and the elements of the plan, as the felicity conditions have become, inferring the nature of the goal is still a problem. The difficulty arises because any state of the world can effectively be a relevant precondition to the accomplishment of a very large number of different goals. To overcome this problem, one must presume that conversational-ists have the ability to speculate on the likely goals of their own conversational partners in any particular context including, of course, the content of the utterance which may contain more or less direct reference to a particular goal. The structured relationship between plan and goal can then be used to assess the relationship between these speculations and the utterance under consideration.

Implications for SST

If these claims are correct, then the implications for SST are straight-forward. In understanding requests, the listener must have a knowledge of the goals which individuals are likely to pursue in different settings, and the ability to relate those goals to utterances via the rationale of plan construction procedures. It is also conceivable that this view can be extended to other types of illocutionary act, particularly those utterances which are offered with the intention of achieving particular outcomes. For example, invitations, warnings, promises, threats, apologies, and the near relatives of requests such as orders and commands are all uttered with the aim of achieving particular states of affairs, and it is quite conceivable that hearers will be able to speculate on the nature of these in much the same way.

Others, though, are more problematic as has often been pointed out, because they do not seemingly result in any subsequent physical or social actions. For example, statements which describe the world, and which are not offered as an indirect way of doing something else come into this category. This view, however, pursues an impoverished conception of what the consequences of an utterance might be, and presumes that speakers will say things without a purpose. There is not room here to explore fully what a richer conception might look like, but it is clear that the description of some state of affairs will at least be offered with the intent of persuading the hearer to believe that the speaker believes that state to be so, and quite possibly with the intent of getting the hearer to believe it to be so also.

Support for this extension, and the general view on the importance of goal perception comes from an analysis by Labov and Fanshel (1977) of a fifteen minute psychotherapy session with an anorexic teenager. They suggest that a critical factor holding an interaction together is the sequential links between the actions which utterances achieve by appealing to the underlying tensions and beliefs in a relationship. They describe the achievement of these actions in a manner not too dissimilar to that on ISAs discussed above. Significantly, though, they draw attention to the fact that any utterance may well involve the pursuit of more than one goal, and that such goals should be thought of in terms of individuals simply raising matters which are central to the relationship between speaker and hearer. Essentially, the goal in raising an issue is the affirmation and maintenance of the relationship

The very restricted focus, which Labov and Fanshel necessarily adopted due to the detail of their analysis, has meant that it is difficult to generalise beyond their particular findings in the same way as researchers have been able to do for work on ISAs. Nevertheless, their work suggests that this goal based analysis does hold promise, and in so doing it is in accord with a movement within some branches of social psychology to this conception of social action, (see, for example, von Cranach, 1982). Therefore, this conception of utterance interpretation might be sensibly extended within an SST framework in at least an experimental fashion.

In the case of the production of requests, the speaker will rely on the mutual knowledge which speakers and hearers have as to how other persons view the world (see Smith, 1982), and in particular how a given hearer will understand an utterance in this fashion to constrain the form any request will take. However, these constraints will not specify a single formulation for an utterance. Instead, they characterise the almost embarrassingly large number of ways a request can be made. For example, (15)–(19) are just a few of the ways one can accomplish the minor goal of getting some salt at the dinner table, and one can add to this list almost *ad nauseam*. (25)–(30) are some suggestions, and seemingly the more significant the goal and the more onerous the imposition contained in the request, the greater the range of ways of saying it there are.

(25) Would you mind passing me the salt?
(26) Could I have the salt?

(27) I don't suppose you could pass the salt could you?
(28) Sorry to trouble you, but I need some salt.
(29) I say, is the salt down your end of the table?
(30) Give me the salt, will you?

Few writers have seriously contemplated this issue, so few suggestions as to how it is resolved are available, but clearly the choice of an appropriate form by the speaker is an important social skill. The most likely reason for the range of circumlocutions available for saying essentially the same thing is politeness. (30) sounds far more abrupt than (25) particularly if one removes the tag question from the end. Specifying what is meant by politeness is far from easy though, but obviously the ability to be appropriately polite is critical because it can mean the difference between social success and social death. As Gumperz (1982) has shown, many cases of inter-ethnic communication failure can be directly attributed to the adoption of the wrong conventions for deferential social behaviour, even though the parties to the communication are initially well-intentioned. A point which demonstrates that in fact this issue is of significance to the hearer also. Also, although the machinery discussed above would ultimately enable the hearer to recognise the speaker's goal, it says nothing about the additional inferences the hearer may draw given the particular form of expression chosen.

The most promising account to emerge so far on how politeness constraints operate in utterance construction is to be found in the work of Brown and Levinson (1978). Their work is only loosely tied to speech act theory, but since it addresses the issue at hand, and since it needs to presume capacities of the type which have been discussed so far it is appropriate to conclude this section with a brief summary of it.[4]

Politeness

Brown and Levinson's account of politeness proposes that individual speakers and hearers are rational beings in pursuit of well-identified social and personal goals, and that an essential part of those pursuits is the maintenance of "face".[5] Their idea of face is Goffmanesque in character (Goffman, 1955), and is not too dissimilar to the common use of the term in expressions such as "losing face" to denote an embarrassment or humiliation. This notion of face has two components. The first is what they call negative face which represents the individual's desire to remain

---

[4]This is a very brief outline of a lengthy and detailed account, and inevitably certain important details have been omitted. Consequently, interested readers are urged to consult the original.
[5]Nothing much should be hung on their assumption of rationality from the SST point of view, since their suggestions will be of value even if it is only the case that members of the speech community presume rationality in the actions of most other people.

unimpeded in his or her actions. The second, which is "positive face", represents the individual's wish or need to be approved of in certain ways, principally through having other persons concur on the desirability of his or her desires.

These notions are obviously very simple, and not particularly novel. Furthermore, one might argue that there are many cases where negative and positive face do not hold. Not everyone wishes to remain unimpeded all the time, nor is it always the case that everyone wishes their desires to be desirable to others, but this does not matter for their account. What they are proposing is a model of human activity to which members of a speech community will orient while assuming that others will do likewise. Also, the simplicity is deceptive. In attempting to pursue specific goals while paying due regard to positive and negative face, a number of conflicts result, and the procedures for dealing with these through the chosen form of expression are anything but simple.

Consider, for example, the case where A wants B to come to dinner at A's new house. In satisfying this desire, A will effectively be dictating B's actions on the evening in question, and will thus threaten B's negative face. This in itself will not matter to A, but A knows that B could retaliate by flatly refusing to come, a move which would threaten A's positive face because it would mark A's desired goal as undesirable to B. Furthermore, such retaliation would be the simplest way for B to neutralise this threat, and therefore its use would be motivated by more than a desire for retribution. Consequently, A will attempt to couch the invitation in a way which will avoid offending B's face to the extent that B will retaliate: (31) is one way in which A may do this. The invitation, which constitutes in Brown and Levinson's terms the face threatening act (FTA) is not directly stated. Instead A asks about the likelihood of B wanting to come to dinner on a specific date, thereby attending to B's negative face wants because the choice of actions is left to B. This form also allows B a way of declining the invitation without offending A's positive face, because B can simply declare that to go would be delightful, but that circumstances do not permit.

(31) Would you like to come to dinner next Friday.

This example is only one of the many ways in which this invitation could have been expressed while paying attention to politeness considerations. Brown and Levinson have described the range of strategies which can be used to pursue this or any FTA in the scheme given in Figure 1.

Essentially, the scheme represents a set of options available to a speaker who wishes to express an FTA. The primary option is between speaking and remaining silent. Clearly, keeping quiet has no linguistic reflexes of any sort, and they do not give it further consideration. Having made the decision to speak, the speaker must then choose between being "off

```
Desire to do something
which constitutes a FTA ======== Don't do it.
          :
          :
          :
      Do it ================== Off record.
          :
          :
          :
   On record ================ Without redressive
          :                   action, baldly.
          :
          :
With redressive action ========= Positive politeness.
          :
          :
          :==================== Negative politeness.
```

FIG 1. Possible Strategies for Doing FTAs.

record" and "on record". The former is the most indirect means which a speaker can employ, and involves constructing an utterance so that more than one intention might be reasonably attributed to the speaker. For example, if I utter (32), and I am a final year undergraduate saying it to my tutor who has just emerged from an examiners' meeting, then I might be interpreted as seeking information about my exam result, or as simply expressing my state of mind for the purpose of passing the time of day. If the tutor takes it to be a request for information, and is offended, I can simply claim the alternative reading to be my true intention, and thereby hopefully defuse the situation.

(32) I'd really love to know what was said in there.

There are many ways in which such utterances might be constructed, and there are many alternatives to (32) in such a context. It is also true that different contexts could easily lead to (32) being quite unambiguous. For example, if it was produced in a context where there was a deep and conspiratorial relationship between myself and the tutor, and there was a mutual expectation that I would receive a report of the meeting, then (32) could function as a straightforward "on-record" request for information.

In such a context, (32) would be only one of many "on-record" ways of making this request. Brown and Levinson divide these "on-record" strategies into three types. The first involves no attention to politeness considerations, and is what they term "baldly, on-record". The corresponding version of (32) under this strategy would be (33) where no consideration is given to the tutor's negative face as it straightforwardly expresses the intention to dictate one of their future actions.

(33) O.K. what's my result?

The second and third involve "redressive action" i.e. the speaker pays attention to the face wants of the hearer by the use of positive or negative politeness. The former caters to the hearer's positive face and can be accomplished in a variety of ways. Typically, positive politeness results in the assertion of the common interests of the speaker and hearer, so that their identification with one another is confirmed, or less commonly in the speaker fulfilling some want of the hearer by offering either social or material goods. Mutual identification can be accomplished through a number of tactics ranging from the use of in-group jargon to specifying the co-operative nature of their joint activities. So, for example, one positive politeness variant of (33) might be (34) where the exam result is specified as being a joint accomplishment, and in a way which foregrounds the importance of the hearer's tutoring.

(34) Well, did I benefit from your excellent coaching?

Negative politeness can also be offered in a wide variety of different ways, but typically one of two tactics is adopted. The first is ostensibly to leave the choice of action open as in (31) or (32) in the unambiguous condition. The second is overtly to recognise the threat to the hearer's negative face, and in so doing account for the affront by reference to some fault on the speaker's part for which an apology is offered, e.g. (35).

(35) I'm sorry for being so rude, but I can't wait any longer. How did I do?

Each of these strategies will have different costs and benefits for the speaker who uses them.[6] Expressing something "baldly without redressive action" will be maximally efficient as a communication, but doing so can cause great offence. Conversely, going "off-record" is least likely to cause an affront, but the speaker runs the risk of being misunderstood. Therefore, choosing between these alternatives is an important matter, and Brown and Levinson argue that the choice is made by consideration of three factors. These are the social distance (D) between the speaker and hearer, the power relationship (P) between them, and the rating of the demand (R) placed upon the hearer. None of these factors is an absolute, and they will vary from society to society. They also subsume many different issues, but clearly these notional headings represent the more

---

[6]Neither this remark, nor any of the preceding discussion should be interpreted as suggesting that there is only one polite utterance on any occasion. The choice a speaker makes between the various options is not simply contingent upon the various aspects of the context such as the social distance between the participants etc. In part the choice will denote the speaker's interpretation of that context, and will contribute towards that speaker's social persona.

important dimensions by which the degree of face threat offered by any utterance will be assessed. For example, if I am close to someone who is my equal i.e. a low value of D and a zero value for P, and I want them to do some moderately onerous task such as collecting some groceries for me, I do not need to do much work to ameliorate the threat to their negative face, and can therefore utter (36), which is a comparatively straightforward and efficient request. However, if the hearer is some prestigous neighbour who I do not know very well i.e. high D, high P, then (37) will be more appropriate.

(36)   Could you do the shopping?

(37)   I'm sorry to trouble you, but would you mind if I asked you to pick up a couple of things for me next time you're at the shops?

This brief summary does not do full justice to Brown and Levinson's account, but it is clear that it has potential for SST. It points out a number of features which are relevant to the choice of utterance, and provides a basis for a general understanding of why individuals may react differently to different ways of achieving the same conversational goal. It is also highly compatible with the machinery discussed above, and the suggestions it makes.

Conversational Analysis

Background

The bulk of the work discussed in the last section is predicated on the intuitions of the analyst as to the interpretation of specially constructed examples. The conclusions it offers place a heavy emphasis on the role of the individual's social knowledge and rational powers. In contrast, work in the tradition commonly referred to as Conversational Analysis (CA) has been based upon the detailed scrutiny of large corpora, and the use of the investigator's intuitions is reduced to the absolute minimum. As a result, CA offers generalisations on the recurring patterns in conversation, and a detailed description of the features which characterise those patterns.

Its origins lie in the Ethnomethodological tradition in Sociology, and is most popularly known for the work on turn-taking systems in conversation by Sacks, Schegloff and Jefferson (1974). It has, however, covered a much wider area of conversation (see, for example, the collections in Atkinson and Heritage, 1985; Psathas, 1979; and Schenkein, 1978), and the techniques have recently been used on video records, thereby allowing the various aspects of non-vocal communication to be analysed in the same way, (see, for example, Goodwin, 1981).

Apart from turn-taking, CA workers have examined various aspects of the sequential structure of conversation such as question-answer, compliment, complaint and request sequences; how preferred next turns can be established by the current speaker, and how the next speaker will mark his or her utterance as being in accord or not with that preference; how the turn-taking system may be suspended when a speaker wishes to take a lengthy turn to tell a joke, story or something similar; how conversations are opened and closed; how laughter is invited and organised; how conversational breakdowns are repaired; how reference is made to other persons; how jokes are told and puns made; and many other facets of conversation.

All the different issues which this literature has touched upon are of potential value to SST because they concern the full content of a skilled social performance. However, realising that potential may not be a simple matter. In the case of Speech Act Theory, the account is for the greater part predicated upon an analysis of the terms which conversationalists use to describe utterances. Consequently, in the extent to which the trainee's understanding of these terms is sound, SST can proceed using this descriptive framework as the medium of exchange. CA does not deal with this level of abstraction because it is ultimately concerned with the minutiae of conversation which make such abstractions possible. Indeed, its practitioners would argue that that kind of abstraction is at best premature and unprincipled because it is not based on such a concern. The consequence of this concern, though, is that in its undigested form, the trainer may feel that this work obscures the interactional wood with its concern for particular conversational trees. An examination of an example of this work will demonstrate why this might be thought to be so, and in turn will enable a consideration of its significance for SST.

Hesitancy

At different times, the levels of hesitancy and pausing in an individual's speech have attracted the attention of various sorts of psychologists. Clinicians have been interested in these levels as an index of anxiety, social psychologists have examined their variation over time as a function of conversationalists' attitudes to one another, and psycholinguists have exploited them as indices of cognitive processing. Apart from one or two writers, (see, for example, Butterworth, 1980) the bulk of this literature has been insensitive to the fact that individual pauses can have an interactional significance which is ignored by their incorporation into aggregated statistics. It is precisely such significances, however, which the techniques of CA reveal by their very attention to issues of structure and pattern.

Consider, for example, (38) a naturally occurring example taken from Levinson (1983).

(38) C: . . . is it — it's all right now — you don't want me to put it out?

R: E::r (1.5) well on the whole I wouldn't bother because er huhuh (2.0) well I mean what — what (0.5) would it involve putting it out? (p. 335).

In this, R has been complaining that C's fire in the apartment below has filled R's apartment with smoke. C's first turn uses the statement "you don't want me to put it out" with a final rising intonation, to ask whether or not R wants the fire extinguished. R then replies, and this is the turn of interest.

If the pauses in this (indicated by the figures in brackets which are in seconds) were considered, for example, from a psycholinguistic perspective, they would be taken to represent the cognitive demands of planning the utterance. Simply put, producing an utterance places a load on the individual's processing capacity, and when this load becomes excessive, the actual process of speaking is interrupted, and silence, and, under some views much filler material as well e.g. "uhm", "er", "well", "well I mean", and the like results, e.g. Beattie (1980). Thus, during the latter part of R's turn, i.e. after "because", R is under a heavy cognitive load as shown by the presence of much pausing and filler material.

From a CA perspective, however, the example would be analysed somewhat differently. Various writers, but most particularly Pomerantz (1985), have shown that there are aspects of utterance form which are contingent upon whether or not the current speaker is conforming to, or deviating from, the preferred content of his or her utterance as indicated by the previous speaker. An example of where this preference constraint operates is when one party offers an assessment of some state of affairs as in (39) and (40). On hearing (39) one would have the sense that the speaker would prefer the next speaker to agree with the assessment offered, and in (40) that disagreement would be preferred.

(39) I think your mother is really nice.

(40) I must be the world's biggest fool.

It is not the case though, that next speakers always conform to these preferences, and Pomerantz has demonstrated that when the dispreferred next turn is produced, it will be marked as such by the speaker. This marking will vary as a function of a number of factors, but a common format is for the speaker to begin the utterance fluently with a phrase or clause which apparently conforms to the preference, often prefacing it with "well" or "er". Then the succeeding clause, which contains the dispreferred material, will be produced very hesitantly, with the pauses coming at specific locations, and often including further instances of "well", "er", and the like. Thus, R's turn in (38) would be analysed as having these particular characteristics, because C's assessment that R would not want him to put it out sets up agreement as C's preference for R's response, but R is producing the dispreferred reply, and is therefore marking it as such. The precise marking will ultimately be a function of many factors since the speaker is also involved in other activities such as managing turn-taking, displaying his understanding of the previous turn, and so on.

Implications

The difference between these two views is quite clear, and it is not surprising given the different assumptions from which they begin. Essentially, the CA worker assumes that until there is reason to believe the opposite, all features of talk are structurally motivated, and must be treated as interactionally relevant if significant generalisations about language use are to be possible.

Unfortunately, the wealth of detail revealed is not necessarily the most useful set of observations for SST because most of it, in all probability, cannot be sensibly communicated in a training exercise. In as much as a tennis coach cannot perfect a player's lob by describing every muscle movement for every lob in every situation, so too, the social skills trainer cannot train by describing the full minutiae of every possible utterance. Consequently, at one level the findings are less than helpful.

However, this analogy also suggests three ways in which CA may be useful to SST. The first concerns the way in which the trainer could specify a particular target for the trainee, for example, an instruction to disagree with some suggestion, and then, using CA results such as these, focus on the inappropriate or inadequate parts of the performance at the level of the fine detail. The second, which could well prove to be part of the first, would essentially involve the trainer in using CA techniques to examine the fine detail of the skills which the trainee already possesses, so as to identify the precise shortcomings or peculiarities. The third would involve the use of such techniques in a joint exercise between trainer and trainee as a way of helping the trainee to understand the particulars of any performance, and thus the conclusions drawn by other observers.

Conclusion

As the analysis of social skills becomes ever more sophisticated, it is certain that a deeper understanding of the conversational processes which lie at the heart of social interaction is going to be needed. In this paper, we have examined two different approaches to this topic, and clearly each has its advantages. As yet, neither is in a sufficiently advanced state for sensible predictions to be made as to their likely value to SST independently of their application in the training process. Initially, it would seem that the descriptive terms employed in Speech Act Theory may render it more valuable, because it is predicated on the study of "talk about talk" as ordinarily conducted in the speech community. However, it is conceivable that this work is pitched at a too general level to be of much use when dealing with the fine grained detail of an individual trainee's difficulties. In which case, the procedures of conversational analysis may be more useful. Indeed in that case, one might suggest that they might be applied to the dialogue between trainer and trainee.

References

Atkinson, J. M. and Heritage, J. (Eds.) (1985) *Structures of social action*. Cambridge: Cambridge University Press.

Allen, J. (1983) Recognizing intentions from natural language utterances. In: M. Brady and R. C. Berwick (Eds.). *Computational models of discourse*. Cambridge, Massachusetts: MIT Press.

Austin, J. L. (1962) *How to do things with words*. Oxford: Oxford University Press.

Beattie, G. (1980) The role of language production processes in the organization of behaviour in face-to-face interaction. In: B. L. Butterworth (Ed.), *Language production: Speech and talk*. London: Academic Press.

Brown, G. and Yule, G. (1983) *Discourse analysis*. Cambridge: Cambridge University Press.

Brown, P. and Levinson, S. C. (1978) Universals in language usage: Politeness phenomena. In E. Goody (Ed.), *Questions and politeness*. Cambridge: Cambridge University Press.

Butterworth, B. L. (1980) Evidence from pauses in speech. In: B. L. Butterworth (Ed.), *Language production: Speech and talk*. London: Academic Press.

Clark, H. H. (1978) Inferring what is meant. In: W. J. M. Levelt and G. B. Flores D'Arcais (Eds.), *Studies in the perception of language*. Chichester: Wiley.

Clark, H. H. and Lucy, P. (1975) Understanding what is meant from what is said: A study in conversationally conveyed requests. *Journal of Verbal Learning and Verbal Behavior*, **14**, 56–72.

Coulthard, M. (1977) *An introduction to discourse analysis*. London: Longman.

Coulthard, M. (1984) Conversation analysis and social skills training. In: P. Trower (Ed.), *Radical approaches to social skills training*. London: Croom Helm.

Forman, D. (1974) The speaker knows best principle. *Papers from the tenth regional meeting of the Chicago Linguistic Society*.

Goffman, E. (1955) On face-work: An analysis of ritual elements in social interaction. *Psychiatry*, **18**. 213–231.

Goodwin, C. (1981) *Conversational organization: Interaction between speakers and hearers*. New York: Academic Press.

Gordon, D. and Lakoff, G. (1971) Conversational postulates. *Papers from the seventh regional meeting of the Chicago Linguistic Society*.

Gumperz, J. J. (1982) *Language and social identity*. Cambridge: Cambridge University Press.

Heringer, J. T. (1972) *Some grammatical correlates of felicity conditions and presuppositions*. Mimeo. Indiana University Linguistics Club.

Hudson, R. A. (1980) *Sociolinguistics*. Cambridge: Cambridge University Press.

Labov, W. (1972) *Sociolinguistic patterns*. Oxford: Blackwell.

Labov, W. and Fanshel, D. (1977) *Therapeutic discourse*. New York: Academic Press.

Levinson, S. C. (1983) *Pragmatics*. Cambridge: Cambridge University Press.

Pomerantz, A. (1985) Agreeing and disagreeing with assessments: Some features of preferred/dispreferred turn shapes. In: J. M. Atkinson and J. Heritage (Eds.), *Structures of social action*. Cambridge: Cambridge University Press.

Power, R. (1979) The organization of purposeful dialogues. *Linguistics*, **17**, 107–152.

Psathas, G. (Ed.). (1979) *Everyday language*. New York: Irvington.

Sacks, H., Schegloff, E. A. and Jefferson, G. (1974) A simplest systematics for the organization of turn taking in conversation. *Language*, **50**, 696–735.

Schenkein, J. (1978) *Studies in the organization of conversation interaction*. New York: Academic Press.

Schmidt, C. F., Sridharan, N. S. and Goodson, J. L. (1978) The plan recognition problem: An intersection of psychology and artificial intelligence. *Artificial Intelligence*, **11**, 45–83.

Searle, J. R. (1969) *Speech acts*. Cambridge: Cambridge University Press.

Searle, J. R. (1975) Indirect speech acts. In P. Cole and J. Morgan (Eds.), *Syntax and semantics volume 3: Speech acts*. New York: Academic Press.

Smith, N. V. (1982) *Mutual knowledge*. London: Academic Press.

Trower, P. (Ed.) (1984) *Radical approaches to social skills training*. London: Croom Helm.

von Cranach, M. (1982) The psychological study of goal directed action: Basic issues. In: M. von Cranach and R. Harré (Eds.), *The analysis of action*. Cambridge: Cambridge University Press.

10

Social Skills Training: Critique and Future Development

CLIVE R. HOLLIN AND PETER TROWER

Whilst every author in both volumes has been concerned with issues particular to their own special field, a number of more general points have been repeatedly raised throughout. These general points are broadly of three types: technical issues concerned with the technique of SST; the practicalities of the use and abuse of SST; and conceptual and theoretical issues connected with SST. In this last chapter we shall summarise each of these general points, and finally make some comments on how we perceive the possible future development of SST.

Technical Issues with SST

Assessment

Bellack (1979) reviewed a number of strategies employed in assessing social skills: these included the clinical interview, self-report and self-monitoring, behavioural observation, peer rating, and physiological monitoring. Of these the most commonly employed assessments, in the literature at least, are self-report and self-monitoring, and behavioural observation. Self-report measures are typically "problem checklists", perhaps with the addition of a rating scale to indicate the severity of the problem (Hersen and Bellack, 1977). With self-monitoring the individual assesses and rates their own performance, perhaps in the form of a diary or more sophisticated scales (e.g. Arkowitz, 1977). Whilst self-report measures, including self-monitoring, can yield valuable data they do have limitations; appropriate eye-contact, for example, would be difficult to self-monitor. Additionally there are other problems of validity and reliability, especially with the latter when over a period of time the individual's self-rating criteria might shift. Bellack (1979) suggests that, at best, self-monitoring is: "An imperfect alternative when behavior cannot be observed by a trained, independent rater" (p. 87).

Clearly Bellack prefers behavioural observation, of which there are several varieties. Whilst naturalistic observation is the most preferable of all, in practice this can be difficult to achieve. Two alternatives to naturalistic observation have been used in social skills assessment. The first is a staged "naturalistic" interaction, for example observing potential trainees' behaviour in a planned waiting-room encounter, with the trainee unaware that assessment is taking place (e.g. Gutride, Goldstein and Hunter, 1973). More commonly, however, a structured role-play is used in which the potential trainee is asked to act a set scene, usually with one or more stooges. This form of assessment has evolved into some highly sophisticated tests such as the Revised Behavioural Assertiveness Test (BAT-R; Eisler *et al.*, 1975). Whilst many experimental-clinical studies have used role-play measures, several recent students have cast some doubt over their validity (Bellack, Hersen and Lamparski, 1979; Bellack, Hersen and Turner, 1978, 1979). Arkowitz (1981) provides a full discussion of the use of role-play assessment and suggests that whilst caution is needed, its use should not be entirely ruled out.

The issues relating to the use of behavioural measures are relatively fully discussed and understood, but in terms of Argyle's model of social behaviour and subsequent information processing models, they form only one part of the system: *perception* of social cues, and translation of this perception into action are integral parts of the model. Bellack (1979) made essentially the same point: "Despite the importance of assessing the various social perception skills . . . no empirically sound assessment techniques currently exist" (p. 99). Bellack notes the development of social perception measures in which the potential trainee observes and comments upon a videotaped social interaction (e.g. Archer and Akert, 1977). This would appear to be a potentially powerful assessment tool, but it is not in general usage as indicated by the social skills literature. Social skills training manuals rely on photographs as a test of ability to perceive facial expressions accurately (e.g. Spence, 1980). Whilst arguably better than nothing, there are obvious limitations inherent in photographs as compared to videotape. This area is one which is ripe for innovation, particularly by drawing on the nonverbal communication and allied literatures where much attention has been devoted to these perceptual skills (e.g. Boice, 1983; Morrison and Bellack, 1981).

The stage of translation might be considered as a "cognitive" stage in which decisions are made, plans of action formulated, consequences of different actions evaluated, and so forth. McFall (1982) suggests a range of cognitive skills which may be particularly required: these include response selection and utility evaluation. As Bellack noted in 1979, and McFall repeated in 1982, few empirically sound assessment methods were available for cognitions. In 1986 there are active developments, but the field is very much in its infancy. Shepherd (1984) has made a number of suggestions which may prove important in developing a reliable test of social cognition: these include standard questionnaires on such phenomena as attributional style, self-monitoring and irrational beliefs; various rating scales; Repertory Grids and semantic differentials (e.g. Osgood, Suci and Tannenbaum, 1957); and the Personal Questionnaire (Shapiro, 1975, cited in Shepherd, 1984). In terms of validity Shepherd notes a number of problems, although two are particularly pressing. The first is simply that as cognitions are not directly observable, how can we check that a "true" assessment has been made? Issues of this kind, however, raise important questions about the epistomological status of "cognitions". Shepherd's second point equally deserves consideration: are the "higher order" cognitive processes involved at the translation stage open to conscious access and inspection? If they are not, then there is a considerable mountain to be climbed before measures of higher order cognition can be formulated.

An area of primary importance but much neglected in the literature is the assessment of the potential trainee's desired goals. In some cases the goal may be apparent as, for example, in hetero-social skills training; but in other instances the aim of training is less obvious. In SST with delinquents, for example, what goal does the training seek to assist the trainee to achieve? It may be the case that the trainer has different goals to the trainee: with delinquents, the trainer may see the goal as reducing offending, whilst the trainee sees the goal as making friends (probably delinquent!) or avoiding detection for criminal acts. Goal assessment is of primary importance but seemingly under-reported in the literature.

Thus assessment of social skills faces difficulty on two fronts: there are technical problems with behavioural assessment, and a lack of valid and reliable measures for perceptual and cognitive processes. The advent of videotape recording may provide an answer to measuring some aspects of social perception, and Shepherd (1984) has made a number of suggestions for progress in cognitive assessment. Following the rapid growth in measures of behaviour, we now seem to have reached a pause in which to consider the next step assessment should take. Social perception would appear to be the most likely candidate for more refined assessment.

Training

The methods used in SST have been fully described by Trower, Bryant and Argyle (1978): these are modelling, role-play, feedback and coaching, practice, and contingent reinforcement. The relative contribution of these methods to the overall effectiveness of training was first examined in a series of studies by McFall and his colleagues (McFall and Lillesand, 1971;

McFall and Marston, 1970; McFall and Twentyman, 1973). It was found that whilst practice and coaching had independent, additive effects, modelling did not significantly enhance the effects of training. However, contrary findings have been reported in which modelling did significantly add to the effectiveness of practice and coaching (Eisler, Hersen and Miller, 1973; Hersen, Eisler and Miller, 1973; Hersen *et al.*, 1973). Further, rather than simply *overt* practice and modelling, it has also been found that *covert* practice and modelling can add to overall training effectiveness (Kazdin, 1974a, 1976).

As was the case with assessment, the vast majority of published work has concentrated upon overt behaviour rather than social perception or cognition. This is not a new point; Curran (1979a) noted: "Inadequate performance may not be the result of an insufficient behavioral repertoire but rather the mis-perception of social cues" (p. 60). Thus, if some individuals are being mis-selected for SST on this basis — and the paucity of social perception assessment measures might suggest that they are — then whilst they may exhibit skilled behaviour during training, the intervention is not addressing the real issue. As stated previously, assessment is the key to understanding a client's difficulties, and McFall (1982) has made some progress in assessment of social perception with efforts to develop "measures for isolating and assessing the abilities of college males and females to detect and interpret social cues emitted by other men and women engaged in social interaction" (p. 27). Looking ahead to the development of training programmes in social perception, it may prove beneficial to examine in detail the training methods successfully used to improve facial memory ability (see Baddeley and Woodhead, 1983), facial affect recognition (Ekman and Friesen, 1975), and nonverbal sensitivity (Rosenthal *et al.*, 1979).

Moving to the translation, or cognitive, stage the position becomes increasingly unsure. We are immediately faced with two problems: exactly what is happening at this translation stage?; and should change at this level be part of the task of SST? To begin to answer the first question Argyle (1967) suggested that translation of social perception was concerned with either "conscious rules and deliberate decisions", or if the task is familiar such processes may be "automatic" in execution. The exact nature of the processes taking place during this phase have been described in a variety of ways: prominent examples include "problem solving" (D'Zurilla and Nezu, 1982), "faulty cognitive-evaluation processes" (Curran, 1979a), and "decision skills" (McFall, 1982). A number of techniques have been developed to attempt to modify translation skills, with social problem solving receiving increasing attention (Bramston and Spence, 1985; Kagan, 1984).

Whilst some researchers and practitioners are developing programmes aimed at modifying cognition, there is an unresolved debate about whether such techniques should form part of SST. Curran (1979a) is to the point: "The term 'social skills' should be limited to behavioural acts and . . . should exclude nonbehavioural components such as cognitive processes" (p. 58).

Other theorists, however, have suggested that cognitions are an integral part of our everyday social behaviour and SST should therefore include cognitive change as part of the programmes. This view was expressed by Trower, Bryant and Argyle (1978), and by Yardley (1979) who argued that SST already includes a much greater emphasis on cognitive change than most researchers and practitioners admit. Yardley expresses the view that: "We cannot simply change complex behaviour, verbal or nonverbal, without recourse to understanding the personal significance of acts" (p. 62).

Yardley (1979) also suggested that "changes of feeling" are of importance in any social interaction. Whilst a definition of "feeling" was not offered, perhaps Yardley was postulating a third system, *emotion*, operating alongside cognition and overt behaviour. Dryden (1984a) has argued that both emotions and cognitions should be included as part of social skills assessment. Following this, Trower (1980) argues for the necessity of two types of training — training in behavioural *component* skills and training in *process* skills (including perception and cognition), depending on the area of deficiency. This point is more fully discussed in the theoretical section.

These arguments for the place of cognition and emotion in SST programmes indicates a radical change in the type of training offered. Traditional skills training which emphasises overt behavioural change would have to be accompanied by cognitive techniques such as "problem solving" (D'Zurilla and Goldfried, 1971) or "self-instructional training" (Camp and Bash, 1981). A number of studies have been carried out comparing the effects of traditional behaviour therapy with behaviour therapy plus some cognitive therapy (e.g. Rossiter and Wilson, 1985), and similar studies have been carried out with assertion training (Stefanek and Eisler, 1983). However, so far comparatively few studies have made this type of comparison with SST as the focus (see Bramston and Spence, 1985; Hollin *et al.*, 1982; Trower, this volume). Dryden's (1984b) suggestion that rational-emotive therapy may be "a powerful adjunct to skills-based social skills training" (p. 343), thus requires more definitive empirical testing. However, we may expect to see shortly studies based on the recent information processing models of SST (e.g. McFall, 1982).

In summary, there is some debate as to the relative effects of each component of training; and also whether cognitive and emotional therapies should be part of, or a separate type of, SST. However, there is little doubt that SST can be an effective means of changing behaviour — the contents of this and other books and research papers testify to that fact. It is this success of the technique which has contributed to its widespread use and popularity. Whilst academic interest, as gauged by research publications, perhaps reached a peak in the late 1970s and early 1980s, Hudson's work (see Volume 1) should leave no doubt that SST is still an immensely popular and widely used technique. Whether this will remain the case will, in part at least, depend upon whether SST is successful as an instrument of manufacturing real-life and long-term change. To consider this issue we move to the generalisation of SST.

Generalisation

It was with the first studies of generalisation that signs of unease began to be displayed about the effects of SST. It appeared that whilst SST was powerful in shaping up new behaviours in the training environment, there were problems with the generalisation of these newly acquired behaviours to the natural environment (Shepherd, 1977, 1978). There are at least three reasons which may explain this "failure" of generalisation: the technique requires some modification; the research is questionable; the technique requires a radical change in theory and practice so as to make it effective. We shall discuss the first two issues here, and the third in the final section of this chapter.

Brown (1982) made the point that if we expect trained skills to generalise to the natural environment, then attempts should be made to bring the natural environment into the training environment. Brown gives ten strategies to achieve this goal, including the use of social reinforcement and instructing relatives and friends in how to continue the training. Additionally, Brown also suggests that training in the provision of self-reinforcement might enhance the prospects of generalisation. This emphasis is clearly one which is liable to be beneficial in terms of generalisation, and it is one which practitioners appear to be using more and more — see for example the SHAPE project as detailed by Hudson in Volume 1. The point has also been made (e.g. Trower, 1982) that *process* skills training would look for a quite different type of generalisation: rather than specific trained skills, assessment of generalisation would test for the trainee's ability to *generate* social skills.

In looking for generalisation, research must first agree on what is meant by the term. Traditionally generalisation is considered in terms of *stimulus* generalisation and *response* generalisation: the relative merits of this dichotomy for SST have been discussed elsewhere with the conclusion that response generalisation is of little value (Hollin and Henderson, 1984). Scott, Himadi and Keane (1983) suggest a more expansive consideration:

they note that generalisation can be across time, settings, persons, responses, and scenes. Accordingly Scott *et al.* reviewed almost 70 studies of generalisation of SST according to these five categories. As might be predicted, the experimental evidence was mixed: a range of variables including type of assessment technique, client population, and sensitivity of the dependent variable all dictated the extent of generalisation of training. However, perhaps the most crucial factor of all is the experimental design employed by the researcher in testing for generalisation. Whilst there are arguments for and against group and single-case designs (Hersen and Barlow, 1976), it is more difficult to understand why follow-up data to determine generalisation across time (sometimes referred to as durability, or maintenance of treatment effects) are not gathered in more studies. Scott *et al.* found that only 37% of the 68 studies they reviewed attempted a follow-up, with the time varying from 2 to 96 weeks (mean time was 21 weeks). So while 88% of studies were able to report generalisation of training on at least one measure, information about long-term effects is not available in the majority of cases. Thus, as this Handbook testifies, whilst there is a vast literature on SST and a considerable weight of favourable evidence on its short-term effects, longitudinal information is sorely lacking. It seems that the problem is not so much the "failure" of SST, rather the failure of research to examine fully the effects of the intervention. Possible reasons for this failure will be discussed in the following section.

Use and Abuse of SST

The Use of SST

As emphasised throughout, from its origins in clinical psychology SST has spread rapidly to influence the work of practitioners in a wide variety of fields. There are a number of related factors which have led, we suggest, to this growth. The first is the relative simplicity of the notion of skills training: compared, say, to concepts within some psychodynamic therapies, skills training can appear quite straightforward. This, in turn, may bestow a degree of face validity to the technique: it is not shrouded in mystery, nor does it require years of study to practice. Further, the model is one with which everyone is familiar through their own experience, say learning to drive a car or being taught some professional skill. The didactic nature of training rather than the specialist skills of therapy may also give the technique a broad appeal.

Whilst there are those rare individuals who appear to be "natural" social skills trainers, most SST practitioners will require training. In the accelerating rush to "give psychology away", SST has been at the forefront with many books and training manuals aimed at non-psychologists (e.g. Spence, 1980). Whilst this may be of benefit in increasing the number of (hopefully) competent trainers, there are also disadvantages with this approach. The first difficulty arises with assessment: there are numerous packages which test for social skills deficits which if administered may well indicate that SST would not go amiss. However, this "cook-book" approach belies the true purpose of assessment which is to understand the issues the client brings to the practitioner. The strategy of fitting clients to SST, rather than SST fitting the need of the client, is one which is liable to occur if the practitioner has only a limited range of assessment skills. To train non-psychologists in cognitive assessment, social perception measurement, functional analysis, family assessment and so forth is to move to a completely different sphere of training rather than "how to run SST groups". This is not to say that such training in refined techniques is impossible or undesirable — it is neither — but rather that it calls for rigorous, highly controlled training involving either full- or part-time academic study alongside supervised practice.

The second issue in the training of non-psychologists as social skills trainers involves evaluation. Like assessment, evaluation can be simple and non-experimental: the client appears to be improving in training sessions, or the client reports improvement, or some observer notices improvement. Whilst these reports may indeed signal a real improvement, they may also be confined to the training environment, or be "halo effects", or be only very short-term changes. Parenthetically, these occurrences may also explain in part the popularity of SST: as most practitioners will testify, SST is highly reinforcing to the trainer in that it "works" — the trainee's behaviour can be seen to improve as training progresses. (Although, as noted above, the question is not whether SST can produce change *per se*, but rather whether it can produce changes which generalise.) To return to evaluation, however, the experimental validation of the effects of training is a complex affair, requiring both knowledge of experimental design and analysis, and the necessary resources to conduct the research. This level of specialist knowledge is outside that of most practitioner groups and so, once again, would demand rigorous training. In addition, many practitioners — nurses, social workers, probation officers — are not employed as researchers, and consequently their work-load does not allow time for the conducting of exhaustive follow-up studies.

Thus whilst it may be possible to train various professional groups in the *practice* of SST — although the style practice will depend on the trainer's individual understanding of SST — assessment and evaluation may prove impossible. The result is obvious: unless a psychologist collaborates in assessment and evaluation, SST programmes will be run for inappropriate clients and without proper evaluation. Paradoxically, training others to run SST programmes may increase rather than decrease the psychologist's workload. In practice it is probably impossible for the psychologist to be able to carry this amount of work, and the partly-trained practitioners are left to fend for themselves. Whilst this might be well and good, there are potential hazards. If the assessment is incorrect or incomplete then the chances are increased that SST will "fail", that is it will not solve the presenting problem. Further, without an appreciation of the finer points of evaluation, SST may be seen as "not working" when, perhaps, the wrong dependent variable is being monitored. In the laudable efforts to offer an improved service to our clients, we must be watchful that we do not foster a disillusionment which either implicity or explicitly creates false expectations of what it is possible to achieve through the use of SST.

The Abuse of SST

In the above section we hinted at one potential abuse of SST, that of indiscriminate training of other professional groups: although it should be noted that if managed correctly this is potentially a greater advantage than disadvantage. In this section we wish to point to three areas of unequivocal abuse: indiscriminate use of the term "social skills training"; indiscriminate application of the technique of SST; the limited approach of some research in evaluating the efficacy of SST.

One of the central problems with SST is the lack of a definition. If, as Curran (1979b) suggests, "everyone seems to know what good and poor social skills are" (p. 321), the lack of a strict definition is not too serious. However, more recently McFall (1982) has commented that the use of SST, "has become so widespread that it begins to strain our credibility and arouse our suspicions. How is it possible for any psychological concept to be invoked so widely and still retain any specificity of meaning or utility?" (p. 2). McFall has pinpointed the gulf between experimental-clinical research and practice and widespread use. In many quarters SST has become the order of the day with the result that much of what is given the title of SST bears little resemblance to what might be thought of as SST in the line advocated by, say, Trower *et al.* (1978). Our own personal experience has revealed all types of therapeutic enterprise, from traditional group therapy to rampant eclecticism, offered under the label of SST. Hudson's chapter in Volume 1 echoes this, with the anguished reference to volleyball as the vehicle for SST. This type of enterprise will never reach the academic journals, but it cannot do other than erode the standing of SST.

Following another of McFall's points, we move to the widespread use of the technique — SST as a universal panacea: how can one technique be so applicable to so many clients? The answer, we suggest, lies in poor theoretical analysis and so will be discussed in the next section.

The final abuse of SST lies not so much in practice but in research. Scott, Himadi and Keane (1983) noted that barely one-third of published studies they reviewed carried out long-term follow-up. Of course knowledge of the immediate effects of training is crucial and not to be discounted, however it is long-term data which are needed as a real test of whether SST is effective. The lack of follow-up data in behavioural research is not a new complaint — Emery and Marholin (1977) made the same point. In an analysis of the forces shaping the researchers' behaviour, Emery and Marholin suggested that such variables as salary, tenure, social and peer acknowledgement, and career development act against any delay in publishing research findings. Therefore, following this line of argument, presumably also against designing long-term studies. Hollin and Henderson (1984) expanded the issue:

> When contemplating a follow-up to our original study . . . we found our study population was scattered over the whole of the British Isles. The financial expense involved in visiting each individual to gather data would have been expensive; and the cost in time would have been expensive; permission to leave other duties would have had to be obtained, further clinical work set aside (p. 338).

Thus, whether for quick publication or lack of time and money, research into the long-term effectiveness of SST is not as thorough as it might be. In some cases it is clearly not being carried out, whilst in other instances broad, easily-measured variables, such as re-hospitalisation, are being monitored whilst more sensitive, relevant variables are not measured. This strategy is more likely to produce negative results as the broad measure is liable to be of dubious value (see Hollin and Henderson, 1984).

The probable result of these abuses of SST is a growing disillusionment with the technique. This has obvious implications for the practice of SST, and may also have repercussions for psychologists who peddle interventions that don't work. The warnings have been spelt out since the beginning of the expansion of SST (e.g. Stravynski, 1978), but it is questionable how much notice has been paid. We agree that psychology should be "given away" but this should be done carefully and with patience: the proverb that we shall reap what we sow is highly appropriate.

Theoretical Issues in SST

To this point our combined efforts as both contributors and editors of this book have been genuinely collaborative, however the point has now arrived where we must diverge. In the next and last part of this chapter, the first section — a radical behaviourist approach — is the work of CH, the second — a cognitive approach — that of PT: these should therefore be read as individual statements. We are in agreement however that a non-theoretical, unsystematic spirit of pragmatism may lead eventually to chaos and disillusionment, and therefore progress in SST requires better and more refined theories to overcome existing problems — particularly in assessment and generalisation.

A Radical Behaviourist Approach to SST

In this section my aim is to show how radical behaviourism and applied behaviour analysis can be used to clarify the issues surrounding the use of SST. The philosophy of radical behaviourism has been fully discussed elsewhere (Blackman, 1980; Skinner, 1974) and will not be repeated here. However, perhaps it is necessary at the outset to state the radical behaviourist position on the vexed question of "cognition". Blackman (1981) has expressed this with perfect clarity:

> Contemporary behaviourists adopt a philosophical position which does not commit them to the assertion that people are no more than puppets, pushed and pulled by forces beyond their control and unable to enjoy or suffer private experiences. Instead, they adopt a way of looking at behavioural phenomena which emphasizes the functional importance of environmental influences on what we do, which seeks to find an appropriate way of incorporating private experiences, and which sets these elements within a dynamic and interactive system (p. 15).

To understand the functional importance of any behaviour, applied behaviour analysis places considerable emphasis on observable behaviour and observable environmental events which influence behaviour. Following this particular emphasis, behaviour modification has traditionally concentrated upon overt behaviour with the development, for example, of techniques such as the token economy (Ayllon and Azrin, 1968). However, this tradition does not exclude private events from a functional analysis: it is a criticism of behaviourists in the past that they have tended to neglect private events but this is less true now. As Lowe and Higson (1981) note: "For radical behaviourists to study the role of private events in controlling behaviour is not to step outside their conceptual boundaries but rather to fulfil the obligations of their theoretical position" (p. 182). Clearly the role of private events should not be ignored in a functional analysis of behaviour, although Blackman's (1981) point that private events are not to be "afforded a role as autonomous causes of behaviour" (p. 24) must be stated.

As behavioural research turned to an understanding private events, so traditional behaviour modification was itself modified to incorporate cognitive functioning. The "new" school of cognitive behaviour modification gave rise to techniques such as problem-solving (D'Zurilla and Goldfried, 1971), coping-skills training (Kazdin, 1974b), cognitive therapy

(Beck, 1976), and self-instructional training (Meichenbaum, 1977). The advent of such interventions sparked a lively debate between its critics (e.g. Ledwidge, 1978, 1979; Wolpe, 1978) and its proponents (e.g. Locke, 1979; Wilson, 1978). The central problem is the definition of "cognitive": if the term is taken to refer to *behaviours* not publicly observable then they fall within the sphere of functional analysis; if, however, the term is used to refer to some hypothetical construct, then this must be rejected in a radical behaviourist analysis. Within this boundary it is therefore important that radical behaviourism continues to attend to the place of private events in controlling behaviour. Further, it is also important that by appropriate behavioural analysis the use of "cognitive" techniques are understood and developed to enhance the effectiveness of behaviour modification — see Lowe and Higson (1981) for a behavioural analysis of self-instructional training.

The next section makes some tentative steps towards such an analysis for SST. This approach considers an analysis and suggestions for practice at the three stages of assessment, training, and evaluation.

Assessment. Skinner's (1953) concept of functional analysis refers to the exercise of observing and understanding the particular behaviour under scrutiny. This involves the behaviour's setting conditions, its parameters such as frequency and duration, and its consequences for the individual. Thus the applied behaviour analyst is concerned with the relationship between setting event and behaviour (i.e. the *operant*), and how the consequences of the operant modify particular antecedent-behaviour relations. In assessment therefore the concern is with antecedents, behaviour, and consequences. If we accept that most behaviour is goal-orientated rather than random, then in assessment the first step should be towards identifying the goals our clients wish to achieve. In many cases these goals are social in nature: "to have more friends", "a heterosexual relationship", "to be a good parent", and so on. Of course, it is the practitioner's task to gain an understanding of these goals, and agree a definition with the individual client.

There are two important points with regard to formulation of the goal of the intervention. The first is that the client may not be able to make a goal, or professes that it is impossible for him or her to achieve any goals, or has unrealistic aims. In such cases the focus of the intervention may shift to some degree, and appropriate counselling, rational emotive therapy, or shaping-up of feasible goals may be required. Secondly, as Frosh and Summerfield particularly noted previously in Volume 1, clinicians should not be seduced into trying to provide remedies for political and economic issues. Examples of such issues include employment — especially job-search training — and some instances of criminal and delinquent behaviour. In offering training as a "remedy" in these areas, the environmental influences are being minimised if not ignored, and individual training slips towards a "medical model" in which the person is to be "cured" rather than the environment modified. It would be anticipated that an accurate behavioural analysis would make such issues clear.

Given these important points, the decision may be made that the client may be assisted to achieve their social goal through individual skill training. The trainer is faced with the task of determining which area of social behaviour should be the focus of the programme. The assessment may be based on a heuristic of the type shown in Fig. 1. It is, however, appreciated that the exact components of each type of social behaviour are open to discussion; and also that assessment measures for each component may be lacking.

	Assess for:
Social Antecedents	Accurate discrimination of social cues
Social Behaviour	Accurate evaluation of antecedents
	Knowledge of response alternatives
	Selection of response alternatives
	Skill level of performance
Social Consequences	Accurate discrimination of consequences of own performance
	Accurate evaluation of consequences of own performance
	Accurate learning of "social rules"
	Decision making for next response

Fig. 1. Suggested Heuristic for Analysis of Social Behaviour

Having carried out the assessment, the client's existing ability can be matched against a model of the abilities required to obtain the agreed goal. Thus the trainer must finally decide which skills will best be modified or constructed to enable the client to attain their goal.

Training. The immediate problem facing social skills trainers is what to include as "social skills". Curran (1979a) has acknowledged this issue: "If we don't put some limitations on our definition of social skills, it will be expanded to include all human behaviour" (p. 58). As McFall (1982) has similarly noted, limitless expansion will render meaningless the concept of SST. The converse, however, is no more appealing: by omitting certain classes of behaviour from skills training the trainees may be participating in programmes which are not of maximum efficacy. A solution to this state of affairs, which I wish to advance here, is to refine the concept of SST into three discrete types — social perception training, social cognition training, and social performance training.

Training methods for *social perception* are not well formulated at present, but there are indications in the literature (e.g. McFall, 1982) that this may soon be remedied. It can be suggested that such training will include modelling and instruction in which social cues to attend to, and how to "decode" their meanings. Training in *social cognition* may follow a number of paths: increasing knowledge of response alternatives may require modelling, coaching, and instruction; enhancing the process of selection and evaluation of response alternatives may call for the use of social problem solving techniques or self-instructional training; accurate learning of social rules and conventions may require coaching and discussion. Training in this area of social cognition is hampered by a lack of empirical data on "appropriate" cognitive processes. Whilst, for example, behavioural "norms" are relatively well understood and so inform the training of appropriate social behaviour, the same cannot be said of "cognitive norms" — if, indeed, they exist. Cognitive research is progressing rapidly, however, and eventually more sophisticated training programmes may be possible. Finally, *social performance* is what is generally now thought of as "social skills training", i.e. the shaping-up of new overt social behaviours using modelling, role-play, coaching, discussion, practice and so forth. As this book testifies, we are relatively knowledgeable and proficient in this area, although the specific area of generalisation requires attention.

In practice it is likely that more than one of the three areas — perception, cognition, performance — will be the focus of training. (Although there may be instances where conceptual problems arise: should, for example, training in cross-cultural skills include how to think like an Italian, Arab, or whatever nationality is appropriate?) Evaluation of the effects of the three types of training should be made both in terms of their cumulative effect and their individual contribution towards the trainee achieving the goal of the training programme.

Evaluation. Much of the research into the effectiveness of SST has been of a group design — SST groups compared against various types of control group. Similarly, research looking at the impact of SST as compared to SST plus some form of cognitive intervention has also used group designs (e.g. Bramston and Spence, 1985; Hollin *et al.*, 1982). Studies conducted using group designs have contributed a great deal to our understanding of the effectiveness of SST. However, there are difficulties with group designs, such as mean group change not accurately reflecting each individual's change, which leads to overall limitations in evaluating training effects. The single-case design is an alternative methodology in which training effects are monitored for each trainee on an *individual* basis. Hersen and Barlow (1976) discuss the available variety of single-case designs. There are some excellent single-case studies in the SST literature which illustrate the utility of the methodology (e.g. Farkas *et al.*, 1981; Gross *et al.*, 1983). Additionally, single-case design would be particularly suited to evaluating the relative and cumulative effects of various types of training, if the training methods are used sequentially. For example, an A-B-C-D-A design would assess baseline levels at some social behaviour, say number of successful heterosexual encounters (A); training would commence with social perception training (B); followed by social cognition training (C); then social performance training (D); a return to baseline conditions would evaluate the generalisation and maintenance of training (A). Any number of dependent variables could be monitored over the duration of the study. It should also be added that evaluation should continue over as long a follow-up period as possible in the client's natural environment. As trainers we are in the business of assisting our clients to achieve *their* goals in their own environment — our evaluation should be towards this end.

A Cognitive Approach to SST

SST has been perhaps the most recent of the "behaviour" therapies to be influenced by the so-termed cognitive revolution, even though the original social skill model had a cognitive stage. The traditional form of SST stressed the assessment and acquisition of discrete behaviours, variously termed verbal and nonverbal components, elements, skills and responses. Trower (1982) clarified the distinction between these social *skills* — the component normative behaviours a person need in their repertoire — and social *skill* — the process by which the individual produces social behaviour. Deficiencies were clearly evident — and training needed — in both areas in clients judged unskilled on global measures in Trower's study. However, though at the time social *skills* training was widely practiced, social *skill* training was generally neglected. It also appeared to have been overlooked that the original Argyle and Kendon (1967) social skill model was a process, not a component model. It advocated a self-regulating, goal-directed system which involved the constant monitoring of performance and making decisions about appropriate responses in the light of this feedback.

The inadequacies of a purely component approach has also been revealed in research on the importance of synchronization in social skills (Fischetti, Curran and Wessberg, 1977; Peterson *et al.*, 1981). However, recent developments towards this more information processing approach have been made, and mark a probable turning point in SST, particularly the models developed by McFall and his colleagues (McFall, 1982; McFall and Dodge, 1982), and by Carver and his colleagues (Carver, 1979; Carver and Scheier, 1984).

Theories from sister disciplines such as cognitive psychology and particularly artificial intelligence (Boden, 1979) are exerting a considerable influence. One such is schema theory, now seen as highly central to cognitive-behaviour therapy in general (Turk and Salovey, 1985) and social skills in particular (Carver & Scheier, 1984). For example "recognitory" schemata guide perception and action in the matching-to-standard process (Carver and Scheier, 1984) and their analysis in unskilled clients has revealed a number of inferential and other cognitive errors which may produce deficient social performance and concomitant emotional distress (see Chapter 2). It is in the area of cognitive blocks in the skill-generating process that cognitive-behaviour therapy has a relevant role to play.

Some of these advances do not fit easily into the traditional paradigms of psychology, and there is a growing trend for a form of "radical" cognitivism which advocates radical reform of the fundamental paradigms of psychology in general (Harré, Clarke and De Carlo, 1985) and SST in particular (Trower, 1984). In brief, these include: (1) the replacement of the familiar parametric methodology (where meaning lies in separate parameters) with a structural or "constructionist" methodology (where meaning lies in structures or context, Gergen, 1985); (2) the adoption of an agency approach in place of the organism-based approach, in which external causal explanation is rejected in favour of an intentional, goal-seeking, rule-following explanation; (3) related to the previous point is the adoption of the central role of a moral order for social behaviour rather than the amoral position of our more familiar "scientific" stance (Howard, 1985). These issues are beyond the scope of this present brief review (see Trower, 1984, for a full review from the SST standpoint), but we can perhaps give the flavour of the debate on the last of these (interrelated) issues.

Put at its simplest, the radical position claims that people attempt to follow rules (or rule-breaking meta-rules) in a matching-to-standard process, and evaluate their success or failure as a *morally* positive or negative event. Skill deficiency matters only if the performer or other judge the performance as morally deficient (stupid, inept, abnormal, wicked etc.), and by means of faulty attributions, judge the *performer* as morally deficient. This inevitably gives rise to emotional distress, further behavioural deviance/avoidance and so on. It is also an essential part of this model that people are viewed as socially constructed objects in which they participate (and try to control by means of self-presentation strategies). Another feature is that behaviour is inseperable from the moral context and moral rules of conduct of the community — the structuring rules that give the behaviour inter-subjective and negotiable meaning. Assessment of the behaviour and its meaning is not a problem intrinsically because such "cognitive" rules are not internal and unverifiable but inter-subjectively agreed, since all such rule-systems operate in an essentially public domain. The problem comes because meanings are negotiated and subject to change — a phenomenon known in parametric terms as unreliability. Compared to the above, the traditional model sees behaviour, including "cognitive behaviour" as the product, not of an individual following rules but of a mechanism bound by causal laws — a system which has no place for decision and moral evaluation. It is hard to predict the outcome of such arguments in the next decade or so. However the direction they do take will have a dramatic effect on the nature of SST.

Concluding Remarks

What will happen to SST over the next decade? We can see at least three potential lines of development. The first, as Barbara Hudson suggested in Volume 1, is that SST will simply be a "fad", to be discarded when the next exciting innovation arrives. Whilst we have argued that too much ill-defined, poorly conceived, and badly carried out SST is taking place, the fault here lies with practitioners, not necessarily the technique. To lose SST on these grounds would be a classic example of throwing out the unfortunate infant with the bathwater.

A slightly less disastrous line of development would be that SST continued in the same, somewhat muddled, vein, some theorists and practitioners arguing for one type of SST, others advocating some other development. Dissatisfaction would rumble on, research and practice would continue in much the same way as in the 1970s and first half of the 1980s, with no clear line of direction or end-point in sight.

The third, ideal, scenario is that researchers and practitioners will agree on a working definition of "social skills" and so direct their efforts towards a common aim. Throughout this Handbook the contributors have, with few exceptions, pointed to the promise of SST; the technique can be highly effective, a valuable addition to the practitioner's battery of techniques. It is time, however, that this promise was fulfilled. We have suggested two ways that a unified theory might be generated. There is some overlap between the suggestions, and future work may extract the communalities and produce a "rapproachement" as is occurring in other areas such as aspects of behaviour therapy and psychoanalysis following Wachtel's (1977) seminal work. This would indeed be progress of the highest order: we await developments.

References

Archer, D. and Akert, R. M. (1977) Words and everything else: Verbal and nonverbal cues in social interpretation. *Journal of Personality and Social Psychology*, **35**, 443–449.
Argyle, M. (1967) *The psychology of interpersonal behaviour.* Harmondsworth: Penguin Books.
Argyle, M. and Kendon, A. (1967) The experimental analysis of social performance. In: L. Berkowitz (Ed.), *Advances in experimental social psychology, Vol. 3.* New York: Academic Press.

Arkowitz, H. (1977) Measurement and modification of minimal dating behavior. In: M. Hersen, R. Eisler and P. Miller (Eds.), *Progress in behavior modification, Vol. 5*. New York: Academic Press.

Arkowitz, H. (1981) Assessment of social skills. In: M. Hersen and A. S. Bellack (Eds.), *Behavioral assessment: A practical handbook*. (2nd ed.). Oxford: Pergamon Press.

Ayllon, T. and Azrin, N. H. (1968) *The token economy: A motivational system for therapy and rehabilitation*. New York: Appleton-Century-Crofts.

Baddeley, A. and Woodhead, M. (1983) Improving face recognition ability. In: S. M. A. Lloyd-Bostock and B. R. Clifford (Eds.), *Evaluating witness evidence*. Chichester: Wiley.

Beck, A. (1976) *Cognitive therapy and emotional disorders*. New York: International Universities Press.

Bellack, A. S. (1979) Behavioral assessment of social skills. In: A. S. Bellack and M. Hersen (Eds.), *Research and practice in social skills training*. New York: Plenum Press.

Bellack, A. S., Hersen, M. and Lamparski, D. (1979) Role play tests for assessing social skills: Are they valid? Are they useful? *Journal of Consulting and Clinical Psychology*, **47**, 335–342.

Bellack, A. S., Hersen, M. and Turner, S. M. (1978) Role play tests for assessing social skills: Are they valid? *Behavior Therapy*, **9**, 448–461.

Bellack, A. S., Hersen, M. and Turner, S. M. (1979) The relationship of role playing and knowledge of appropriate behavior to assertion in the natural environment. *Journal of Consulting and Clinical Psychology*, **47**, 670–678.

Blackman, D. E. (1980) Images of man in contemporary behaviourism. In: A. J. Chapman and D. M. Jones (Eds.), *Models of man*. Leicester: British Psychological Society.

Blackman, D. E. (1981) The experimental analysis of behaviour and its relevance to applied psychology. In: G. Davey (Ed.), *Applications of conditioning theory*. London: Methuen.

Boden, M. A. (1979) The computational metaphor in psychology. In: N. Bolton (Ed.), *Philosophical problems in psychology*. London: Methuen.

Boice, R. (1983) Observational skills. *Psychological Bulletin*, **93**, 3–29.

Bramston, P. and Spence, S. H. (1985) Behavioural versus cognitive social-skills training with intellectually-handicapped adults. *Behaviour Research and Therapy*, **23**, 230–246.

Brown, M. (1982) Maintenance and generalization issues in skills training with chronic schizophrenics. In: J. P. Curran and P. M. Monti (Eds.), *Social skills training: A practical handbook for assessment and treatment*. New York: The Guilford Press.

Camp, B. W. and Bash, M. A. (1981) *Think aloud: Increasing social and cognitive skills — a problem solving program for children*. Champaign, Illinois: Research Press.

Carver, C. S. (1979) A cybernetic model of self-attention processes. *Journal of Personality and Social Psychology*, **37**, 1186–1195.

Carver, C. S. and Scheier, M. F. (1984) A control-theory approach to behaviour and some implications for social skills training. In: P. Trower (Ed.), *Radical approaches to social skills training*. London: Croom Helm.

Curran, J. P. (1979a) Pandora's box reopened? The assessment of social skills. *Journal of Behavioral Assessment*, **1**, 55–71.

Curran, J. P. (1979b) Social skills: Methodological issues and future directions. In: A. S. Bellack and M. Hersen (Eds.), *Research and practice in social skills training*. New York: Plenum Press.

Dryden, W. (1984a) Social skills assessment from a rational-emotive perspective. In: P. Trower (Ed.), *Radical approaches to social skills training*. London: Croom Helm.

Dryden, W. (1984b) Social skills training from a rational-emotive perspective. In: P. Trower (Ed.), *Radical approaches to social skills training*. London: Croom Helm.

D'Zurilla, T. J. and Goldfried, M. R. (1971) Problem solving and behavior modification. *Journal of Abnormal Psychology*, **78**, 107–126.

D'Zurilla, T. J. and Nezu, A. (1982) Social problem solving in adults. In: P. C. Kendall (Ed.), *Advances in cognitive behavioral research and therapy*. New York: Academic Press.

Eisler, R. M., Hersen, M. and Miller, P. M. (1973) Effects of modelling on components of assertive behavior. *Journal of Behavior Therapy and Experimental Psychiatry*, **4**, 1–6.

Eisler, R. M., Hersen, M., Miller, P. M. and Blanchard, E. B. (1975) Situational determinants of assertive behavior. *Journal of Consulting and Clinical Psychology*, **43**, 330–340.

Ekman, P. and Friesen, W. V. (1975) *Unmasking the face: A guide to recognising emotion from facial expressions*. New York: Prentice-Hall.

Emery, R. E. and Marholin, M. J. (1977) An applied behavior analysis of delinquency: The irrelevancy of relevant behavior. *American Psychologist*, **6**, 860–873.

Farkas, G. M., Sherick, R. B., Matson, J. C. and Loebig, M. (1981) Social skills training for a blind child through differential reinforcement. *The Behavior Therapist*, **4**, 24–26.

Fischetti, M., Curran, J. P. and Wessberg, H. W. (1977) Sense of timing: A skill deficit in heterosexual-socially anxious males. *Behavior Modification*, **1**, 179–194.

Gergen, K. J. (1985) The social constructionist movement in modern psychology. *American Psychologist*, **40**, 266–275.

Gross, A. M., Helmann, L., Shapiro, R. and Schultz, R. M. (1983) Children with diabetes: Social skills training and hemoglobin A_1c levels. *Behavior Modification*, **7**, 152–164.

Gutride, M. E., Goldstein, A. P. and Hunter, G. F. (1973) The use of modeling and role playing to increase social interaction among asocial psychiatric patients. *Journal of Consulting and Clinical Psychology*, **40**, 408–415.

Harré, R., Clarke, D. and De Carlo, N. (1985) *Motives and mechanisms*. London: Methuen.

Hersen, M. and Barlow, D. H. (1976) *Single case experimental designs: Strategies for studying behaviour change*. Oxford: Pergamon Press.

Hersen, M. and Bellack, A. S. (1977) Assessment of social skills. In: A. R. Ciminero, K. S. Calhoun and H. E. Adams (Eds.), *Handbook for behavioral assessment*. New York: Wiley.

Hersen, M., Eisler, R. M. and Miller, P. M. (1973) Development of assertive responses: Clinical measurement and research considerations. *Behaviour Research and Therapy*, **11**, 505–521.

Hersen, M., Eisler, R. M., Miller, P. M., Johnson, M. and Pinkston, S. (1973) Effects of practice, instructions, and modelling in components of assertive behaviour. *Behaviour Research and Therapy*, **11**, 447–451.

Hollin, C. R. and Henderson, M. (1984) Social skills training with young offenders: False expectations and the "failure of treatment". *Behavioural Psychotherapy*, **12**, 331–341.

Hollin, C. R., Huff, G. J., Clarkson, F. and Edmondson, A. C. (1982, July) Social skills training with young offenders in a borstal: An evaluative study. Paper presented at the International Conference on Psychology and Law, Swansea, Wales. (Also in press, *Journal of Community Psychology*).

Howard, G. S. (1985) The role of values in the science of psychology. *American Psychologist*, **40**, 255–265.

Kagan, C. (1984) Social problem solving and social skills training. *British Journal of Clinical Psychology*, **23**, 161–173.

Kazdin, A. E. (1974a) Effects of covert modelling and model reinforcement on assertive behavior. *Journal of Abnormal Psychology*, **83**, 240–252.

Kazdin, A. E. (1974b) The effect of model identity and fear relevant similarity on covert modeling. *Behavior Therapy*, **5**, 624–636.

Kazdin, A. E. (1976) Effects of covert modeling, multiple models, and model reinforcement on assertive behavior. *Behavior Therapy*, **7**, 211–222.

Ledwidge, B. (1978) Cognitive-behavior modification: A step in the wrong direction? *Psychological Bulletin*, **85**, 353–375.

Ledwidge, B. (1979) Cognitive-behavior modification: A rejoinder to Locke and Meichenbaum. *Cognitive Therapy and Research*, **3**, 133–139.

Locke, E. A. (1979) Behavior modification is not cognitive and other myths: A reply to Ledwidge. *Cognitive Therapy and Research*, **3**, 119–125.

Lowe, C. F. and Higson, P. J. (1981) Self-instructional training and cognitive behaviour modification: A behavioural analysis. In: G. Davey (Ed.), *Applications of conditioning theory*. London: Methuen.

McFall, R. M. (1982) A review and reformulation of the concept of social skills. *Behavioral Assessment*, **4**, 1–33.

McFall, R. M. and Dodge, K. A. (1982) Self-management and interpersonal skills learning.

In: P. Karoly and F. H. Kanfer (Eds.), *Self-management and behavior change: From theory to practice.* New York: Pergamon.

McFall, R. M. and Lillesand, D. B. (1971) Behavior rehearsal with modeling and coaching in assertion training. *Journal of Abnormal Psychology*, **77**, 313–323.

McFall, R. M. and Marston, A. R. (1970) An experimental investigation of behavior rehearsal in assertive training. *Journal of Abnormal Psychology*, **76**, 295–303.

McFall, R. 'M. and Twentyman, C. T. (1973) Four experiments on the relative contributions of rehearsal, modeling and coaching to assertion training. *Journal of Abnormal Psychology*, **81**, 199–218.

Meichenbaum, D. (1977) *Cognitive behavior modification: An integrative approach.* New York: Plenum Press.

Morrison, R. L. and Bellack, A. S. (1981) The role of social perception in social skill. *Behavior Therapy*, **12**, 69–71.

Osgood, C. E., Suci, G. J. and Tannenbaum, P. M. (1957) *The measurement of meaning.* Urbana: University of Illinois Press.

Peterson, J., Fischetti, M., Curran, J. P. and Arland, S. (1981) Sense of timing: A skill deficit in heterosocially anxious women. *Behavior Therapy*, **12**, 195–201.

Rosenthal, R., Hall, J. A., Archer, D., DiMatteo, M. R. and Rogers, P. L. (1979) *Sensitivity in nonverbal communication: The PONS test.* Baltimore, Maryland: John Hopkins University Press.

Rossiter, E. M. and Wilson, G. T. (1985) Cognitive restructuring and response prevention in the treatment of bulimia nervosa. *Behaviour Research and Therapy*, **23**, 349–359.

Scott, R. R., Himadi, W. and Keane, T. M. (1983) A review of generalization in social skills training: Suggestions for future research. In: M. Hersen, R. M. Eisler and P. M. Miller (Eds.), *Progress in behavior modification, Vol. 15.* New York: Academic Press.

Shepherd, G. (1977) Social skills training: The generalization problem. *Behavior Therapy*, **8**, 1008–1009.

Shepherd, G. (1978) Social skills training: The generalization problem — some further data. *Behaviour Research and Therapy*, **16**, 287–288.

Shepherd, G. (1984) Assessment of cognitions in social skills training. In: P. Trower (Ed.), *Radical approaches to social skills training.* London: Croom Helm.

Skinner, B. F. (1953) *Science and human behavior.* New York: Macmillan.

Skinner, B. F. (1974) *About behaviorism.* New York: Knopf.

Spence, S. H. (1980) *Social skills training with children and adolescents: A counsellor's manual.* Windsor: NFER.

Stefanek, M. E. and Eisler, R. M. (1983) The current status of cognitive variables in assertiveness training. In: M. Hersen, R. M. Eisler and P. M. Miller (Eds.), *Progress in behavior modification, Vol. 15.* New York: Academic Press.

Stravynski, A. (1978) The "Emperor's Clothes" — revealed, or social skills versus research skills. Which are needed most? *Behavioural Psychotherapy*, **6**, 91–96.

Trower, P. (1980) Situational analysis of the components and processes of behavior of socially skilled and unskilled patients. *Journal of Consulting and Clinical Psychology*, **48**, 327–339.

Trower, P. (1982) Toward a generative model of social skills: A critique and synthesis. In: J. P. Curran and P. M. Monti (Eds.), *Social skills training: A practical handbook for assessment and treatment.* New York: Guilford Press.

Trower, P. (1984) *Radical approaches to social skills training.* London: Croom Helm.

Turk, D. C. and Salovey, P. (1985) Cognitive structures, cognitive processes, and cognitive-behavior modification: 1. Client issues. *Cognitive Therapy and Research*, **9**, 1–18.

Trower, P., Bryant, B. and Argyle, M. (1978) *Social skills and mental health.* London: Methuen.

Wachtel, P. (1977) *Psychoanalysis and behavior therapy.* New York: Basic Books.

Wilson, T. (1978) Cognitive behavior therapy: Paradigm shift or passing phase. In: J. Foreyt and D. Rathjen (Eds.), *Cognitive behavior therapy: Research and application.* New York: Plenum Press.

Wolpe, J. (1978) Cognition and causation in human behavior and its therapy. *American Psychologist*, **33**, 437–446.

Yardley, K. M. (1979) Social skills training — a critique. *British Journal of Medical Psychology*, **52**, 55–62.

Author Index

Subject Index